OXFORD ENGLISH MONOGRAPHS

General Editors

JOHN CAREY   STEPHEN GILL

DOUGLAS GRAY   ROGER LONSDALE

RUSKIN'S MYTHS

DINAH BIRCH

CLARENDON PRESS · OXFORD

1988

Oxford University Press, Walton Street, Oxford OX2 6DP

Oxford New York Toronto
Delhi Bombay Calcutta Madras Karachi
Petaling Jaya Singapore Hong Kong Tokyo
Nairobi Dar es Salaam Cape Town
Melbourne Auckland
and associated companies in
Berlin Ibadan

Oxford is a trade mark of Oxford University Press

Published in the United States
by Oxford University Press, New York

British Library Cataloguing in Publication Data
Birch, Dinah.
Ruskin's myths,—(Oxford English monographs).
1. Ruskin, John—Knowledge—Folklore, mythology. 2. Mythology in
literature.
I. Title
828'.809   PR5267.M82
ISBN 0–19–812872–X

Library of Congress Cataloging in Publication Data
Birch, Dinah.
Ruskin's myths/by Dinah Birch.
p.   cm.—(Oxford English monographs)
Bibliography: p.   Includes index.
1. Ruskin, John, 1819–1900—Knowledge—Folklore,
mythology.   2. Mythology in literature.   3. Myth in literature.
I. Title.   II. Series.
PR5267.M83B57 1988
828'.809–dc19
ISBN 0–19–812872–X

Set by Downdell Ltd.
Printed in Great Britain
at the University Printing House, Oxford
by David Stanford
Printer to the University

For Neil and Rowena Baggaley

ACKNOWLEDGEMENTS

My first thanks must go to Mr Paul Turner, who has warmly encouraged every stage of my research. Many Ruskinians have helped me: I would like especially to thank Mr James S. Dearden, Curator of the Ruskin Galleries at Bembridge, Mr Robert Hewison, Mr Michael Simmonds, and Dr Jeanne Clegg. Mr Tim Hilton gave much generous assistance. I have profited greatly from the kindness and learning of Professor Marilyn Butler. Dr Nicola Bradbury and Miss Jane Havell patiently read early drafts. Special thanks are due to Mrs Valerie Burns and Miss Teresa Bonasera, without whose skilled help this book could not have been written. To all these people, I am most grateful.

Thanks are also due to Unwin Hyman Ltd. as the Literary Trustees of John Ruskin for allowing me to quote from the unpublished writings of Ruskin. For permission to quote material in their care I thank The Education Trust Ltd., The Ruskin Galleries, Bembridge School, Isle of Wight. Permission to quote from unpublished material has been kindly granted by the Bodleian Library, Oxford, the Syndics of the Fitzwilliam Museum, Cambridge, the Trustees of the National Library of Scotland, and the Harry Ransom Humanities Research Center at the University of Texas at Austin.

Finally, I would like to record my gratitude to my husband, Sid, who makes things possible.

CONTENTS

1
Introduction

Mythology and Mythography

My subject is the growth of Ruskin's myths. What myth might mean to us must therefore matter less for my purposes than what it meant to Ruskin. But the study of myth has been one of the major growth-points of our culture, and this is in itself a reason to be interested in Ruskin's changing ideas on the subject. Is it an encoded body of spiritual wisdom? Is it a kind of primitive science? Or disguised history? Does it reveal the hidden structure of human thought? The only indisputable conclusion to be drawn from the proliferating answers to such questions is that myth is multiple. It has taken widely different forms at different times in different cultures. No single method of analysis is likely to be equally effective for all mythological traditions, nor can myth be claimed as the legitimate territory of any one intellectual discipline. Philosophers and historians, theologians, linguists, political theorists, anthropologists, literary critics—all have reason to be interested in the material of myth. It is unsurprising, then, to find their researches leading to divergent conclusions, laden with the values and presuppositions of their starting-points.

The word 'myth' itself has acquired a sort of glamour. Those who wish to oppose *mythos* to *logos* often interpret the former as the regenerative action of the imagination taking a proper precedence over the rational mind. Hungry for the hallowed, artists and scholars alike have been eager to turn to the magical resonance of myth. But this modern reverence coexists with modern contempt. For if myth is a denial of fact, it may be a lie. In everyday usage this is often the primary meaning of the word. Such a split in the idea of a myth— exciting and creative on the one hand, dangerous and specious on the other—has a history which is engaged with fundamental conflicts of belief. Myth may be presented as the enemy of science, and the rising interest in myth is in part a reaction against the triumph of science. But it may also be seen as a refutation of established religion. It has often proved attractive to those who reject both modern rationalism and the traditions of faith, and this accounts for its reputation as the territory of intellectual mavericks, charismatic thinkers, or eccentrics. The study of myth has never quite been part of an academic mainstream, though the issues it raises have repeatedly proved to be of central importance.

Myth has thus provided a persistent focus for ideological debate in the twentieth century. We may think of these controversies as peculiarly modern. But mythography, or writing about myth, has never been neutral. Differing views of its ancient history and fluid significance had been current among thinkers for at least three centuries before Ruskin came to the subject. His earliest thoughts on myth, dating from his years as schoolboy and undergraduate in the 1830s, were formed by the conventions of his education. During his lifetime, however, mythography acquired new sophistication and urgency, as the need to find ways of reconciling the material and the spiritual became pressing. As religion declined, the investigation of mythology gathered pace. Ruskin's view of myth changed, sometimes in unexpected ways, in response to these explorations. Like many Victorians, he discovered languages which others had made out of myth, and used them to interpret the fragmentation of his own world.

One of the first reasons for the accommodating character of myth, and its vitality, is that it has no fixed or final form. There can be no agreed text of a myth. The mythology of Greece in particular, perpetually attractive to scholars and poets, has acquired a shifting identity as generations of writers have imposed their biases on its interpretation. The diversity and abundance of Greek myth contributed to its close association with literary tradition: that tradition has continued to enrich its variety. Greek mythology gained a status closely identified with that of ancient literature. Yet it presented no obstructive authorial precedent to those who wanted to borrow its authority. Its literary weight, coupled with its anonymity, is one of the most telling reasons for Ruskin's almost exclusive concern with the myths of Greece rather than the less familiar mythologies of other cultures.

But Ruskin's preoccupation with the Greeks is not wholly typical of the mythography of his age. Other mythical traditions —the American, the Hindu, the Norse—were increasingly attracting attention. An important motive for the widening interest in diverse mythological material lay in its much-debated relation with religion, and more specifically with Christianity. Myth might be, and often was, seen as a religious phenomenon. But whether its religious nature was viewed positively or not depended on the position of the interpreter. Sceptics of the seventeenth and eighteenth centuries used their analyses of myth, in which they often perceived evidence of both religious instinct and primitive error in the mind of early man, as an oblique means of undermining the dignity of the Christian faith. If it could be demonstrated, or hinted, that the forms and beliefs of Christianity were not wholly distinct from those of pagan mythologies which were characterized as at best mistaken, at worst depraved, then the supremacy of Christian faith was threatened. If, on the other hand, it could be shown that mythology was quite separate from divinely revealed religion, the sacred status of Christianity was preserved. The contention between those who wanted to identify myth with religion, and those who did not, continued throughout the nineteenth century and well into the twentieth.

The issue of religion is at the heart of Ruskin's interest in the subject. He consistently saw myth as religion: but, as his own spiritual experience darkened, the perspective from which he did so changed. Here as elsewhere Ruskin's position is conditioned by his family history. His close ties with his parents were cemented by shared religious conviction. His mother was a devoted Evangelical Christian; his father, more actively interested in literature and painting, was no less firm in his faith. Their son inherited their beliefs to an extent that made him at first reluctant to grant any kind of religious dignity to the mythology which, in his early years, he termed 'heathen'. The difference between the pure monotheistic beliefs of the Christian—the Protestant Christian—and the polytheistic delusions of the pagan seemed absolute. Mythology was a religion, but a degraded and mistaken one. Ruskin had no wish to denigrate Christianity by comparing its traditions with those of other or lesser faiths. It follows that he had, in fact, only a limited interest in mythology during the years of his firmest adherence to Christian belief. What concern he did show grew out of the study of the Greek literature that was for him and his peers a central part of his education.

In later years Ruskin was to reject the aims and methods of this education as energetically as he was to reject his dismissal of mythology. Many related assumptions crumbled as he grew into the world outside the safe walls of his parents' home in Denmark Hill. The complex association between education, religion, and myth in Ruskin's mature work is formed by a reaction against the patterns of his own youthful experiences. In freeing himself from what came to seem the confinements of childhood assumptions, however, Ruskin had no desire to free himself from the habit of reverence which he felt to be the truly valuable thing that he had learnt as a child, and the motive of all healthy thinking and teaching. The habit was right; to circumscribe its action had been wrong. To recognize religious aspiration or wisdom in the forms of mythology need imply, after all, no demotion of Christianity. Certainly Ruskin, in urging that myth should be both studied and valued, intended no such implication. Yet what he finally created for himself out of his analysis of myth has less to do with public religious controversy than with the needs of his troubled imagination. Myth gave Ruskin a much-needed means of integrating broken belief into new patterns, combining political conviction and social action with an obsessive inward language.

Ruskin's Greek Education

When Ruskin began to write, he was either indifferent or hostile to mythology. This was partly due to the religious training that motivated his work throughout his life. But it was also due to his classical training. The education of a young gentleman was inevitably based on the study of the classics. Ruskin was taught within this tradition and came to reject it. His lifelong interest in educational reform grows out of disillusionment with the kind of schooling that he had

himself received. Ten years after leaving Oxford, he wrote
about the 'present European system of so-called education'
in the third volume of *The Stones of Venice* (1853):

By a large body of the people of England and Europe a man is
called educated if he can write Latin verses and construe a Greek
chorus. By some few more enlightened persons it is confessed that
the construction of hexameters is not in itself an important end of
human existence; but they say, that the general discipline which a
course of classical reading gives to the intellectual powers is the
final object of our scholastical institutions.

But it seems to me there is no small error even in this last and
more philosophical theory. I believe that what it is most profitable
to know, it is also most profitable to learn; and that the science
which it is the highest power to possess, it is also the best exercise to
acquire.[1]

These remained the grounds of Ruskin's work for changes in
education throughout his life. 'Classical reading' had been
his diet as a boy: he had no training in natural history or
politics, the subjects he came to feel it most essential that all
should be taught. He had, as a matter of course, been schooled
in the elements of theology: but not, in terms of his later convictions, in religion. Ruskin's first teachers were clergymen.
It is one of the paradoxes of history that during what is now
seen as a pious age the ministers of the Church into whose
hands the business of education, or at least the education of
boys, had largely fallen should have been chiefly concerned
with instructing their pupils in a literature that was not
Christian. Ruskin was sharply aware of the contradiction:

That English ministers of religion should ever come to desire rather
to make a youth acquainted with the powers of Nature and of God,
than with the powers of Greek particles; that they should ever think
it more useful to show him how the great universe rolls upon its
course in heaven, than how the syllables are fitted in a tragic metre;
that they should hold it more advisable for him to be fixed in the
principles of religion than in those of syntax; or, finally, that they
should ever come to apprehend that a youth likely to go straight out
of college into parliament, might not unadvisably know as much of

---

[1] *The Works of John Ruskin*, ed. E. T. Cook and Alexander Wedderburn, 39
vols. (London, 1903–12), xi. 258. Subsequent references to this edition will give
volume- and page-numbers only.

the Peninsular as of the Peloponnesian War, and be as well acquainted with the state of modern Italy as of old Etruria; all this, however unreasonably, I *do* hope, and mean to work for. (xi. 261)

The vehemence of Ruskin's reaction is partly explained by peculiarities in his position within the orthodox system. He was a precocious and talented child, but his early training had not equipped him to win academic honours. The root of the problem lay in the fact that he was a 'home boy'. Because they had no wish to lose his company, and because they felt they could themselves provide a sounder education, Ruskin's parents had not sent him to a public school. Ruskin's mother saw no reason to regret the decision. She wrote to his father:

But tho' John should take no class I shall never regret his having been kept at home good Morals, good habits, and the various knowledge and acquirements which may be attained in a private education must be cheaply rated, indeed, if they are not considered of more value than the mere knowledge of Greek and Latin grammar.[2]

She was right in that Ruskin had been allowed to develop his own interests—in drawing, in the natural world—to an extent that would not have been possible amid the restrictions of a public school. There was, however, a price to pay. He was not unpopular at Christ Church, and he was recognized as one of the most gifted of his generation. But there is no doubt that, having been haphazardly taught by a series of private tutors, he had been left with an uncertain grasp of the 'Greek and Latin grammar' he needed to distinguish himself in classical studies. This mattered to him, for both he and his parents wanted formal public success. After matriculating at Christ Church in 1836, Ruskin made heroic efforts to overcome his disadvantages through hard application. His labours contributed to a breakdown of health in the early summer of 1840, shortly before he was to take his final examinations. All hopes for high honours were abandoned. He at last went up only for a pass degree. This seemed a defeat, and was cer-

[2] *The Ruskin Family Letters: The Correspondence of John James Ruskin, his Wife, and their Son, John, 1801–1843*, ed. Van Akin Burd, 2 vols. (Ithaca and London, 1973), ii. 543.

tainly a blow to his self-esteem. Ruskin could not easily forget it.

The effects of this unhappy period in Ruskin's life were pervasive and long-lasting. Not all were negative: he made friendships in Oxford that were to be important to him throughout his life—notably with Henry Acland and Henry Liddell. And it was in Oxford that he made his first acquaintance with the classical authors who were to be important in his mature work: Aristophanes, Thucydides, Herodotus, Aristotle, Euripides, Homer, Pindar, and, most significantly, Plato. But what Ruskin remembered best was a system of education built on misplaced ambition and wasted toil. In 1840, at the end of his Oxford career, he wrote of his feelings to one of his boyhood tutors, Thomas Dale:

> It is not without considerable bitterness that I can look back on the three years I spent at the University—three years of such vigorous life as I may never know again, sacrificed to a childish vanity, and not only lost themselves, but breaking down my powers of enjoyment or exertion, for I know not how long. If I ever wished to see the towers of Oxford again, the wish is found only in conjunction with another—Rosalind's—that I had 'a thunderbolt in mine eye'.[3] (i. 382–3)

These were the feelings that prompted Ruskin's repudiation of classical studies, and for many years they led to hostility towards anything that could be called pagan, classical, heathen, Greek, or 'mythic'. Not only were such studies coloured with the competitive spirit of scholarly ambition that Ruskin came to despise, partly because he was ashamed of having succumbed to it himself, they were also tainted with infidelity, for they were not Christian. Ruskin embarked on his career in a crusading spirit. He intended to rewrite the concept of criticism. If the clergymen who had taken charge of his education with such questionable results had combined their vocation with a worldly preoccupation with the heathen world, was it not his duty to make himself into a different and more truly Christian kind of teacher?

---

[3] In fact this is Celia's phrase: 'If I had a thunderbolt in mine eye, I can tell who should down' (*As You Like it*, I. ii. 202).

Writing and Preaching

Ruskin's mother had always hoped and intended that her son should become a minister of religion. Though he was never to enter the Church, there is a sense in which he fulfilled her ambition. In 1844, the year after the publication of the first volume of *Modern Painters*, he wrote to Osborne Gordon, a clerical don who had taught Ruskin at Christ Church and who now doubted whether the fine arts could provide an appropriate career for a devout young man. Understandably under these circumstances, Ruskin's reply is oppressively pious. He explains that his object as a critic will be to direct 'the public to expect and the artist to intend—an earnest and elevating *moral* influence in all that they admire and achieve' (iii. 665). This sounds like Victorian sentiment at its least enticing. But in fact Ruskin's ambition is more Romantic than his terms here might suggest. His early passion for nature, and for the art that celebrated nature, had been an experience far more intense than anything inspired by the course of classical reading which had made up his formal education. It was this passion that he now wanted to bring to God's service, in a way that would combine his mother's religious devotion with his father's literary aspiration.

Ruskin's schoolboy duties had lain with classical literature, but the pleasure he had found in books had chiefly derived from the literature of the Romantics. His father, an enthusiastic and discerning reader, had shown the way. He had introduced his son to the hills of the Lake District and the poetry of Wordsworth; to Scotland and the novels of Scott. Ruskin's feeling for Romantic literature was inseparable from his love for his father: both were intimately bound up with his veneration for nature. He had found more food for the imagination in Wordsworth than in Aristotle, and, like many of his contemporaries, he intended to translate the Wordsworthian idiom into his own langauge. He points out to Gordon that he feels himself to be 'quite as capable of *preaching* on the beauty of the creation, of which I know something, as of preaching on the beauty of a system of salvation of which I know nothing' (iii. 666). Ruskin was still far from breaking free from the religion of his childhood:

that rift would not come until the late 1850s. But he already knew that the Christian ministry would confine his work in ways that would be intolerable to him. The natural truths of creation, not the dogmas of Evangelical religion or the classics of Oxford, increasingly seemed appropriate texts for the writer who wished, as Ruskin always did, to follow Wordsworth in finding his own spiritual growth in promoting that of others. Nature would provide the texts; the writer, as preacher, would expound them to readers eager for an 'earnest and elevating *moral* influence in all that they admire or achieve'. The epigraph of each of the five volumes of *Modern Painters* came from Wordsworth's *Excursion*, that sober statement of writing as preaching which has so offended modern literary taste but which haunted Ruskin all his life.

> Accuse me not
> Of arrogance, . . .
> If, having walked with Nature,
> And offered, far as frailty would allow,
> My heart a daily sacrifice to Truth,
> I now affirm of Nature and of Truth,
> Whom I have served, that their Divinity
> Revolts, offended at the ways of men,
> Philosophers, who, though the human soul
> Be of a thousand faculties composed,
> And twice ten thousand interests, do yet prize
> This soul, and the transcendent universe,
> No more than as a mirror that reflects
> To proud Self-love her own intelligence.[4]

The mystic fusion of nature with divinity was the starting-point of Ruskin's serious interest in mythology. Such a link is a truism of the Romantic view of religious history; but it is a truism whose origin predates Romanticism. For the notion of a natural religion had been the basis of much of the mythography of the pre-Romantic period. The philosophers of the Enlightenment had interpreted myth as a form of benighted superstition from which the progress of reason had rescued mankind. Myth was evidence of primitive man's incapacity to free his thinking from the restrictions of the purely physical

---

[4] Wordsworth, *The Excursion*, iv. 978–92.

circumstances of his circumscribed life. Holbach's analysis of myth was prominent in the tradition of Enlightenment thought that had seen a worship of nature as the origin of ancient mythologies:

The elements of nature were, as we have shown, the first divinities of man; he has generally commenced with adoring material beings; each individual, as we have said, and as may be still seen in savage nations, made to himself a particular God of some physical object, which he supposed to be the cause of those events in which he was himself interested; he never wandered to seek out of visible nature the source either of what happened to himself, or of those phenomena to which he was a witness.[5]

Other Enlightenment thinkers had taken comparable views of ancient mythology. Charles Dupuis, writing at the time of the Revolution, had attributed particular importance to the heavenly bodies. He may be seen as one of the earliest solar mythologists. Bolder than most, he had not hesitated to suggest that Christ himself might be seen simply as another solar myth. Dupuis's claims have a vigorously polemical edge:

When we shall have shown,—that the pretended history of a God, born of a Virgin at the winter solstice, who resuscitates at Easter or at the equinox of spring, after having descended into hell; of a God, who has twelve apostles in his train, whose leader has all the attributes of Janus; of a God-conqueror of the Prince of Darkness, who restores to mankind the dominion of Light, and who redeems the evils of Nature—is merely a solar fable, like all those, which we have analysed, it will be quite as indifferent, or of as little consequence to examine, whether there ever existed a man by the name of Christ, as it would be to enquire, whether some Prince was called Hercules, provided it will be conclusively demonstrated, that the being, consecrated by worship under the name of Christ, is the Sun, and that the marvellousness of the legend or of the same poem, has that luminary for its object, because it would seem then to be proved, that Christians are mere worshippers of the Sun, and that their priests have the same religion as those of Peru, whom they have caused to be put to death.[6]

[5] Paul Henri, Baron d'Holbach, *The System of Nature* (London, 1770), trans. Burton Feldman and Robert D. Richardson in *The Rise of Modern Mythology 1680–1860* (Bloomington and London, 1972), 180.

[6] Charles Dupuis, *The Origin of all Religious Worship*, 7 vols. (Paris, 1795), trans. Feldman and Richardson in *The Rise of Modern Mythology*, pp. 286–7.

Such theories could hardly be further from Ruskin's Christian certainties in the 1840s; nor is there any evidence or likelihood that he was directly influenced by these sceptical writers of the Enlightenment. Yet his view of myth was shaped by their speculations. The idea that ancient mythology involved some form of nature worship had become commonplace in the 1820s and 1830s, and Ruskin was never to reject this basic premiss. Mythology could be defined as a manifestation of reverence for the natural world: this is one of the ways in which it had been used as a weapon in an attack on Christianity. But Ruskin, formed by Wordsworthian Romanticism, came to see this very reverence as fundamental to the life of all religions, including Christianity. The study of myth seemed to have been appropriated by the secularists. It became Ruskin's aim to reinterpret their conclusions in the light of a faith still wider than Christianity.

As Ruskin's Christian belief faltered over the seventeen years which encompassed the publication of *Modern Painters*, his arguments tended more and more to the conclusion that the Greeks were not, after all, superstitious pagans; their mythological religion of nature was wiser than the arrogant materialism of the nineteenth century.

With us, observe, the idea of the Divinity is apt to get separated from the life of nature; and imagining our God upon a cloudy throne, far above the earth, and not in the flowers or waters, we approach these visible things with the theory that they are dead; governed by physical laws, and so forth . . . But the Greek never removed his god out of nature at all; never attempted for a moment to contradict his instinctive sense that God was everywhere. (v. 231)

The Greeks, in other words, could be claimed as prestigious authority for the Romantic wish to endow nature with spirituality. This concept of classical mythology as an expression of a sense of God in nature had, for Ruskin, more than one important recommendation. It enabled him to associate myth with the art that meant most to him—the art of the Romantic poets and, above all, the art of Turner, defined by Ruskin as the greatest painter of truth in nature. And such truth had, for Ruskin, a reassuringly permanent quality. Exempt from change and constituted by God, it stood apart from the bewildering flux and uncertainties of the human world. Even the authority of Christian religion, which had seemed established for all time, had become vulnerable to the restlessly destructive powers of the human intellect. Only a religion built on nature, a religion such as Ruskin discovered in mythology, could offer a fixed body of spiritual truth. Ruskin's claims that mythology did constitute such a natural religion are first made in *Modern Painters*. They are elaborated throughout the 1860s, and culminate with *The Queen of the Air*, the book in which Ruskin finds that

all guidance to the right sense of the human and variable myths will probably depend on our first getting at the sense of the natural and invariable ones. The dead hieroglyph may have meant this or that —the living hieroglyph means always the same; but remember, it is just as much a hieroglyph as the other; nay, more,—a 'sacred or reserved sculpture,' a thing with an inner language. (xix. 361)

Natural myth, the 'living hieroglyph', is constant, and lies behind the multiplicity of the 'dead' myths of human art and literature. But neither natural nor human myth could be understood without the intervention of sympathetic interpretation.

This sense of a concealed fixity of meaning in mythology is central to Ruskin's celebration of its power to sustain the spirit in a world of threat. Pained by a sense of personal weakness, he was to claim the curse of Reuben as his own: 'Unstable as water, thou shalt not excel.'[7] But the sanctioned work of the preacher is set apart from the imperfections of his nature. His intelligence, devoted to the service of God rather than to the uncertainties of self-expression, is the medium through which the meaning of divine texts becomes available to the people. For the Christian preacher, the sacred texts are those of the Bible. Ruskin's writing remains full of biblical reference, allusion, and exposition—long after his Christian faith had disintegrated. But sacred authority need not, Ruskin came to believe, he confined to the Bible. The texts of nature—the skies, the mountains, the seas—might carry equal weight. The obscurities of mythology were to be seen as interpretive expressions of these texts, expressions

---

[7] Gen. 49: 4; see xxviii. 275.

which themselves stood in need of moral elucidation amid the corruptions of the nineteenth century. No more weighty responsibility awaited the secular preachers of the new age. Its implications were for Ruskin both personal and polemic, and they were vital to his developing work as a critic.

2
Rediscovering Myth (1843–1860)

Ruskin's Early Hostility to the Greeks

Ruskin's mission as an art critic began as his official introduction to the Greeks ended. When the first volume of *Modern
Painters* appeared in May 1843, its anonymous author was
about to complete a final term of residence at Oxford.[1] His
disillusionment with the training he had received at Christ
Church was deeply felt. Yet his first book was published as
the work of 'A Graduate of Oxford'. Ruskin's early writing is
marked by curiously ambivalent feelings about conventional
learning. In order to challenge its assumptions, he felt that he
must prove his command of its disciplines. His experience of
traditional scholarship had been closely connected with his
study of the Greeks. Allusions to Aristotle, Aeschylus, Plato,
or Homer help to give the desired air of intellectual authority
in the first two volumes of *Modern Painters*.[2] But he also
associated the Greeks with the stultifying 'classical' approach
that it was his aim to discredit. The 'classical poison' (iii.
233), later to be separated and identified more specifically with
neo-classicism and the Renaissance, is initially implied in the
Greeks themselves. 'The manner of Nicolo Poussin is said to
be Greek—it may be so; this only I know, that it is heartless
and profitless,' Ruskin remarks in his first volume (iii. 230).
At once respectful and dissident, Ruskin's thinking about the
ancient world lay outside the imaginative impulses which led
him to defend Turner. By June 1860, however, when the fifth
and final volume of *Modern Painters* appeared, the Greeks
had assumed a positive importance in Ruskin's work. Rather
than representing 'classical' conformity to sterile principles,

[1] He had taken his BA degree in April 1842, but returned to Oxford to fulfil
residence requirements for his MA degree. See *Family Letters*, ii. 741.

[2] Many such references disappear from later editions of *Modern Painters*. 'I have
cut out here a quotation from Aristotle—which was only put in to show that I had
read him,' Ruskin notes of one such excision from the 1883 edition of the second
volume of *Modern Painters* (iv. 97 n.).

their mythology had come to suggest insights that were central in his massively expanded scheme of thought. Seventeen years after leaving Oxford, Ruskin was able to turn to the Greeks for confirmation of his vision of a moral universe.

The transformation in Ruskin's religious position made this possible. His changing doctrinal viewpoint between 1843 and 1860 gave him the freedom to see the Greeks in a new light. He had begun to write *Modern Painters* in the Evangelical faith of his parents. His mother's hope that he might become a clergyman had been disappointed, but not her expectation that he would choose a pious life.[3] In the first volume of *Modern Painters*, Ruskin recommends that his reader should spend a day and a night 'upon the peak of some isolated mountain' (iii. 415) in order to prove whether Turner or Claude had most effectively rendered on canvas the various beauties of nature that such a vigil would reveal: 'When you can look no more for gladness, and when you are bowed down with fear and love of the Maker and Doer of this, tell me who has best delivered this His message unto men!' (iii. 419). The answer is of course Turner—but, by implication at least, the answer is also Ruskin. It is not intended that the reader should literally spend twenty-four hours on the top of a mountain with 'neither breakfast nor dinner'; as Ruskin pointed out, with the self-mockery characteristic of his later years, when the passage was reprinted in 1875 (iii. 415 n.). The experience of divine revelation through nature is conveyed through Ruskin's own recreation of natural beauty. In defending Turner through opening his readers' eyes to the splendour of creation and its meaning as it is expressed in Turner's painting, Ruskin is furthering his purposes as a Christian writer.

The second volume of *Modern Painters* appeared, three years after the first, in 1846. It is less concerned with the vindication of Turner. But Ruskin's interpretation of nature and art is still assertively Christian. He continues to stress the divine benevolence of nature, claiming that 'it is not possible for a Christian man to walk across so much as a rood of the

---

[3] Margaret Ruskin, comparing herself to the biblical Hannah, had dedicated her only son to the service of the Lord as an Evangelical clergyman in the Church of England. See xxxv. 24.

natural earth, with mind unagitated and rightly poised, without receiving strength and hope from some flower, leaf, or sound, nor without a sense of a dew falling upon him out of the sky' (iv. 215–16). Only Christian art could interpret such holiness. Ruskin's diary shows that he did not consider classical culture to be capable of the 'earnest and elevating *moral* influence' that he demanded. 'Consider the great want of real and deep seriousness in classical poetry and design. Grasp of outward things, and shallow, philosophical emotion, only—a constant superiority attempted and believed of the man over nature . . . The great sense of eternity upon us constantly—a wider knowledge'.[4] From Ruskin's Evangelical point of view, the gulf between classical and Christian understanding seemed profound.

Ruskin encountered his most influential predecessor in his wish to define a Christian approach to the study of art in the figure of Lord Lindsay, whose *Sketches of the History of Christian Art* he reviewed in the *Quarterly Review* of June 1847. Lord Lindsay places stern emphasis on the higher rank of Christian over classic art: 'Herein then lies our vantage—not in our merit, not our genius, but in that we are Christians, that we start from a loftier platform, that we are raised by communion with God to a purer atmosphere, in which we see things in the light of Eternity.'[5] Ruskin declared himself entirely in agreement:

Yet let us not be misunderstood:—the great gulf between Christian and Pagan art we cannot bridge—nor do we wish to weaken one single sentence wherein its breadth or depth is asserted by our author. The separation is not gradual, but instant and final—the difference not of degree, but of condition; it is the difference between the dead vapours rising from a stagnant pool, and the same vapours touched by a torch. (xii. 184)

These are views that colour Ruskin's attitude to the Greeks in the first two volumes of *Modern Painters*. What he was

---

[4] Bodl. MS Eng. Misc. c. 214, fo. 102. That this passage was not included in the *Diaries* may have been due to the difficulty in dating it precisely. It occurs in the volume that Ruskin used as his diary in 1847 and 1848, and its place in the book suggests that it dates from the early months of 1848.

[5] Alexander William Crawford (Lord Lindsay), *Sketches of the History of Christian Art* (London, 1847), vol. i, p. xv.

later to describe as the 'Protestant egotism and insolence' (xxix. 90) of his early works touches a high point in the second volume. In 'The Superhuman Ideal', it reaches a supremely confident statement of Christian superiority:

Gather what we may of great from Pagan chisel or Pagan dream, and set it beside the orderer of Christian warfare, Michael the Archangel . . . It is vain to attempt to pursue the comparison; the two orders of art have in them nothing common, and the field of sacred history, the intent and scope of Christian feeling, are too wide and exalted to admit of the juxtaposition of any other sphere or order of conception; they embrace all other fields like the dome of heaven. (iv. 330–1)

Ruskin was to grow yet more convinced of the inferiority of Greek religious thought. In the early 1850s, his attack on the art of the Renaissance gave him particular reason for hostility towards the Greeks. His rejection of Renaissance ideals necessarily implied a questioning of the classical culture that the Renaissance had aspired to emulate. In *The Stones of Venice* (1851–3), classical culture is confused with its neo-classical issue. The estimate of the Greeks expressed in this work is often surprisingly irreverent. In the third volume of *The Stones of Venice*, Ruskin argues that

a people may take so definite a lead over all the rest of the world in one direction, as to obtain a respect which is not justly due to them if judged on universal grounds. Thus the Greeks perfected the sculp-ture of the human body; threw their literature into a disciplined form, which has given it a peculiar power over certain conditions of modern mind; and were the most carefully educated race that the world has seen; but a few years hence, I believe, we shall no longer think them a greater people than either the Egyptians or the Assyrians. (xi. 188)

Given the traditions of his day, his prediction would have seemed little less than perverse.

Distrust of ancient Greek religion in *The Stones of Venice* accompanies a distaste for classical Greek art. Here, Ruskin's position is complicated by his view of the relation between Greek and Byzantine work. In the first volume, he spoke simply of 'three principal styles of architecture in Venice,—the Greek or Byzantine, the Gothic, and the Renaissance' (ix.

425). In so far as Greek architecture could be identified with the Byzantine monuments of Venice, Ruskin implied praise for the Greek in his celebration of Byzantine design. But he had already made a clear distinction between the Christian Byzantine and the pagan Greek in *The Seven Lamps of Architecture* (1849). Byzantine ornament had seemed to him to show a sense of the divine power of nature:

The rolling heap of the thunder-cloud, divided by rents, and multiplied by wreaths, yet gathering them all into its broad, torrid, and towering zone, and its midnight darkness opposite; the scarcely less majestic heave of the mountain side, all torn and traversed by depth of defile and ridge of rock, yet never losing the unity of its illumined swell and shadowy decline; and the head of every mighty tree, rich with tracery of leaf and bough, yet terminated against the sky by a true line, and rounded by a green horizon, which, multiplied in the distant forest, makes it look bossy from above; all these mark, for a great and honoured law, that diffusion of light for which the Byzantine ornaments were designed; and show us that those builders had truer sympathy with what God made majestic, than the self-contemplating and self-contented Greek. I know that they are barbaric in comparison; but there is a power in their barbarism of sterner tone, a power not sophistic nor penetrative, but embracing and mysterious; a power faithful more than thoughtful, which conceived and felt more than it created; a power that neither comprehended nor ruled itself, but worked and wandered as it listed, like mountain streams and winds; and which could not rest in the expression or seizure of finite form. It could not bury itself in acanthus leaves. Its imagery was taken from the shadows of the storms and hills, and had fellowship with the night and day of the earth itself. (viii. 120–1)

Though Ruskin describes the Byzantine conception of St Mark's as 'Greek', he refers to a Christian rather than a pagan Greek spirit. For it seemed to Ruskin that classical Greek art had paid small heed to the richness of organic form. The Greek had been blind to grace in nature: 'Pagan sculptors seem to have perceived little beauty in the stems of trees; they were little else than timber to them; and they preferred the rigid and monstrous triglyph, or the fluted column, to a broken bough or gnarled trunk. But with Christian knowledge came a peculiar regard for the forms of vegetation, from the root upwards' (ix. 277). In 'The Nature

of Gothic', Ruskin sets Greek art against the vision of a
Christian age. The 'Servile ornament' (x. 189) of the Greeks
could not allow for the creativity of the workmen employed
to produce it, which it seemed the peculiarly Christian strength
of Gothic architecture to do. Neither the Greek master-
workman 'nor those for whom he worked could endure the
appearance of imperfection in anything; and, therefore, what
ornament he appointed to be done by those beneath him was
composed of mere geometric forms,—balls, ridges, and perfectly symmetrical foliage,—which could be executed with
absolute precision by line and rule, and were as perfect in their
way, when completed, as his own figure sculpture' (x. 189).

Ruskin showed an Evangelical temper in his emphasis on
the value of the individual, for the assertion of merit in
separate effort for salvation was fundamental to Noncon-
formist belief. But in seeing a rigidly mechanical exactitude in
Greek monuments, hostile to such expression of individual
aspiration, he was basing his judgement on second-hand
evidence. Though Ruskin had seen a great deal of Gothic architecture, he had never seen a Greek building, for he had never
been to Greece. Others had more direct knowledge of classical
remains, and he was glad to learn from their experience.
Charles Newton, a fellow graduate of Christ Church, was a
pioneer in the developing science of archaeology.[6] Ruskin
respected his knowledge without sharing his enthusiasm. Newton
contributed a scholarly appendix on 'Ancient Representations
of Water' to the first volume of *The Stones of Venice* (ix.
460–9). But the degree of insight, and indeed interest, which
Ruskin showed in any subject depended on the extent of his
personal experience. Conversation with Charles Newton was
no substitute. Ruskin's views on the Parthenon might well
have been different if he had been able to examine it in the way
that he had studied the Gothic monuments of Venice. But his
response to classical Greek architecture was shaped rather by
the buildings that had revived its principles in other ages and
other countries.

[6] Charles Newton (1816–94) enjoyed a long and distinguished career as an archae-
ologist, becoming keeper of the Greek and Roman antiquities at the British Museum
in 1861.

They were not limited to the neo-classical constructions of the Renaissance that he so disliked; nor to the Venetian Byzantine buildings that he loved. The early stirrings of archaeology in the forty years preceding Ruskin's birth had prompted an attempt to recreate a purely classical architecture, bypassing Palladio and Vitruvius in a search for their ancient sources. The Greek Revival had been particularly active in Britain. It had reached its height long before Ruskin began to publish *The Stones of Venice*, but it was by no means dead. Charles Cockerell's prize-winning classical design for the new Ashmolean Museum and Taylor Institution in Oxford had been completed in 1845, only ten years before the foundation stone of the Oxford Museum of Natural History, its rival Gothic style largely inspired by the work of Ruskin, was laid. Sir Robert Smirke's vast Ionic design for the British Museum was finished in 1847. In Scotland the influence of the Greek ideal was particularly widely felt. Its prevalence in Edinburgh, the 'Athens of the North', continued throughout a period when the revived Gothic style had become fashionable elsewhere. Ruskin's enmity towards the ideal of ancient Greek architecture was not directed at a merely historical phenomenon.

Looking at the measured detail of Smirke's learned design or recalling the stern Greek buildings of Edinburgh, it seemed to Ruskin that the Greeks themselves had denied the humanity of art. Nor had his experience of Greek art other than architecture served to convince him otherwise. Such experience had, indeed, been limited. At this time Ruskin knew little of the sculpture, vases, or coins of the classical Greek period. Just as his concept of ancient Greek architecture was formed by buildings which were inspired by its revival in other ages, so his idea of Greek sculpture was largely restricted to the Hellenistic copies or Roman pieces then still commonly accepted as the best Greek work. In speaking of the lifeless 'polished limbs' of the Apollo Belvedere in the Vatican, Ruskin was speaking of a Roman copy of a Greek work now lost (iii. 118). He felt a similar lack of power in the sculpture which had become, through the writings of Winckelmann, almost a symbol of the Greek spirit—the Laocoön. But the tortured Laocoön is a late, Hellenistic work, far from typical of the serene sculpture of fifth-century Athens. Ruskin loathed it. 'I suppose that no group has exercised so pernicious an influence on art as this; a subject ill-chosen, meanly conceived, and unnaturally treated, recommended to imitation by subtleties of execution and accumulation of technical knowledge' (iv. 120). Here, Ruskin is comparing the Laocoön with the Theseus from the Elgin Marbles. These were among the very few examples of classical Greek work that he knew well. The Theseus earned his admiration and respect largely by virtue of its 'calmness'[7] (iv. 119). In the first draft of the second volume of *Modern Painters*, however, Ruskin had chosen to contrast the Laocoön with a Roman copy of another Hellenistic work—the Dying Gladiator of the Capitoline Museum in Rome.[8] Far better preserved than the Theseus, and far more naturalistically finished, this later statue seemed to Ruskin to express a similar quality of repose: 'The dying gladiator—though the statue of a vanquished slave—a mere victim of some butcher of the arena—is yet noble and exalted in its whole tone and character, for the very reason—strange as it may appear—that in its numbing clasp the right hand has already forgotten its cunning, and death has stamped upon the seared and disgraced brow the nobility of its repose' (iv. 119 n.). Ruskin is pleased by the Dying Gladiator largely because of its expressive realism, a realism which he saw in more restrained form in the Elgin Marbles. The Greek vases and coins which he knew at this time must have seemed to him, in contrast, thin and stereotyped. Though he was later to develop a keen interest in this art, he never considered it to be beautiful. He was to be concerned with the moral symbolism that he came to see in its mythological iconography. But in the 1840s and early 1850s, the mythological faith of the Greeks seemed to him the most vicious element in their culture, and this above all prevented him from looking sympathetically at their art.

Ruskin continued to see disparagement of the Greeks as part of his duty as a Christian writer. He was forthright in his condemnation of their beliefs. In the first volume of *The Stones of Venice*, he argued that the moral and artistic

---

[7] The piece is now thought to represent Dionysus.
[8] This piece is also known as the Dying Trumpeter or the Dying Gaul.

collapse that he perceived in the Renaissance was at least partly due to the loss of the vital Christianity that had inspired the achievement of Gothic architecture. This decay seemed to him revealed in the resuscitation of the dead forms of paganism. The Renaissance is characterized by

a return to pagan systems, not to adopt them and hallow them for Christianity, but to rank itself under them as imitator and pupil. . . . Instant degradation followed in every direction,—a flood of folly and hypocrisy. Mythologies ill understood at first, then perverted into feeble sensualities, take the place of the representations of Christian subjects, which had become blasphemous under the treatment of men like the Caracci. Gods without power, satyrs without rusticity, nymphs without innocence, men without humanity, gather into idiot groups upon the polluted canvas, and scenic affectations encumber the streets with preposterous marble. . . . And thus, Christianity and morality, courage, and intellect, and art all crumbling together in one wreck, we are hurried on to the fall of Italy, the revolution in France, and the condition of art in England (saved by her Protestantism from severer penalty) in the time of George II. (ix. 45)

Implied in this passage is the idea that, though the 'pagan systems' are inherently of a lower order than Christianity, it is in their corruption that the real evil lies. Ruskin makes this distinction more explicit in the second volume of *The Stones of Venice*, published in 1853:

For there is a wider division of men than that into Christian and Pagan: before we ask what a man worships, we have to ask whether he worships at all. Observe Christ's own words on this head: 'God is a spirit and they that worship Him must worship Him in spirit, *and* in Truth.' The worshipping in spirit comes first, and it does not necessarily imply the worshipping in truth. Therefore, there is first the broad division of men into Spirit worshippers and Flesh worshippers; and then, of the Spirit worshippers, the farther division into Christian and Pagan,—worshippers in Falsehood or in Truth. (x. 67)

Here, the word 'pagan' in part means 'Catholic'; Ruskin has Mariolatry rather than Greek mythology in mind. Whether modern-day Catholic or ancient Greek, the pagan is a worshipper 'in Falsehood'. Yet Ruskin admits that he is to be preferred to the entirely godless man. The unbelievers of the

Renaissance were, however, to be reviled as worshippers in neither spirit nor truth. They are, in Ruskin's uncompromising phrase, 'Flesh worshippers'.

His analysis of the second fall from grace produced by their infidelity is the product of a vigorously Protestant point of view. The third volume of *The Stones of Venice*, which followed the second in 1853, is simply entitled 'The Fall'. Ruskin wrote no other book so hostile towards Greek culture. It contains his most severe denunciation of the revival of classical mythology, and, by implication, of the mythology itself. The renewed study of classical writers at the time of the Renaissance necessarily involved a corresponding falling away in the study of Christian religion, for

what was heartily admired and increasingly contemplated was soon brought nigh to being believed; and the systems of Pagan mythology began gradually to assume the places in the human mind from which the unwatched Christianity was wasting. Men did not indeed openly sacrifice to Jupiter, or build silver shrines for Diana, but the ideas of Paganism nevertheless became thoroughly vital and present with them at all times; and it did not matter in the least, as far as respected the power of true religion, whether the Pagan image was believed in or not, so long as it entirely occupied the thoughts. The scholar of the sixteenth century, if he saw the lightning shining from the east into the west, thought forthwith of Jupiter, not of the coming of the Son of Man; if he saw the moon walking in brightness, he thought of Diana, not of the throne which was to be established for ever as a faithful witness in heaven; and though his heart was but secretly enticed, yet thus he denied the God that is above. (xi. 129)

Ruskin's position here is intransigently partisan. But his perception is acute. He was right to see conflict between pagan and Christian ideals in the Renaissance. In 1853, however, he saw the tension in terms of a simple pattern of antagonism that he was later to reject. His censure of Renaissance worship inevitably suggested a similar contempt for their chosen idols. In this final volume of *The Stones of Venice*, the distinction that he had previously suggested between ancient religion as it had originally been practised, and its altered and degraded forms in later ages, is overwhelmed by his repudiation of both. 'The characters of the heathen divinities were as suitable to the manners of the time as their forms were agreeable to its taste; and Paganism again became, in effect, the religion of Europe' (xi. 131–2).

It now seemed to Ruskin that the study of classical literature and art had results that were comprehensively disastrous. In undermining the moral and religious fabric of the age, it destroyed its intellectual integrity. It led, he felt, to a concentration on the outward shell of things; on forms, systems, words. His denunciation is in part the result of mixed feelings about his own classical education, now ten years past. He argues that through 'this study of words, that of forms being added, both as of matters of first importance, half the intellect of the age was at once absorbed in the base sciences of grammar, logic, and rhetoric; studies utterly unworthy of the serious labour of men, and necessarily rendering those employed upon them incapable of high thoughts or noble emotion' (xi. 127–8). The 'base sciences of grammar, logic, and rhetoric' had formed Ruskin's education, as indeed they had shaped all higher education since the medieval foundation of the universities. It is in *The Stones of Venice* that Ruskin's condemnation of this system is most explicit. A classical education is deficient above all because it is not a Christian education; and what Ruskin saw as the evil of paganism had continued unchecked into his own age. He points out that

In the very institutions of which the administration may be considered as the principal test of the genuineness of national religion—those devoted to education—the Pagan system is completely triumphant; and the entire body of the so-called Christian world has established a system of education for its youth, wherein neither the history of Christ's Church, nor the language of God's law, is considered a study of the smallest importance; wherein, of all subjects of human inquiry, his own religion is the one in which a youth's ignorance is most easily forgiven; and in which it is held a light matter that he should be daily guilty of lying, of debauchery, or of blasphemy, so only that he write Latin verses accurately, and with speed. (xi. 133)

It is on Aristotle that Ruskin focuses his sharpest attack. His suspicion of Aristotle had always been strong. It had not previously been so public. His denunciation is now bold and unequivocal. He declares that 'it is impossible to overrate the mischief produced in former days, as well as in our own, by the mere habit of reading Aristotle, whose system is so false, so forced, and so confused, that the study of it at our universities is quite enough to occasion the utter want of accurate habits of thought, which so often disgraces men otherwise well-educated' (x. 373–4). This attack forms part of a passage in which Ruskin challenges the whole academic tradition on the grounds that it embodies a threat to Christianity. He describes the resulting tendency to 'throw all religion into forms and ciphers' (x. 359) as 'that root of the Renaissance poison-tree, which, of all others, is deepest struck; showing itself in various measures through the writings of all the Fathers, of course exactly in proportion to the respect which they paid to classical authors, especially to Plato, Aristotle, and Cicero' (x. 370). Aristotle and Cicero are singled out for especial blame. 'Plato, indeed, studied alone, would have done no one any harm. He is profoundly spiritual and capacious in all his views, and embraces the small systems of Aristotle and Cicero, as the solar system does the Earth' (x. 370). The grounds on which Ruskin chooses to praise Plato are revealing.

Plato is seen as the most valuable ancient philosopher because he is closest to the Christian spirit. Ruskin notes that Plato seems to him 'especially remarkable for the sense of the great Christian virtue of Holiness, or sanctification; and for the sense of the presence of the Deity in all things, great or small, which always runs in a solemn under-current beneath his exquisite playfulness and irony' (x. 370). He chooses the famous passage from *Alcibiades I* as a perfect expression of the ethical values of the ancient world. Socrates describes how a Persian king is educated by four tutors—the wisest, the bravest, the most just, and the most temperate of men.[9] However, Ruskin claims that reverence for this system has harmed the Christian Church. 'All this is exceedingly beautiful, so far as it reaches; but the Christian divines were grievously led astray by their endeavours to reconcile this system with the nobler law of love' (x. 372). In their attempt to preserve the 'pagan' order in the institution of four cardinal virtues—justice, prudence, temperance, and fortitude—by

---

[9] Plato, *Alcibiades I*, 121 E.

merely adding the three exclusively Christian or 'theological' virtues of faith, hope, and charity to complete the system, Ruskin felt that the early Christian theologians were 'productive of infinite confusion and error', partly because 'Faith is classed with its own fruits', and partly because the meaning of terms used to express the virtues by the ancients was confused with the meaning of these terms as they are used in the Bible (x. 372–4). Veneration of the classics, even of Ruskin's favourite Plato, is seen in *The Stones of Venice* both as a threat to Christianity and as a pursuit intellectually suspect in itself.

Ruskin's reaction against the Aristotelian system must in part be seen as a reaction against the character of his own early writings. Despite his declared distaste for Aristotle, Ruskin had been influenced by Aristotle's process of argument and logic, not merely as a source of authority or ideas, but more generally in methods of organization. Aristotle was not the only figure behind the orderly, point-by-point succession of themes which characterizes the first two volumes of *Modern Painters*. But Ruskin's approach to the task of logical analysis frequently showed a specifically Aristotelian tendency. In the first volume of *Modern Painters*, he begins to defend his claim that particular truths are more important than general premises with a reference to Aristotle: 'Now, if we are to begin our investigation in Aristotle's way, and look at the φαινόμενα of the subject' (iii. 149). Ruskin's instinct for beginning the study of a subject with an examination of its φαινόμενα or appearances is deep-rooted. In later works, however, the framework within which he does so loses its Aristotelian bias. Reproving early Christian thinkers for their emphasis on classical models in the second volume of *The Stones of Venice*, Ruskin indirectly expresses misgivings he had begun to feel over the form of his own early work:

And, indeed, the study of classical literature, in general, not only fostered in the Christian writers the unfortunate love of systematizing, which gradually degenerated into every species of contemptible formulism, but it accustomed them to work out their systems by the help of any logical quibble, or verbal subtlety, which could be made available for their purpose, and this not with any dishonest intention, but in a sincere desire to arrange their ideas in systematical groups, while yet their powers of thought were not accurate enough, nor their common sense stern enough, to detect the fallacy, or disdain the finesse, by which these arrangements were frequently accomplished. (x. 374–5)

The self-imposed restrictions of his early works had begun to chafe. An emancipation is demonstrated in the scheme of the third volume of *Modern Painters*, which appeared three years after the completion of *The Stones of Venice*, in 1856. The frank subtitle of this volume, 'Of Many Things', declares the relinquishment of the book's previously strict and methodical pattern of organization. Ruskin explains that he no longer intends

to pursue the inquiry in a method so laboriously systematic; for the subject may, it seems to me, be more usefully treated by pursuing the different questions which arise out of it just as they occur to us, without too great scrupulousness in marking connections, or insisting on sequences. Much time is wasted by human beings, in general, on establishment of systems; and it often takes more labour to master the intricacies of an artificial connection, than to remember the separate facts which are so carefully connected. (v. 18)

Ruskin had outgrown his first plans for *Modern Painters*. He had also begun to outgrow the attitude to the Greeks that had helped to form that work.

Ruskin's Revaluation of Greek Religion

The third volume of *Modern Painters* marks a turning-point in Ruskin's thinking about Greek culture. He now begins to make a consistent dissociation between the Greeks and the 'paganism' and false art of the neo-classical Renaissance. In particular, the volume contains an important preliminary attempt to formulate a new concept of Greek mythology. This undertaking is closely bound up with changes in Ruskin's own religious position. In 1877, Ruskin gave 1858 as the date of the crisis point in his movement away from the Evangelical convictions of his youth. A well-known passage from *Fors Clavigera* (1871–84) describes it as the result of attending a drab service in a Waldensian chapel and experiencing the 'God-given power' of Paul Veronese's painting on the same Sunday morning in Turin (xxix. 89). However, as often in recalling events from the vantage-point of age, Ruskin conveys a picture that is simpler and more dramatic than it is accurate. Speaking of the event in *Praeterita* (1885–9), he points out that the 'hour's meditation in the gallery of Turin only concluded the courses of thought which had been leading me to such end through many years' (xxxv. 496). Changed attitudes to Greek mythology in the third volume of *Modern Painters* reveal that Ruskin had in 1856 begun to question his formerly dogmatic condemnation of 'pagan' religion. In his chapter on classical landscape, he gives his first sympathetic consideration of the meaning of the mythological imagination of the Greeks. Three years after his assertion, in the third volume of *The Stones of Venice*, that the 'characters of the heathen divinities' made them especially suitable objects of worship in the corrupt years of the Renaissance, Ruskin denounces the 'bitter short-sightedness of Puritanism, holding the classical gods to be either simply an idol,—a block of stone ignorantly, though sincerely, worshipped—or else an actual diabolic or betraying power, usurping the place of God' (v. 233). This passage accompanies what amounts to an apology for Ruskin's own past confusion between genuine Greek religion and the distorted reflection that had its origins in the Renaissance:

We are so accustomed to the modern mockeries of the classical religion, so accustomed to hear and see the Greek gods introduced as living personages, or invoked for help, by men who believe neither in them nor in any other gods, that we seem to have infected the Greek ages themselves with the breath, and dimmed them with the shade, of our hypocrisy; and are apt to think that Homer, as we know that Pope, was merely an ingenious fabulist . . . (v. 223)

Ruskin's rejection of his own previous position is qualified. The Puritan attitudes he denounces for their 'bitter short-sightedness' are also described as 'to some extent true. The corruption of classical worship is barren idolatry; and that corruption was deepened, and variously directed to their own purposes, by the evil angels' (v. 223). But the distinction between original Greek worship and its perversion in later centuries is now clear.

In the second volume of *Modern Painters*, Ruskin had defined and condemned Greek mythology as the product of an essentially materialistic religion. 'The Greek could not conceive a spirit; he could do nothing without limbs; his God is a finite God, talking, pursuing, and going journeys' (iv. 329). Only in the field of battle might the Greek be touched with a true spirituality; and even then, in only a limited sense, for 'what were the Greek's thoughts of his God of Battle? No spirit power was in the vision; it was a being of clay strength, and human passion, foul, fierce, and changeful; of penetrable arms, and vulnerable flesh' (iv. 330). In a deprecatory note of 1883, Ruskin points out that the 'false bias' of this passage is corrected by *The Queen of the Air* (1869) (iv. 330 n.). But he had already moved a long way from such a position in 1856. 'Mythic' remains a derogatory term when used in the context of a painting by Raphael: 'It is all a mere mythic absurdity, and faded concoction of fringes, muscular arms, and curly heads of Greek philosophers' (v. 82). In the context of classical Greek culture, however, mythology has become a religious phenomenon demanding careful and respectful consideration. Having lost at least part of the support of his early and more rigid faith, Ruskin had begun to think that other religions may have had access to moral and spiritual truths.

Yet there is a continuity in Ruskin's interpretation of Greek myths. He had always seen a fundamental materialism in Greek mythology. What he had at first deplored now came to attract him. Ruskin saw that the Greek conception of a god is firmly founded on the physical world. Mythology, like the art of Turner, or indeed his own art as a writer, might provide a means of expressing the relation between man, nature, and the divine. In *The Stones of Venice*, he had condemned Greek art as irreligious, inhuman, and unnatural. But a Greek god had now come to seem nothing less than the embodiment in human form of the divine power in a natural element. In 'Of Classical Landscape', he points out that an understanding of the Greek mind depends upon a realization of

the tangible existence of its deities;—blue-eyed—white-fleshed—
human-hearted,—capable at their choice of meeting man absolutely
in his own nature—feasting with him—talking with him—fighting
with him, eye to eye, or breast to breast, as Mars with Diomed; or
else, dealing with him in a more refined spirituality, as Apollo
sending the plague upon the Greeks, when his quiver rattles at his
shoulders as he moves, and yet the darts sent forth of it strike not as
arrows, but as plague; or, finally, retiring completely into the
material universe which they properly inhabit, and dealing with
man through that, as Scamander with Achilles, through his waves.
(v. 227)

Ruskin's emphasis on the natural basis of Greek mythology
is unchanging. But he now suggests that the meaning of the
Greek gods was not less spiritual because their existence had a
material basis. Such a concept of divinity expressed an insight
that the modern world had lost—the sense of the universal
presence of God in the natural world. Greek mythology affirms
what Ruskin had been urging throughout *Modern Painters*.
Since first he began to write, Ruskin had been attempting to
imbue his readers with the 'instinctive sense that God was
everywhere' (v. 231). The realization that the Greeks possessed
this religious instinct to such a degree that they could not be
dismissed as in every way the moral inferiors of Christians is
the first basis of his revaluation.

Ruskin's conclusions in 'Of Classical Landscape' are largely
determined by his reading of Homer. Aware that his case
might seem to rest on insufficient foundation, he defends the
narrow range of his evidence on the grounds that Homer's art
is of sufficient stature to be representative of the Greek spirit
as a whole. 'And without doubt, in his influence over future
mankind, Homer is eminently the Greek of Greeks' (v. 245).
In this representative character, Homer was for Ruskin comparable to Dante and Sir Walter Scott. Ruskin claims that in
studying these three figures alone an accurate impression of
the Greek, medieval, and modern ages may be achieved. 'But
I believe the true mind of a nation, at any period, is always
best ascertainable by examining that of its greatest men; and
that simpler and truer results will be attainable for us by
simply comparing Homer, Dante, and Walter Scott than by

attempting . . . an analysis of the landscape in the range of contemporary literature' (v. 244). In believing history to be most faithfully reflected in its great men, Ruskin shared in a contemporary fashion and showed his debt to Carlyle. The taste for Homer, particularly, had grown widespread in the first half of the nineteenth century. Martial and stoical, adventurous and authoritarian, Homer seemed to many an expression of the age. The vogue for Homer has complex origins and may be seen as a Romantic rather than Victorian phenomenon. But the Victorians had incorporated Romantic enthusiasm into institution and establishment. In his *Homer and the Homeric Age* (1858), W. E. Gladstone suggests the university reforms at Oxford as a reason for increased interest in Homer. Gladstone, an eager advocate of a Homeric slant in classical education, notes with satisfaction the result of specifying Homer as an author required in the first public examination in classics. 'When, however, the University of Oxford brought to maturity, in the year 1850, a new Statute of examinations, efforts were made to promote an extended study of Homer. Those efforts, it happily appears, have produced a considerable effect.'[10] Gladstone may be confusing cause with effect. The popularity of Homer had been established long before Oxford had incorporated it into its statutes. In his essay 'On Translating Homer' (1861), Matthew Arnold felt that he could take the supreme position of Homer for granted: 'The study of classical literature is probably on the decline; but, whatever may be the fate of this study in general, it is certain that, as instruction spreads and the number of readers increases, attention will be more and more directed to the poetry of Homer, not indeed as part of a classical course, but as the most important poetical monument existing.'[11] The selection of Homer as the central voice in Greek literature seemed less strange in 1856 than it would today.

Peculiarly personal circumstances, however, had more to do with Ruskin's choice of Homer than contemporary fashion. Homer, like Sir Walter Scott, had been a childhood favourite.

[10] W. E. Gladstone, *Studies on Homer and the Homeric Age*, 3 vols. (Oxford, 1858), i. 11.
[11] *The Complete Prose Works of Matthew Arnold*, ed. R. H. Super, 11 vols. (Ann Arbor, 1960–77), i. 97.

Ruskin's Scottish ancestry made it easy for him to associate himself with Sir Walter Scott. He extended this association to Homer, oddly suggesting something approaching a Scottish identity for the Greek poet. Such a link is implied in a passage intended for *Fors Clavigera*:

It has curiously happened to me also to have been educated in many particulars under the same conditions as Scott, and often in the same places. My father was a High School lad of Edinburgh; the first picture I ever saw with conscious eyes was of Edinburgh Castle; the earliest patriotic delight I can remember in my life, distinctly, is the delight of crossing the Tweed into Scotland; and I was educated —to all intents and purposes—by my Puritan mother and aunt, first by thorough training in the Bible, secondly by being let loose into Homer and Scott. (xxix. 539)

Homer and Scott are connected in Ruskin's mind, each as the voice of an ideally ordered society and as his own spiritual ancestor. So, to take a familiar instance, they appear in the opening sentences of *Praeterita*: 'I am, and my father was before me, a violent Tory of the old school;—Walter Scott's school, that is to say, and Homer's. I name these two out of the numberless great Tory writers, because they were my own masters' (xxxv. 13). Ruskin's childhood reading of Homer made him feel especially attracted towards a Homeric ideal. The association between this Homeric ideal and its Scottish counterpart is marked in the comparison that he makes, in concluding his analysis of classical landscape, between the Greek mind as it is expressed in Homer, and

that of a good, conscientious, but illiterate Scotch Presbyterian Border farmer of a century or two back, having perfect faith in the bodily appearances of Satan and his imps; and in all kelpies, brownies, and fairies. Substitute for the indignant terrors in this man's mind, a general persuasion of the *Divinity*, more or less beneficent, yet faultful, of all these beings; that is to say, take away his belief in the demoniacal malignity of the fallen spiritual world, and lower, in the same degree, his conceptions of the angelic, retaining for him the same firm faith in both, . . . and I think we shall get a pretty close approximation to the vital being of a true old Greek . . . (v. 245–8)

Ruskin links the Border farmer and the 'true old Greek' first in terms of their religion. He may have acquired his belief that the Borderer, unlike the Greek, would have seen spiritual beings other than angels as creatures of evil from the stories of his mother, or his old nurse, Anne Strachan. A more literary source might be seen in Walter Scott's essay on fairies, published in his *Minstrelsy of the Scottish Border* (1802) as an introduction to the Tale of Tamlane, a ballad of the supernatural. Scott points out that the Christian religion

admits only of two classes of spirits, exclusive of the souls of men—angels, namely, and devils. This doctrine had a necessary tendency to abolish the distinction among subordinate spirits, which had been introduced by the Scandinavians. The existence of the fairies was readily admitted, but as they had no pretensions to the angelic power, they were deemed to be of infernal origin. The union, also, which had been framed betwixt the elves and the Pagan deities was probably of disservice to the former; since every one knows that the whole synod of Olympus were accounted demons. [12]

The specific connection between Scottish superstition and classical religion, hinted at above, is made explicit elsewhere in Scott's essay:

Greece and Rome had not only assigned tutelary deities to each province and city, but had peopled with peculiar spirits, the seas, the rivers, the woods, and the mountains. The memory of the pagan creed was not speedily eradicated, in the extensive provinces through which it was once universally received; and in many particulars, it continued long to mingle with, and influence, the original superstitions of the Gothic nations. [13]

Ruskin compares the appearance of the river-god Scamander in the *Iliad* with the voice of the river-spirit in Scott's *The Lay of the Last Minstrel*, [14] claiming that Scott's river-spirit 'is accurately the Homeric god, only Homer would have believed in it,—Scott did not: at least not altogether' (v. 225 n.). Scott differs from Homer in his approach to the natural world only in what Ruskin considered to be a taint of modern infidelity. Yet Ruskin asserts elsewhere in the third volume of *Modern Painters* that Scott was 'entirely incapable of entering into the

---

[12] Sir Walter Scott, *Minstrelsy of the Scottish Border*, 2 vols. (London and Edinburgh, 1802), ii. 200–1.

[13] Ibid. 188.

[14] *The Poetical Works of Sir Walter Scott*, ed. J. Logie Robertson (Oxford, 1904), 5.

spirit of any classical scene' (v. 391). What may be described as 'classical' in the traditional sense has now for Ruskin little connection with what is of value in the Greek world. The association between the Greek and the Scot is one of the ways in which Ruskin succeeded in detaching his concept of the Greeks from the impersonal classicism and unimaginative scholarship that he had experienced at Oxford.

The relation in Ruskin's mind between the ideal Greece to be seen in Homer and the ideal Scotland represented by Sir Walter Scott may have been furthered by his friendship with John Stuart Blackie, who became Professor of Greek at Edinburgh in 1852. There existed a long tradition of hostility between the universities of Oxford and Edinburgh, and academics at Edinburgh had long been scornful of the approach to classical scholarship at Oxford. Sir William Hamilton's attacks on Oxford in the *Edinburgh Review* of the 1830s had been influential.[15] Blackie's own views on education, vigorously opposed to a pedantically exclusive study of the classics at the expense of natural history, are in accordance with those of Ruskin. In 1848 Blackie published a pamphlet on the subject of university reform which would have found a sympathetic reader in Ruskin:

In the two largest, most celebrated, and best frequented Universities of Scotland, while Greek grammars and Latin dictionaries are worked through and through with mole-like assiduity, the academical eye is altogether blind to the multifarious luxuriance and the teeming wealth of God's glorious outer world. This grand living panorama of things *may* be looked at, in passing, if the boy, or his guardian, takes the whim; the Latin grammar *must* be studied whether the boy will or not, and a host of mute pedants must be crammed periodically—for what purpose it is hard to see—with the sounding sentences of Cicero. So true is it that the perverse principles of Oxford, however in argument denied, are only too frequently affirmed by the educational practice of Scotland.[16]

Blackie believed that Greek could not properly be studied as a dead language. In his introductory lecture as Professor of

[15] Ruskin met this energetic campaigner against the Oxford education while he was in Edinburgh in 1853. See vol. xii, p. xxxv. If they discussed university reform, they must have found common ground.

[16] John Stuart Blackie, *University Reform: Eight Articles Reprinted from the Scotsman Newspaper; with a Letter to Professor Pillans* (Edinburgh, 1848), 44.

Greek at Edinburgh, he suggests that the close relationship between classical Greek and the language of modern Greece could provide the means for young students to approach Greek as a living tongue. They should read modern Greek literature or newspapers, or travel to Greece.[17] The idea must have been refreshing for those who had undergone the toilsome process of a conventional classical education. It seemed so to Ruskin, and he wrote to the Professor to express his appreciation:

I can't tell you how much delighted I am with your lecture*—and how happy in the idea of the Greek being come alive again. I shall even join in any triumphal processions proposed round *new Parthenons* if ever I am in Greece at the time of their creation . . .

   * I most heartily admire and agree with every word of your lecture—and consider myself to have been first taught *Greek* in Edinburgh.[18]

Ruskin sympathizes with Blackie's contempt for 'those sleek Hellenists on the banks of Cam and Isis'[19] in a letter of 31 December 1853. He refers again to the 'exceeding pleasure I had in hearing *Greek* tongue and Greek spirit examined by a *Living* man with a living temper—and not dealt with in the dim and dusty way I have been used to. You taught me more Greek in the little while I was with you than I learned at Oxford in three years.'[20] There is no evidence that Ruskin put into serious practice Professor Blackie's theories on the value of approaching classical literature through the medium of modern Greek, though he does write to his father of his delight in being given by Professor Blackie 'a Greek *newspaper*, about a week

---

[17] See John Stuart Blackie, *On the Living Language of the Greeks and its Utility to the Classical Scholar: An Introductory Lecture Delivered in the University of Edinburgh* (Edinburgh and London, 1853).

[18] Unpubl. letter, National Library of Scotland, Edinburgh, MS 2643, fo. 136. The letter is not dated, but its reference to Blackie's lecture suggests that it may have been written in 1853. Ruskin spent some time in Edinburgh during the summer of that year and delivered the *Lectures on Architecture and Painting* there in November 1853. I am most grateful to Tim Hilton for drawing my attention to the correspondence between Ruskin and Blackie.

[19] So described in Blackie's inaugural lecture of 1852. John Stuart Blackie, *Classical Literature in its Relation to the Nineteenth Century and Scottish University Education: An Inaugural Lecture Delivered in the University of Edinburgh* (Edinburgh and London, 1852), 23.

[20] Unpubl. letter, National Library of Scotland, Edinburgh, MS 2624, fo. 15 (31 Dec. 1853).

old, printed at Athens, and in good old Attic Greek hardly differing in a syllable from the language of Alcibiades, except in its subject-matter' (vol. xii. p. xxxv). His experience at Edinburgh seems to have hardened his rejection of the 'dim and dusty' way of looking at the Greeks that he had found at Oxford. It may have contributed to the rethinking of Greek civilization that we find in 'Of Classical Landscape'.

Greek mythology and Homer were both popular topics in scholarly circles during the 1850s. Ruskin characteristically makes no reference to the enormous proliferation of literature on these subjects, and it is difficult to measure the extent to which he was aware of it. Hostility towards the academic conventions of classical studies did not make him receptive to currents of contemporary research. He makes no mention of the active controversy over the 'Homeric question' in these years.[21] Ruskin would, however, have come into contact with standard works of reference on Homer. George Grote's major *History of Greece*, which made its first appearance in 1846, might seem an obvious source of material on Homer and Greek mythology. The first two volumes of Grote's *History* deal with Homer and with Greek religion in some detail. In later years Ruskin was to make his contempt for Grote as a 'vulgar materialist' public.[22] Though he may have used Grote's work, there is little to suggest that it could ever have been an important source for his views of Homeric religion. Grote, a liberal meliorist, sees little or no spiritual value in the myths of the Greeks. 'To us these now appear puerile, though pleasing fancies', he remarks of the myths of Apollo.[23] Describing the gradual decline of a literal belief in mythology, he comments that 'this change was the result of a silent alteration in the mental state of society,—of a trans-

---

[21] The debate as to whether Homer was one man or many began with Friedrich August Wolf's *Prolegomena ad Homeron* in 1795 and reached no conclusion during the century which followed.

[22] So described in a letter to Acland of the autumn of 1864. See vol. xvii, p. xxxiv. Twenty-two years later, Ruskin wrote to the *Pall Mall Gazette* to explain why he felt Grote's *History* ought to be removed from the list of the hundred best books prepared for the Working Men's College by Sir John Lubbock: 'Because there is probably no commercial establishment, between Charing Cross and the Bank, whose head clerk could not write a better one, if he had the vanity to waste his time on it' (xxxiv. 586). The letter is dated February 1886.

[23] George Grote, *A History of Greece*, 8 vols. (London, 1846–56), i. 465–6.

ition on the part of superior minds (and more or less on the part of all) to a stricter and more elevated canon of credibility, in consequence of familiarity with recorded history and its essential tests. . . . To us these mythes are interesting fictions.'[24] Grote claims a radical difference between myth and history. This premiss was essential to Ruskin's argument. But in interpreting Greek myths as no more than 'interesting fictions', Grote was typical of the modern tendency to 'think that Homer, as we know that Pope, was merely an ingenious fabulist'[25] (v. 223). Ruskin held such condescension in contempt. Grote's reductive analysis of mythology suggests that, if Ruskin used him as a source of information, it can have been with little pleasure.

Other works of scholarly research published during the 1840s and 1850s might seem to parallel Ruskin's position more closely. In Carl Otfried Müller's great *Ancient Art and its Remains*, translated in 1847, we find a definition of Greek religion which is close to Ruskin's views in 1856: 'A religion in which the life of deity is blended with that which exists in nature and finds its consummation in man'.[26] The idea of a religion based on spontaneous reverence of nature and personification of its phenomena in the ancient world had, however, become a commonplace which Ruskin might have encountered in countless texts. An anonymous article on 'The Principles of the Grecian Mythology: Or, How the Greeks Made their Gods', which appeared in *Fraser's Magazine* in January 1854, serves to suggest the extent to which the idea of a physical basis in Greek religion had become conventional in the 1850s. The author expects his readers to be acquainted with current theories of mythology: 'It may be assumed that most persons are familiar with what is meant by the mythical or mythopoeic stage of a nation's mental progress. It is that stage in which the concrete or poetical mode of thought prevails universally over the abstract or scientific; . . . The essential characteristic of this mode of thought is the habit of *personification*.'[27] He goes on to describe the natural world

24 Ibid. i. 479–81.   25 See above, p. 28.
26 Carl Otfried Müller, *Ancient Art and its Remains: Or a Manual of the Archaeology of Art*, trans. John Leitch (London, 1847), 11.
27 'The Principle of the Grecian Mythology: Or, How the Greeks Made their Gods', *Fraser's Magazine*, 49 (Jan. 1854), 71.

as the first inspiration of the deifying instinct of the ancient Greeks. At first all nature seemed divine. Later only the more powerful natural phenomena survived as gods in the Greek imagination: 'The sun, the earth, the sea, the winds, the thunder—long after the minuter objects and substances which constitute the larger part in the filling up of nature had been killed down to impersonality, these mightier bulks and agencies would necessarily survive in all the pomp of will and intelligence.'[28] The article suggests that contemporary interest in mythology was not limited to that of the Greeks. The question of comparative mythology, soon to become of controversial importance, was already topical: 'A comparison of the mythologies of different nations would serve a double purpose—it would give a clearer insight into the mythical process in general and it would reveal, in a more vivid way than any other species of investigation, the characteristic differences of those separate masses of the human family by whose activity, contemporaneously or successively, the historic evolution has been conducted.'[29] Friedrich Max Müller's seminal essay on comparative mythology, which was to have an appreciable influence on Ruskin's own thinking about Greek mythology, appeared in April 1856, four months after the publication of the third volume of *Modern Painters*.

As we have seen, Ruskin had emphasized the close relation between Greek mythology and the natural world as early as 1844. Neither he nor his readers would have seen innovation in his continuing to stress the connection between Greek gods and natural phenomena in 'Of Classical Landscape'. Many of the ideas about the Greeks which Ruskin works out in the third volume of *Modern Painters* had, in fact, occurred to him years before. His diary for the years 1847–8 records a comment on the Homeric epithet—'note these passionless epithets having nothing to do with the feeling of the utterer'[30] —that foreshadows his analysis of such an epithet in his chapter on 'The Pathetic Fallacy'. Commenting on Homeric similes in the same volume of his diary, Ruskin records his admiration for the passage in the *Odyssey* which describes

[28] Art. cit., *Fraser's Magazine*, 49 (Jan. 1854), 75.
[29] Ibid. 72.
[30] Bodl. MS Eng. Misc. c. 214, fo. 99. See v. 213.

Ulysses covering himself with fallen leaves for protection against the night's cold: 'Ulysses wrapt up in the leaves like fire among the ashes is again fine.'[31] Ruskin returned to this image as a representative illustration of Homeric landscape. In 'Of Classical Landscape', he picks on the image of the fiery strength and heroism of Ulysses 'lulled under the brown dead heap, as embers under ashes' (v. 241) as an example of the way in which Homer's feeling about landscape is concentrated on its relation to the human rather than on its beauty. 'The wreathed wood is admired simply as being a perfect roof for it; the fallen leaves only as being a perfect bed for it; and there is literally no more excitement of emotion in Homer, as he describes them, nor does he expect us to be more excited or touched by hearing about them, than if he had been telling us how the chambermaid at the Bull aired the four-poster, and put on two extra blankets' (v. 241). Ruskin now implies admiration for this passionless, utilitarian attitude to nature at least in so far as it avoids the emotionalism and 'cloudiness' of modern ideas about landscape;[32] though he had previously condemned the Greeks for their tendency to appreciate only the practical beneficence of nature. His perception about the Greek's matter-of-fact feeling about nature has not changed; his interpretation could hardly be more different.

What is remarkable in Ruskin's analysis in 'Of Classical Landscape' does not derive from contemporary scholarship, or from a wider reading in the Greeks, but from a new readiness to admit value in characteristics of Greek culture that he had perceived long before. No longer prejudiced by adverse associations between the Greeks and disappointing experiences in his education, or by the conviction that they were the enemies of faith, Ruskin was now willing to see a direct relation between Greek culture and his own beliefs. The Greeks were not, after all, either 'classical' or 'pagan'. In the close relationship between their religion and the natural world, they were in possession of a spiritual instinct that Ruskin hoped to revive in a materialistic age. An enlarged concept of

---

[31] Bodl. MS Eng. Misc. c. 214, fo. 108. See Homer, *Odyssey*, v. 481–90.

[32] Ruskin turns to the Greeks to confirm his view, quoting Aristophanes' description of clouds as 'mistresses of disputings, and logic, and monstrosities, and noisy chattering' (v. 318). See Aristophanes, *Clouds*, 317–18.

religion suggested that Greek mythology, like the paintings of Turner, had expressed the divine revelation of nature.

Turner's Mythological Art

Three events combined to intensify Ruskin's interest in myth in the years immediately following the publication of the third and fourth volumes of *Modern Painters* in 1856. The first was the appearance of Max Müller's essay on comparative mythology in 1856. Secondly came Ruskin's renewed experience of Turner in 1857 and 1858. The third event was a crisis in Ruskin's religious thought. In the final volume of *Modern Painters*, published in June 1860, Ruskin's interpretation of Greek mythology begins to take new forms.

Ruskin's approach was given a wider perspective by the theories of Max Müller. In the third volume of *Modern Painters*, he had focused on the nature of Homeric divinities. Now, like Müller, he deals with myths associated with the gods, rather than the gods themselves, no longer limiting himself to Homeric material. The etymological slant of his allegorical method of analysis also suggests the influence of Müller, who had used philological evidence to trace a common root in mythological traditions. Ruskin and Müller agree in finding an association between natural phenomena and mythology. Müller, however, argued the origins of all myths to have been 'almost always solar'.[33] In the fifth volume of *Modern Painters*, Ruskin does perceive solar influence in mythic tradition in a way that may have been suggested by Müller. He sees, for instance, the myth of Danaë enclosed in a brass tower as 'only another expression for the cumulus or Medusa cloud; and the golden rain for the rays of the sun striking it' (vii. 185). But Ruskin did not wholly accept the German scholar's position.

Müller, eager to establish the pre-eminence of the sun as the inspiration of all mythology, had counselled his readers not to connect myths 'too exclusively with the fleeting phenomena of clouds, and storms, and thunder'.[34] Ruskin, with

[33] Friedrich Max Müller, 'Comparative Mythology', in *Oxford Essays: Contributed by Members of the University* (London, 1856), 87.
[34] Ibid.

no such case to prove, in fact gives most of his attention to cloud, storm, wind, and rain in his interpretation of myth. In analysing the myth of Danaë, he associates the birth of Perseus with a cycle of storm-legends connected with the hero's slaying of Medusa. He sees the Gorgons as storm-clouds, and Medusa as 'essentially the highest storm-cloud; therefore the hail-cloud or cloud of cold, her countenance turning all who behold it to stone' (vii. 184). Ruskin points out that Acrisius, the father of Danaë, is killed by a gust of wind that accidentally carries Perseus' discus against his head, and suggests this as a further link between the wind and storm of the Medusa legend and the myth of Perseus' birth.[35] Nor do the associations with storm end with the death of Medusa. When Perseus has killed the monster, the offspring that rise from her blood are storm-deities—Chrysaor, whose name means 'golden sword' and whom Ruskin identifies with the lightning, and Pegasus, 'the fastest flying or lower rain-cloud; winged, but racing as upon the earth' (vii. 185). Ruskin sees storm, not sun, as the natural phenomenon under-lying the complex cycle of myths which surrounds Perseus and Medusa.

Ruskin shows an awareness of Müller's methods in an attempt to use etymological grounds to associate this theme of storm and rain with other myths. Yet he continues to claim such an association without discovering a satisfactory etymo-logical basis for it. He links the myth of Danaë, mother of Perseus, with the story of Danaüs, who was made king of Argos in return for bringing water to the land, though he finds no evidence in etymology for such a link:

we have not only this rain of Danaë's to remember in connection with the Gorgon, but that also of the sieves of the Danaïdes, said to represent the provision of Argos with water by their father Danaüs, who dug wells about the Acropolis; nor only wells, but opened, I doubt not, channels of irrigation for the fields, because the Danaïdes are said to have brought the mysteries of Ceres from Egypt. And though I cannot trace the root of the names Danaüs and Danaë, there is assuredly some farther link of connection in the

---

[35] See Hyginus, *Fabulae*, 63. This was the fulfilment of the prophecy that Acrisius would be killed by Danaë's son. Acrisius had shut Danaë in the brass tower in an attempt to avoid his fate.

deaths of the lovers of the Danaïdes, whom they slew, as Perseus Medusa.[36] (vii. 185)

Etymology might provide peripheral evidence, but is not at the centre of Ruskin's argument.

Ruskin's acceptance of solar or etymological methods of interpreting myth was qualified. But this was not the most important way in which he differed from Müller. Müller's essay on comparative mythology attempts to suggest a common basis for the different mythological traditions of the world. The full development of his famous theory that all mythology is no more than a 'disease of language' did not come until 1861, when the first series of his *Lectures on Language* was published. This curious idea is, however, already present in his first essay on comparative mythology. Müller sees little value in Greek myths:

Although later poets may have given to some of these fables a charm of beauty, and led us to accept them as imaginative compositions, it is impossible to conceal the fact that, taken by themselves, and in their literal meaning, most of these ancient mythes are absurd and irrational, and frequently opposed to the principles of thought, religion and morality which guided the Greeks as soon as they appear to us in the twilight of traditional history. By whom, then, were these stories invented?—stories, we must say at once, identical in form and character, whether we find them on Indian, Persian, Greek, Italian, Slavonic, or Teutonic soil. Was there a period of temporary insanity, through which the human mind had to pass, and was it a madness identically the same in the south of India and in the north of Iceland?[37]

Ruskin shows little interest in comparing the origins of different national mythologies. To suggest that the myths of the Greeks were opposed to their 'principles of thought, religion and morality' could hardly be further from his own position. The rain, cloud, and storm which he discerned in the Medusa cycle of myths were in his view the agents of a powerful moral force. His analysis of the Medusa myth is inspired by his belief that the 'renovating and purifying work'

---

[36] Ruskin's editors suggest δανός, meaning burnt or parched, as a common root. According to Appollodorus, Acrisius, the father of Danaë, was the great grandson of Danaüs. Appollodorus, *The Library*, II. ii. 1.

[37] F. M. Müller, 'Comparative Mythology', p. 7.

(vii. 178) done by rain, the 'Angel of the Sea', led to the superiority of the forest and mountain peoples of the North over the peoples of the Southern tropical jungles. The beauty of the storm-cloud, with its 'strange golden lights and purple flushes before the morning rain' (viii. 181), is a reminder of God's beneficence; its violence and terror teach the certainty of his judgement. The Greeks recognized the moral vitality of cloud. Their cloud-myths, far from being at variance from their thought and religion, are an expression of reverence for the spiritual guidance of nature. Indeed, this teaching can be seen as the foundation of their art. Pegasus, the fast-flying rain-cloud, produced the fountain of poetic inspiration, the Hippocrene, with a stroke of his foot. Such acknowledgement seemed to Ruskin an appropriate model for his English readers:

> Wherein we may find, I think, sufficient cause for putting honour upon the rain-cloud. Few of us, perhaps, have thought, in watching its career across our own mossy hills, or listening to the murmur of the springs amidst the mountain quietness, that the chief masters of the human imagination owed, and confessed they owed, the force of their noblest thoughts, not to the flowers of the valley, nor the majesty of the hill, but to the flying cloud. (vii. 186)

The Greek myth may be more relevant to the English than to the people who created it; for 'they never saw it fly, as we may in our own England. So far, at least, as I know the clouds of the south, they are often more terrible than ours, but the English Pegasus is swifter' (vii. 186). What for Müller are merely 'extraordinary stories of gods and heroes,—of gorgons and chimaeras,—of things that no human eye had ever seen, and that no human mind in a healthy state could ever have conceived'[38] are now for Ruskin a source of wisdom for England in the nineteenth century as they had been for the golden age of Athens. No longer heathen or academic in his eyes, Greek mythology seemed to represent the divine made manifest in the natural world.

Ruskin illustrates this chapter on the Angel of the Sea with an engraving of the advancing rain-cloud from Turner's *Slaver Throwing Overboard the Dead and Dying: Typhoon*

[38] Ibid. 33.

Coming on. In the preface to the final volume of *Modern Painters*, Ruskin describes how he had renewed and extended his experience of the painter who had first inspired his work. He had spent months sorting and arranging more than nineteen thousand Turner drawings in the National Gallery.[39] Now, for the first time, he associates Turner with the Greeks. Ruskin had previously regretted anything that might be termed 'classical' in Turner's art; believing, as he declared in the second volume of *Modern Painters* (1846), 'that there is not only deficiency, but such difference in kind as must make all Greek conception full of danger to the student in proportion to his admiration of it' (iv. 328–9). Even in 1856 Ruskin had seen the Greeks as a distorting influence on Turner's art. Speaking of Turner's teachers in the third volume of *Modern Painters*, Ruskin asserts that he is not 'able to conceive what would have been the result, if his aims had been made at once narrower and more natural, and he had been led in his youth to delight in Gothic legends instead of classical mythology; and, instead of the porticoes of the Parthenon, had studied in the aisles of Notre Dame'[40] (v. 392). By 1860 Ruskin felt that Greek mythology shared Turner's power of uniting natural and moral truth. Turner's greatness derived from an understanding of the moral lessons of nature, an understanding to be compared with that which the Greeks showed in their myths. He was Greek in that cloud, wind, and storm were more than weather to him. Such wisdom was not to be gained from formal study. Ruskin assures his readers that in various byways Turner

had gained a knowledge of most of the great Greek traditions, and that he felt them more than he knew them; his mind being affected, up to a certain point, precisely as an ancient painter's would have been, by external phenomena of nature. To him, as to the Greek,

[39] On the death of Turner on 19 Dec. 1851, Ruskin had been appointed executor of his will. He renounced his executorship, but undertook the work of examining and arranging the works which Turner had bequeathed to the nation. The task began in Oct. 1857 and was completed in May 1858.

[40] Turner had in fact studied Gothic architecture in his youth. Ruskin admits his mistake in the fifth volume of *Modern Painters*. See vii. 390 n. This may well have been something that he learned in the course of his work on Turner's drawings in 1857–8.

the storm-clouds seemed messengers of fate. He feared them, while he reverenced; nor does he ever introduce them without some hidden purpose, bearing upon the expression of the scene he is painting. (vii. 189)

The Greek myths had expressed the ambiguity of meaning in the rain-cloud, which represents both God's blessing and his judgement, by balancing such images as the terror of Medusa against Pegasus' rapturous flight. Ruskin describes how Turner expresses the same double truth in his water-colour drawings of Salisbury and Stonehenge. The picture of Salisbury is dominated by its Christian cathedral. Rain is falling, but it is 'the rain of blessing—abundant, but full of brightness; golden gleams are flying across the wet grass, and fall softly on the lines of willows in the valley—willows by the water-courses; the little brooks flash out here and there between them and the fields' (vii. 190). The drawing of Stonehenge pictures the contrasting storm of judgement. The Christian cathedral is replaced by the great Druidical monument: 'That, also, stands in great light; but it is the Gorgon light— the sword of Chrysaor is bared against it. The cloud of judgement hangs above. The rock pillars seem to reel before its slope, pale beneath the lightning. And nearer, in the darkness, the shepherd lies dead, his flock scattered' (vii. 190–1). Ruskin had begun *Modern Painters* with the claim that Turner's art possessed the ability to express the Christian morality in nature. Seventeen years later, he attributed the same faculty to Greek mythology and used the religious imagery of the Greeks to demonstrate the Christian message of Turner.

Ruskin returns to the relation between Greek myths and Turner's art in his analysis of *The Goddess of Discord Choosing the Apple of Contention in the Garden of the Hesperides*—a subject he had formerly despised for its classicism. This painting now seemed to him the culmination of Turner's early period, and his discussion is detailed. It is prefaced with an examination of the myth which had inspired the painting: 'The fable of the Hesperides had, it seems to me, in the Greek mind two distinct meanings; the first referring to natural phenomena, and the second to moral' (vii. 392).

Ruskin argues that the winds, rather than the sun, had shaped the physical meaning of the myth:

The nymphs of the west, or Hesperides, are, therefore, I believe, as natural types, the representatives of the soft western winds and sunshine, which were in this district most favourable to vegetation. In this sense they are called daughters of Atlas and Hesperis, the western winds being cooled by the snow of Atlas. The dragon, on the contrary, is the representative of the Sahara wind, or Simoom, which blew over the garden from above the hills on the south, and forbade all advance of cultivation beyond their ridge. (vii. 392–3)

Ruskin finds such a natural meaning in the painting of the well-watered garden, with the dragon watching from the cliff 'wrapped in flame and whirlwind' (vii. 393). It is not, however, what fascinated him. In myth, as in nature and in art, his concern is to define a hidden moral text. He maintains that 'both in the Greek mind and in Turner's, this natural meaning of the legend was a completely subordinate one. The moral significance of it lay far deeper' (vii. 393). It is in this second and more important moral meaning that Ruskin makes the association that would have seemed to Max Müller the obvious inspiration of the myth—its connection with the sunset. But for Ruskin, this setting sun does not represent the 'tragedy of nature' that haunted Max Müller.[41] As a natural and moral phenomenon, it suggests the brightness of hope; 'a light in the midst of a cloud' (vii. 393). The golden apples of the Hesperides typify earthly wealth, and Juno has placed two kinds of guard on them. We see the first in the nymphs of the Hesperides, who embody domestic order, brightness, and peace. The second guard is represented by the Dragon of the Hesperides. Ruskin devotes the larger part of his mythological analysis of Turner's picture to this more sinister keeper.

Ruskin connects the physical dimension of the dragon's significance with the complex of storm-myths that he had examined in 'The Angel of the Sea'. All clouds and storms belong to the same family, with Phorcys and Ceto as their parents. 'Phorcys and Ceto, in their physical characters (the grasping or devouring of the sea, reaching out over the land,

---

[41] F. M. Müller, 'Comparative Mythology', p. 66.

and its depth), beget the Clouds and Storms—namely, first, the Graiæ, or soft rain-clouds; then the Gorgons, or storm-clouds; and youngest and last, the Hesperides' Dragon,—Volcanic or earth-storm, associated, in conception, with the Simoom and fiery African winds' (vii. 397). The volcanic, earth-bound character of the dragon's physical meaning is repeated in his moral significance. He represents the 'consuming (poisonous and volcanic) passions—the "flame backed dragon", uniting the powers of poison, and instant destruction'[42] (vii. 397–8). Like Pegasus, though in a more ominous way, the Dragon of the Hesperides may be more relevant to the English nation than he was to the Greek. Ruskin claims that Turner has painted the dragon in exact accordance with the Greek myth. 'How far he had really found out for himself the collateral bearings of the Hesperid tradition I know not; but that he had got the main clue of it, and knew who the Dragon was, there can be no doubt; the strange thing is, that his conception of it throughout, down to the minutest detail, fits every one of the circumstances of the Greek tradition' (vii. 401–2). Yet neither Turner's painting nor the Greek myth can wholly account for the dragon that Ruskin describes. This dragon, as 'the evil spirit of wealth' (vii. 403) set to keep the golden apples of the earth, has become the chosen guardian of the English people, who have placed themselves under the protection of the covetousness and sulphurous smoke of the industrialism of the nineteenth century. Though not Christian in theme, Turner's painting is in Ruskin's account spiritual in meaning: 'In each city and country of past time, the master-minds had to declare the chief worship which lay at the nation's heart; to define it; adorn it; show the range and authority of it. Thus in Athens, we have the triumph of Pallas; and in Venice the Assumption of the Virgin; here, in England, is our great spiritual fact for ever interpreted to us—the Assumption of the Dragon' (vii. 408). The year in which Ruskin wrote of the Dragon of the Hesperides, 1860, was also the year in which he published the four articles which were to comprise *Unto This Last* in the *Cornhill Magazine*. His interests had begun to diverge and

---

[42] For δράκοντα πυρσονωτον, the 'flame-backed dragon', see Euripides, *Hercules Furens*, 398.

expand. But the moral imagery provided by Greek mythology was shaping Ruskin's concept of social criticism as it influenced his criticism of art. His interpretation of Turner's dragon shows how such imagery might simultaneously formulate both.

Turner's interest in myth can hardly, in fact, be seen in terms of the syncretic and monotheistic allegories that Ruskin elaborates in the last volume of *Modern Painters*: it has much more to do with a vividly Romantic denial of Christian supremacy. Ruskin is, characteristically, appropriating the painter for his own purposes. The pictures are seen as texts, and Ruskin's exegesis is dictated by his own conviction of spiritual value in mythology, a conviction by no means identical with the views of Turner. In weaving an elaborate network of mythological associations round Turner's painted dragon, Ruskin makes an explicit connection between this Greek myth and its biblical counterpart. 'Now the reader may have heard, perhaps, in other books of Genesis than Hesiod's, of a dragon being busy about a tree which bore apples, and of crushing the head of that dragon' (vii. 398). Interest in the interpretation of the Bible as mythology had become a mark of liberal religious thinking in the mid-nineteenth century, and Ruskin demonstrates a growing doctrinal tolerance through his willingness to consider such parallels. Yet he cannot properly be considered part of any cohesive religious movement in so doing. For Ruskin never lost his faith in the Bible as a repository of human and divine wisdom, as others had lost or were losing such faith; indeed he grew yet closer to the Bible during these years. The change in his position was not that he came to value the Bible less, but that he grew to revere mythology more.

Thus Ruskin sets himself apart from German theories of 'higher criticism'. He had, of course, come into contact with such works as Strauss's *Das Leben Jesu*, translated 1842–4. Ruskin held, however, a stubborn distaste for all things German. In an appendix on German philosophy attached to the third volume of *Modern Painters*, he makes his attitude plain: 'The reader must have noticed that I never speak of German art, or German philosophy, but in depreciation' (v. 424). The work of Strauss was specifically included in

Ruskin's comprehensive scorn: 'I have often been told that any one who will read Kant, Strauss, and the rest of the German metaphysicians and divines, resolutely through, and give his whole strength to the study of them, will, after ten or twelve years' labour, discover that there is very little harm in them; and this I can well believe; but I believe also that the ten or twelve years may be better spent' (v. 425). When Ruskin wrote this, in 1856, he had scarcely been in Germany: a fact which was soon to prove an embarrassment.[43] Before the completion of *Modern Painters*, he remedied the omission in his summer tour of 1859. His experiences did not make him more sympathetic either to German art or to German philosophy. While staying at Cologne, he wrote to his protégées at Winnington Hall[44] to warn them of the danger in German thinking:

I had not 'intended to write anything of a lesson in this letter':—but I happen to receive this afternoon, a line from Miss Bell—in which she speaks with some anxiety about some German ideas which have got 'into your little minds' respecting *myths*. I have always had an acute dread of this Germanism: and here from Cologne—I cannot but protest against it in all seriousness. . . . so let me close these letters, till you return to Winnington, with one entreaty:—that you will not any of you—until you are much older, allow yourselves to be troubled with the talk going on at present in the world of so called philosophers, respecting the typical or mythical meaning of portions of the Bible—Be assured that God will never blame you for taking His words too simply or literally: He will only blame you for not attending to them, when they are explicit—or for not obeying them, when they are imperative.[45]

Ruskin wrote this letter with the peace of mind of the pupils at Winnington as his first consideration. His dislike for German

---

[43] In 1857 the National Gallery Site Commission, hearing evidence from Ruskin, had enquired whether he had 'recently been at Dresden', or 'was acquainted with the Munich Gallery' (vii. 1). Ruskin had to confess that he had no experience of either town.

[44] In March 1859 Ruskin had visited Winnington Hall, a girls' school in Cheshire, for the first time. He took a keen interest in the education of the girls he met there and continued to be associated with the school for a number of years. For an excellent account of the importance of Winnington Hall in his life, see *The Winnington Letters: John Ruskin's Correspondence with Margaret Alexis Bell and the Children at Winnington Hall*, ed. Van Akin Burd (London, 1969).

[45] Ibid. 187.

thought should not conceal the fact that he had himself moved away from a simple or literal interpretation of the Bible. It was largely through the medium of Carlyle that German idealism took its place among the factors that had influenced this movement. But there were a number of other factors; and the movement was gradual and uncertain. Ruskin's enthusiasm for geology made him particularly vulnerable to the religious implications of works such as Lyell's *Principles of Geology* (1830–3). He knew Furnivall, Maurice, and Kingsley, men who had abandoned orthodox theology. He was soon to be familiar with the biblical criticism of the ill-famed *Essays and Reviews* (1860). When, in 1862, a bitter storm broke over the publication of Colenso's *Critical Examination of the Pentateuch and the Book of Joshua,* he gave unequivocal support to the heretical bishop. But through all this, his trust in the Bible as a supreme guide for human conduct did not waver. The value of the Bible seemed to him neither affected nor threatened by research into the historical circumstances of its composition. His interest in such research was not long-standing. It was irrelevant to the issues of morality and art that asked all his energy during these years.

Ruskin stood aloof from those who would seem to discredit the Bible in comparing it with mythology. Nor did he share the position of those who would degrade mythology in making the same comparison. Among this second group of scholars was W. E. Gladstone, whose *Studies on Homer and the Homeric Age* appeared, in three stout volumes, in 1858. Gladstone's fervent devotion to Homer made it seem to him no slur on the Christian faith to suggest that Greek poetry partook of the divine wisdom that is revealed in the Bible. The Holy Trinity, Gladstone suggested, is echoed in the combination of trinity with unity represented by the three sons of Cronos—Zeus, Poseidon, and Hades. The idea of the son of God as a healer and a redeemer from death is foreshadowed in Apollo. The divine wisdom or Logos is suggested by Athena. Latona, mother of Apollo and Artemis, reflects the tradition of the woman from whom the Deliverer was to be descended. But Gladstone felt that, lacking the support of Holy Scripture, the originally true religion of the Greeks had been corrupted over the years into falsehood and decay. It is

not strictly a false theology, but a true theology falsified: a true
religion, into which falsehood has entered, and in which it is gradually overlaying and absorbing the original truth, until, when the
process has reached a certain point, it is wholly hidden and borne
down by countervailing forces, so that the system has for practical
purposes become a false one, and both may and should be so termed
and treated.[46]

This is not a view which Ruskin would have shared. However, Gladstone's work is a reminder that Ruskin need not
have turned to German scholarship to find explicit association
between the imagery of Greek and biblical theology.

In 1846 Ruskin had compared the influence of nature over
the receptive Christian mind with a 'sense of a dew falling
upon him out of the sky' (iv. 215–16). Nature seemed less
kindly in 1860. In 'The Lance of Pallas',[47] Ruskin describes
the human suffering beside the beauty of the poverty-stricken
Scottish Highlands: 'Truly, this Highland and English hill-
scenery is fair enough; but has its shadows; and deeper
colouring, here and there, than that of health and rose'
(vii. 270–1). The Greeks and Venetians are equally to be
admired in that they had recognized and expressed this sorrow,
for 'all great and beautiful work has come of first gazing
without shrinking into the darkness. If, having done so, the
human spirit can, by its courage and faith, conquer the evil, it
rises into conceptions of victorious and consummated beauty.
It is then the spirit of the highest Greek and Venetian art'
(vii. 271). Not only in their art, but also in their mythology,
the Greeks had seen and expressed the darkness and sorrow
of the world, and the victory still possible to the human spirit.
Turner's picture *Apollo and the Python*, the second of the
great mythically inspired paintings that Ruskin analyses in
detail, is seen as an expression of this understanding. Like the
myth which is its theme, the picture expresses both the beauty
and the decay of nature. The light of Apollo is in conflict with
the darkness of Python: 'It was a far greater contest than that
of Hercules with Ladon. Fraud and avarice might be overcome

---

[46] Gladstone, *Studies on Homer*, ii. 9.

[47] An allusion to Achilles' spear, which Pallas Athena treacherously gives back to
Achilles after he has missed his first throw, thus becoming the agent of Hector's
death. See Homer, *Iliad*, xxii. 273–7.

by frankness and force; but this Python was a darker enemy, and could not be subdued but by a greater god. . . . Apollo's contest with him is the strife of purity with pollution; of life with forgetfulness; of love with the grave' (vii. 419–20). The picture is heightened by what Ruskin perceived as the radiance and colour of Apollo, and here Turner is the painter of 'the loveliness and light of the creation' (vii. 410). Yet he could not see Apollo's victory over the Python as final. He paints a 'smaller serpent-worm rising out of his blood' (vii. 420) beside the slain dragon. In the midst of his celebration of the triumph of light, he confesses the indestructibility of darkness. For Ruskin, this ambiguity is essential to Turner's art. 'He is distinctively, as he rises into his own peculiar strength, separating himself from all men who had painted forms of the physical world before,—the painter of the loveliness of nature, with the worm at its root: Rose and cankerworm,—both with his utmost strength; the one *never* separate from the other'[48] (vii. 421–2). In talking about Turner, Ruskin is talking about himself. The rose and the worm were now for him inextricably associated. As he had first seen his task as a Christian author in equalling Turner's teaching of the divine glory of nature, so he came to feel the need to follow Turner's expression of darker implications in nature's morality and man's corruption. In Greek mythology he found the imagery to do so. Throughout the 1860s myth becomes increasingly important to Ruskin's vocation as a writer, evangelical now in a wider sense than in 1843.

[48] In 1860 the word 'rose' may already have been acquiring the resonance of his love for Rose La Touche. Ruskin here gives the word a capital letter evoking the girl's name.

3
The Greek Precedent (1860–1863)

Modern Painters was at last complete in 1860. In November of that year Ruskin wrote to Elizabeth Barrett Browning: 'What I am now to do, I know not. I am divided in thought between many things, and the strength I have to spend on any seems to me nothing' (xxxv. 350). For the first time since the immense labour of *Modern Painters* had begun seventeen years previously, no major project demanded attention. It seemed a turning point. Notes for Oxford lectures of 1877 recall the arrival of the final volume of *Modern Painters*: 'I got this bound volume in the Valley of St. Martin's in that summer, and in the Valley of Chamouni I gave up my art-work and wrote this little book, the beginning of the days of reprobation' (xxii. 512). The 'little book' was *Unto This Last*, and in 1860 Ruskin began to think of himself as primarily a social critic.

There is a tempting over-simplification in a division which falls so tidily on the turn of a decade. Ruskin had been thinking about political economy long before 1860. He had indeed written about it, notably in *The Stones of Venice* (1851–3) and *The Political Economy of Art* (1857). Political and social issues had become important in the final defence of Turner. For Ruskin's economic thinking was not unconnected with his criticism of art, nor was the renunciation of 'art-work' either complete or permanent. Yet his life and writing after 1860 does change in a way that marks the completion of *Modern Painters* as a watershed. A changing concept of mythology shapes and is shaped by this development.

The end of what must have come to seem an endless task in *Modern Painters* brought freedom. It also created new perplexity in Ruskin's life. His 'days of reprobation' were to be both long and difficult. In terms of quantity of published work, the four years that followed the appearance of the fifth volume of *Modern Painters* in 1860 are among the least productive in his career. From the point of view of self-confidence and sense of purpose, they are among the most troubled. Ruskin wrote to Charles Eliot Norton in February 1861 of the intense 'scorn of all I had hitherto done or thought, still intenser scorn of other people's doings and thinkings, especially in religion' (xxxvi. 356) that haunted him. The conclusion of *Modern Painters* had coincided with the dissolution of Ruskin's religious certainty, and in this lay much of his difficulty. In 1861 his only publication was a catalogue of Turner drawings presented to the Fitzwilliam Museum at Cambridge. The year 1862 saw three essays in *Fraser's Magazine*, later to be published as the first four chapters of *Munera Pulveris* (1862–3), together with the publication in one volume of *Unto This Last*, which had first appeared as four separate essays in *Cornhill Magazine* in 1860. In 1863 the fourth and last essay in the *Fraser's Magazine* series appeared; in 1864, nothing at all.

The short, controversial, and polemical essays that now occupied Ruskin's attention differed from his previous books in both character and form. Published in periodicals rather than as complete volumes and dealing with political economy rather than art, they met with a mixed reception. Both *Cornhill* and *Fraser's* eventually suspended publication. While Ruskin was breaking away from the pattern of his first writing, he was also trying to change his earlier way of life. Much of his time during these years was spent on the Continent, away from the parental home, and Ruskin seriously thought of living abroad permanently. Neither development met with the approval of John James Ruskin. Though Ruskin's father was in complete accordance with his son's political arguments, he feared any suggestion of threat to his reputation. And he dreaded the idea of Ruskin's leaving England for good. It was only after his father's death in 1864 that Ruskin gave up the idea of making his home on the Continent and began to write about art again. The years between 1860 and 1864 must be seen as a time in which Ruskin was asserting intellectual and personal independence and attempting to reshape both his public and private life in the face of considerable uncertainty and tension.

The continuing and increasingly serious attention that Ruskin paid to his Greek studies during these years might also reflect a movement away from the control of his father. John James Ruskin, a competent Latin scholar, seems to have had little knowledge of Greek.[1] In his study of Greek language and literature Ruskin must have felt that he had found a means of moving outside the range of his father's influence, as in a different way he had challenged his authority by his plan to settle abroad and by his writing on political economy. Indeed, much of Ruskin's work on the Greeks during these years was carried out on the Continent and directed towards political economy. In a preface written for *Unto This Last* in 1862, Ruskin claimed Xenophon and Plato among the classical precursors of his economic thinking, particularly in his definition of wealth: 'The real gist of these papers, their central meaning and aim, is to give, as I believe for the first time in plain English,—it has often been incidentally given in good Greek by Plato and Xenophon, and good Latin by Cicero and Horace,—logical definition of WEALTH: such definition being absolutely needed for a basis of economical science' (xvii. 18). The reference to Plato and Xenophon gives a reassuring air of ancient authority to Ruskin's controversial speculations. Nor was an allusion to Greek precedent inappropriate. Ruskin's insistence on justice as the central issue in political economy[2] suggests the influence of the *Republic*, Plato's great attempt to define the nature and operation of justice in human affairs. The *Hipparchus*, which deals with love of gain or profit ($\phi\iota\lambda o\kappa\acute{\epsilon}\varrho\delta\epsilon\iota\alpha$), might have provided a source for Ruskin's examination of the real nature of value.[3] Parts of Xenophon's *Economist* bear a close relation

[1] John James Ruskin attended the Royal High School at Edinburgh, where an emphasis on Latin studies was traditional. For an account of John James's education, see Helen Gill Viljoen, *Ruskin's Scottish Heritage: A Prelude* (Urbana, Ill., 1956).

[2] Ruskin declares that the 'whole question, therefore, respecting not only the advantage, but even the quantity, of national wealth, resolves itself finally into one of abstract justice' (xvii. 52).

[3] See Plato, *Hipparchus*, 231 D: Δεῖ ἄρα, ὡς ἔοικε, τῷ κέρδει τοῦτο προσεῖναι, τὴν ἀξίαν. 'Socrates: So gain, it seems must have this addition of *worth*.' Most scholars would doubt whether this dialogue was in fact written by Plato. However, it is included in the edition of Plato which Ruskin used: *Platonis Scripta Graece Omnia*, ed. E. Bekker, 11 vols. (London, 1826). Ruskin's copy of this edition is now preserved in the Ruskin Galleries at Bembridge, Isle of Wight. Some pages of the *Hipparchus* are marked, suggesting that Ruskin thought the dialogue worth reading, whether or not he was aware of doubts as to its authenticity.

to his theory of wealth.[4] Ruskin makes, however, no specific citation of either Plato or Xenophon in *Unto This Last*. His acknowledgement refers to a mode of approach rather than to details of analysis.

In fact, it may be that the idea of naming Plato and Xenophon as classical authorities for his economic theories was largely confirmed, if not suggested, by studies which had occupied Ruskin after the essays had first appeared in the *Cornhill Magazine*.[5] Plato's *Republic* and Xenophon's *Economist* are obvious sources for Greek influence on the economic thought of *Unto This Last*. Yet Ruskin does not seem to have given sustained attention to these works before 1861. Letters written from the Continent testify to the classical reading which was occupying him at the time. He writes to his father in November: 'I fully intend finishing Political Economy, but otherwise than as I began it. I have first to read Xenophon's *Economist* and Plato's *Republic* carefully, and to master the economy of Athens. I could not now write in the emotional way I did then' (vol. xvii, p. xlix). The letter implies that Ruskin had not given thorough study to either work, though he may of course have been acquainted with both. Two days after writing to his father he repeated his plans in a letter to the Carlyles: 'When I've read Xenophon's *Economist*, and Plato's *Republic*, and one or two more things carefully, I shall finish, if I can, my political economy' (xxxvi. 391). A note in his diary suggests that Ruskin's reading of Xenophon's *Economist* was not complete until October 1862—two years after *Unto This Last* had first appeared, and six months after the publication of the 1862 preface.[6] Ruskin's reference to Plato and Xenophon among the classical authorities that had inspired *Unto This Last* is not the simple attribution of influence that it might seem. It is in part an

[4] See Xenophon, *Economist*, i. 10–12. Xenophon's *Economist* continued to be important to Ruskin. Translated by his pupils Alexander Wedderburn and W. G. Collingwood, it was published in 1876 as the first of the chosen series of classical books under the general title *Bibliotheca Pastorum*. See xxxi. 7–98.

[5] Robert Hewison has remarked on the misleading nature of the reference in the 1862 preface to *Unto This Last* in his unpublished B.Litt. thesis 'Some Themes and their Treatment in the Work of John Ruskin 1860–71, with Special Reference to *Unto This Last, Sesame and Lilies*, and *Queen of the Air*' (Oxford, 1972), 25 n.

[6] See *The Diaries of John Ruskin*, ed. Joan Evans and J. H. Whitehouse, 3 vols. (Oxford, 1956–9), ii. 571.

attempt to dispel the impression of 'emotional' writing on a potentially explosive subject.

Yet the image of rectitude in the ancient world, a virtue lost in the materialist and mechanistic nineteenth century, is important in *Unto This Last*; and it is a rectitude which mythology had expressed as fully as classical literature. The first direct mention, in the peroration of his second essay, 'The Veins of Wealth', Ruskin refers to Roman virtue rather than to Greek:

Nay, in some far-away and yet undreamt-of hour, I can even imagine that England may cast all thoughts of possessive wealth back to the barbaric nations among whom they first arose; and that, while the sands of the Indus and adamant of Golconda may yet stiffen the housings of the charger, and flash from the turban of the slave, she, as a Christian mother, may at last attain to the virtues and the treasures of a Heathen one, and be able to lead forth her Sons, saying,—

'These are MY Jewels.'[7] (xvii. 56)

Other references turn to Greek myth as a repository of economic wisdom. These allusions are concentrated in 'Ad Valorem', the fourth, last, and by far the longest of the essays published in the *Cornhill Magazine*.[8] The Greeks provide an example of the use and abuse of a property in which Ruskin felt a particular interest—wine, his father's trade:

Thus, wine, which the Greeks, in their Bacchus, made rightly the type of all passion, and which, when used, 'cheereth god and man' (that is to say, strengthens both the divine life, or reasoning power, and the earthy, or carnal power, of man); yet, when abused, becomes 'Dionusus,' hurtful especially to the divine part of man, or reason.[9]

[7] The story to which Ruskin refers is given by Valerius Maximus. Cornelia, mother of the Gracchi, on being asked to show her ornaments, shows her sons instead. See Valerius Maximus, IV. iv. 1–7.

[8] It was the longest because Thackeray, editor of the *Cornhill*, insisted that it should be the last.

[9] Ruskin's editors append a disparaging footnote to this passage: 'The actual meaning of the word Dionysus is, however, matter of uncertainty. "Zeus of Nysa" (a supposed place) was the favourite derivation among the ancients. Of modern guesses, "son of Zeus" seems as good as any . . . Ruskin's derivation is not clear' (xvii. 88n). The etymology of 'Dionysus' remains uncertain. However, Ruskin's derivation, though unconventional, is quite clearly based on δῖος, meaning of Zeus, or the divine, and νόσος, meaning sickness or disease.

And again, the body itself, being equally liable to use and abuse, and when rightly disciplined, serviceable to the State, both for war and labour;—but when not disciplined, or abused, valueless to the State, and capable only of continuing the private or single existence of the individual (and that but feebly)—the Greeks called such a body an 'idiotic' or 'private' body, from their word signifying a person employed in no way directly useful to the State; whence finally, our 'idiot,' meaning a person entirely occupied with his own concerns. (xvii. 87–8)

Here an associative mode of analysis gives Greek language and mythology a range of economic implications. Such an approach differs from the more convential acknowledgement of the authority of Plato and Xenophon in the 1862 preface. In 'Ad Valorem' Ruskin is not merely giving substance to his own authority by claiming classical precedent. He is using the Greeks to expand the field of his perception, exposing the narrow inhumanity of utilitarian political economy through reference to the imaginative understanding of a wiser people.

Ruskin's interest in etymology, and some aspects of his approach to the interpretation of mythology, may have been influenced by a reading of Max Müller. But Ruskin, like Carlyle, gives etymological and mythological argument a moral rather than a historical weight. Such studies are essential in his concept of political economy as an ethical science. The Greeks represent the right way of approaching economic theory, and their understanding of the nature of labour and its value is embodied in their myths:

Labour which is entirely good of its kind, that is to say, effective, or efficient, the Greeks called 'weighable', or ἄξιος, translated usually 'worthy', and because thus substantial and true, they called its price τιμή, the 'honourable estimate' of it (honorarium): this word being founded on their conception of true labour as a divine thing, to be honoured with the kind of honour given to the gods; whereas the price of false labour, or of that which led away from life, was to be, not honour, but vengeance; for which they reserved another word,[10] attributing the exaction of such price to a peculiar goddess, called Tisiphone, the 'requiter (or quittance-taker) of death'; a person versed in the highest branches of arithmetic, and

---

[10] τίσις, meaning payment by way of return; recompense, retribution, or vengeance.

punctual in her habits; with whom accounts current have been opened also in modern days.[11] (xvii. 95 n.)

In this footnote Ruskin finds more than economic meaning in the grim figure of Tisiphone. The image introduces mythological analysis of the complex syncretic type with which readers of the fifth volume of *Modern Painters* would have been familiar. Discussing the question of capital, Ruskin notes that if its operation involves the destruction rather than the creation of life, 'it is merely an advance from Tisiphone, on mortgage—not a profit by any means' (xvii. 99). He refers this insight to the Greek myth of Ixion. In his desire for Juno, Ixion typifies the lust for power of wealth. He is deceived into coupling with a cloud rather than the goddess. From this union issues the centaur, 'human in sagacity,—using both intellect and arrow—but brutal in its body and hoof, for consuming, and trampling down' (xvii. 100–1). Ruskin associates the myth with layers of meaning in the Bible, Dante, Aristophanes, and Bunyan, and with the iconography of the Middle Ages. His eclectic interpretation ends with an image drawn at once from biblical, mythological, and medieval sources. He describes how, as punishment for the sin of desiring Juno,

Ixion is at last bound upon a wheel—fiery and toothed, and rolling perpetually in the air;—the type of human labour when selfish and fruitless (kept far into the Middle Ages in their wheel of fortune); the wheel which has in it no breath or spirit, but is whirled by chance only; whereas of all true work the Ezekiel vision is true, that the Spirit of the living creature is in the wheels, and where the angels go, the wheels go by them; but move no otherwise. (xvii. 101)

Like the myth of the Gorgons and of Pegasus, the story of Ixion is for Ruskin resolved by the moral significance of its imagery of wind and cloud. These insights, not the cynical theory of utilitarian economics, disclose the 'real nature of capital' (xvii. 101). For the modern capitalist, like Ixion desiring a cloud in the shape of Juno, desires the power of wealth without understanding its nature. Again Ruskin sees this in images of cloud and storm:

for capital is the head, or fountain head, of wealth—the 'well-head' of wealth, as the clouds are the well-heads of rain: but when clouds

[11] Tisiphone, the Avenger of blood, was one of the Erinyes.

are without water, and only beget clouds, they issue in wrath at last, instead of rain, and in lightning instead of harvest; whence Ixion is said first to have invited his guests to a banquet, and then made them fall into a pit filled with fire; which is the type of the temptation of riches issuing in imprisoned torment. (xvii. 99–100)

Greek myth, like the art of Turner, seemed to Ruskin to use natural imagery to express a judgement on human folly and greed. The use of such imagery in serious economic debate must have seemed no less eccentric to his first readers than to us today. Yet Ruskin is tacitly defending himself against the charge of idiosyncrasy. His analysis of Greek literature and myth implies that not only he, but all great and wise traditions of thought have reached the same conclusions on the subject of economy. The utilitarian economists do indeed seem insular beside the august and ancient authorities that Ruskin evokes, though his interpretation of Greek precedent in economic thinking is often extremely personal. His view of Aristophanes' *Plutus*, one of the sources in *Unto This Last*, shows how he reads myth on his own terms.

Ruskin made a careful study of the *Plutus* in 1858. In *Praeterita* he records the difficulty he had with it, recalling his disgust with himself 'for not yet knowing Greek enough to translate the *Plutus*' (xxxv. 494). Nevertheless, the play made an impression on him. It is an attempt to answer a question at the heart of Ruskin's political economy—why do the unworthy grow wealthy while the virtuous remain poor?[12] Because Plutus, the god of Wealth, is blind, Aristophanes suggests. In this light-hearted play, Plutus is cured of his blindness by a night in Asclepius' shrine.[13] He is then able to distinguish between the just and the vicious, and confers his favour only on the former. The result is that all men become both virtuous and rich; for once wealth is no longer blind, the wicked see the material benefits of honesty and mend their ways. Poverty is represented as a terrifying harridan, compelling men to spend their lives at the mundane toil without which society cannot function. She opposes the plan to restore the sight of

[12] Not, of course, a new question for Ruskin, whose study of the New Testament was as thoughtful as it was detailed.

[13] Asclepius, son of Apollo and Coronis, was in Greek mythology the god of healing.

Plutus, for if wealth can see, her power is threatened. Chremylus, the hero of the play, is quite unable to overcome her logic. Poverty's arguments are unassailable. It is simply impossible for all men to become rich: for, as Ruskin recognized, 'rich' is a relative term. But in the dream world of the *Plutus*, logic is overcome by magic, and poverty is silenced. This made Ruskin uneasy. In his notes on the *Plutus* he remarks:

In the plan of the *Plutus*, it is difficult to understand what the author really intended to convey. He makes the happiness and reward of the just persons consist finally in becoming rich, while yet the arguments of Poverty are excellent. His hero cannot answer her in the least, but only mocks her and abuses her; and one sincerely wishes that the prophecy with which she leaves the stage— $\hat{\eta}$ μὴν ὑμεῖς γ᾽ἔτι μ᾽ἐνταυθοῖ μεταπέμψεσθον . . .—may be accomplished; to make the play at all complete, I think it should.[14] (xxxiv. 688)

In his references to the play Ruskin makes no recognition of its exuberant, fairy-tale quality of wishes come true. He treats it as a source of texts, not as a drama. His scattered allusions, taken as a whole, would suggest the *Plutus* as a measured eulogy of virtue in poverty. In the fifth volume of *Modern Painters*, for instance, he refers to the *Plutus* in noting that the Venetians saw no advantage in poverty: 'nor did the grave spirit of poverty rise at his side to set forth the delicate grace and honour of lowly life' (vii. 285). In 'Ad Valorem' Ruskin names the 'entirely wise' among those who remain poor and gives in a footnote two untranslated quotations from the *Plutus*: ' "ὁ Ζεὺς δήπου πένεται."—Arist. *Plut*. 582. It would but weaken the grand words to lean on the preceding ones:—"ὅτι τοῦ Πλούτου παρέχω βελτίονας ἄνδρας, καὶ τὴν γνώμην, καὶ τὴν ἰδέαν." ' (xvii. 90 n.). The first phrase notes the supposed poverty of Zeus.[15] Ruskin gives the second quotation again in *Aratra Pentelici* (1870) in a discussion of Greek sculpture and provides a translation. He claims that 'you can have Greek sculpture only on that Greek theory: shortly expressed by the words put into the mouth of Poverty

---

[14] Poverty leaves with the words, 'You who send me away today will soon wish for me back' (Aristophanes, *Plutus*, 608–9).

[15] 'For Zeus must be poor' (*Plutus*, 582).

herself, in the *Plutus* of Aristophanes' (xx. 296) and translates: 'I deliver to you better men than the God of Money can, both in imagination and feature.'[16] Though the proper use of riches is a recurring topic in Greek thought, one may question whether Poverty's speech can safely be taken as the expression of a 'Greek theory'. In the *Plutus*, it is balanced and qualified by the views of Chremylus, the hero, and by the picture of universal wealth and happiness with which the play ends.

The title of *The Crown of Wild Olive* (1866) embodies Ruskin's most prominent reference to the *Plutus*. Poverty claims that Zeus' lack of wealth is demonstrated by his giving only a crown of wild olive, not of gold, to the victor in his games.[17] Ruskin alludes to this prize in the title of his book. Having lost faith in immortality, he makes the crown of olive an image of the modest rewards which he had come to see as the highest prize of a virtuous life. The heathen

knew that life brought its contest, but they expected from it also the crown of all contest: No proud one! no jewelled circlet flaming through Heaven above the height of the unmerited throne; only some few leaves of wild olive, cool to the tired brow, through a few years of peace. It should have been of gold, they thought; but Jupiter was poor; this was the' best the god could give them. Seeking a better than this, they had known it a mockery. (xviii. 398)

Chremylus has a different explanation for the crown of wild olive. Zeus is not poor, but avaricious—he wants to keep all the gold for himself.[18] He is represented as a spiteful and revengeful tyrant throughout the *Plutus*, and in the final scene he is left abandoned without sacrifice or honour. Ruskin's image of the crown of wild olive shows the extent to which he is now shaping his own myths out of the texts of classical literature.

Ruskin's difficulty in reading the *Plutus* in 1858 suggests that fluency in Greek still escaped him.[19] Once *Modern Painters* was finished, he made the acquisition of this skill a priority. References to Greek studies in letters of this period are frequent. They often suggest that such work provided at

[16] See *Plutus*, 558–9.
[17] Ibid. 581–6.
[18] Ibid. 587–9.
[19] Few readers, however, find the language of Aristophanes easy.

least a partial solution to the personal problems that he faced in these years as he tried to redefine his writing in the face of parental opposition, religious difficulties, and an uncertain sense of purpose. The study of Greek seemed to represent a means of withdrawal from the troubles and perplexities of his situation. In the summer of 1861 Ruskin wrote to Mrs Simon:

Read Pope's essay on man. I believe after all it's the only bit of good divinity in the English language, but I'm finding some also in Greek.

I don't know what I'm going to do.—I'm a good deal stronger—by no means merrier—If I can go on reading Greek and going nowhere and feeling nothing it will be best for me.[20]

Some weeks later he wrote again: 'I'm getting to hate people, and I'm not going to be kind or philanthropic any more. I'm going to learn Greek accents—and save money—and be a monster—.'[21] In November he wrote to the Reverend W. L. Brown, formerly his tutor at Oxford:

I'm trying to learn a little Latin and Greek accurately—. . . . The Greek I perceive to be quite infinite when one opens Liddell's Dictionary and reads—half a column anywhere—to think that one must know all the book—before one knows Greek! Still, plodding on and making out a sentence now and a sentence then—I find I get good though I shall never know Greek—and perhaps if I take another three years of 'College' life—in Switzerland—it may do me some good even at 42.—though I wish I had my old tutor to ask, at lecture, about imperfects and aorists. I find the Imperfect is the great tense of my life—quite an intense tense—but it shall not at least be aoristic any longer.[22]

Six days later he wrote again to Mrs Simon: 'I wonder what you *will* do, or say when I have become nothing but a Grammarian —and won't read letters—nor come and see anybody—and only care about my dinner, and Greek accents—which I'm

[20] Unpubl. letter, Bodl. MS Eng. Lett. c. 34, fo. 324 (21 July 1861). Jane Simon (1816–1901) was the wife of Dr John Simon (1816–1904), pathologist and sanitary reformer. Ruskin had become friendly with the Simons in 1856.

[21] Unpubl. letter, Bodl. MS Eng. Lett. c. 34, fo. 332 (5 Aug. 1861).

[22] Unpubl. letter, Bodl. MS Eng. Lett. c. 34, fo. 344 (18 Nov. 1861). The point of Ruskin's grammatical joke is that the aorist tense has the sense of a completed action with no implication of continuance or repetition.

fast on the way to?'[23] Ruskin's absorption in 'Greek accents' was not only a necessary preliminary to the reading of Plato and Xenophon, but also provided an avenue of escape from personal difficulties.

The study of Greek language may have distracted Ruskin from his problems, but the study of Greek literature only increased his sense of life's perplexity. In October 1862 he wrote to his father from Mornex:

I have been reading the *Odyssey* tonight with much delight, and more wonder. Everything now has become a mystery to me—the more I learn, the more the mystery deepens and gathers. This which I used to think a poet's fairy tale, I perceive to be a great enigma—the Apocalypse, in a sort, of the Greeks. . . . But what it all means, or meant, heaven only knows. I see we are all astray about everything—the best wisdom of the world has been spoken in these strange enigmas—Dante's, Homer's, Hesiod's, Virgil's, Spenser's—and no one listens, and God appoints all His best creatures to speak in this way: 'that hearing they may hear, and not understand'; but *why* God will always have it so, and never lets any wise or great man speak plainly—Ezekiel, Daniel, St. John being utter torment to anybody who tries to understand them, and Homer scarcely more intelligible—there's no guessing. (vol. xvii, pp. lxii–lxiv)

Ruskin's sense of the unintelligibility of things becomes important in his second series of essays on political economy, which first appeared in *Fraser's Magazine* in 1862 and 1863, and was given the title *Munera Pulveris* when published in a collected form in 1872. The solution to the enigma may be found in close attention to words:

The reader must not, therefore, be surprised at the care and insistence with which I have retained the literal and earliest sense of all important terms used in these papers; for a word is usually well made at the time it is first wanted; its youngest meaning has in it the full strength of its youth; subsequent senses are commonly warped

---

[23] Unpubl. letter, Bodl. MS Eng. Lett. c. 34, fo. 345 (24 Nov. 1861). Ruskin continued in this frame of mind for a number of months. On 6 Jan. 1863 he wrote from Mornex to Eliza Fall, the sister of his boyhood friend Richard Fall: 'You will have no news in return, unless you care to hear how deep the snow is on the mountain paths, or are interested in the discoveries I make respecting the relative forces of Prepositions. (I find this last a most interesting study—only perhaps of too exciting a character.)' (Unpubl. letter, Bem. MS BXIII).

and weakened; and as all careful thinkers are sure to have used their words accurately, the first condition, in order to be able to avail themselves of their sayings at all, is firm definition of terms. (xvii. 148)

For Ruskin, the etymology made fashionable by Max Müller was attractive because it suggested that words, like myths or the paintings of Turner, had an unchanging meaning to be revealed by the critical interpreter.

Ruskin repeats the lament he had made to his father in an extended footnote[24] to the third of his essays:

It is a strange habit of wise humanity to speak in enigmas only, so that the highest truths and usefullest laws must be hunted for through the whole picture-galleries of dreams, which to the vulgar seem dreams only. Thus Homer, the Greek tragedians, Plato, Dante, Chaucer, Shakespeare, and Goethe, have hidden all that is chiefly serviceable in their work, and in all the various literature they absorbed and re-embodied, under types which have rendered it quite useless to the multitude. (xvii. 208)

It seemed to Ruskin that the interpreter might explain, but could not properly simplify the obscurity of these types. Dante, Homer, Goethe, Herbert, Virgil, Bacon, Spenser, and the Bible are all called on to confirm Ruskin's economic views. The great thinkers of the past support Ruskin's desire to understand political economy in moral terms, but they do so in an ambiguous way. Homer and Plato, revered by Ruskin as the first moralists, provide no clear beginning, for they seem to contradict each other: 'What is worse, the two primal declarers of moral discovery, Homer and Plato, are partly at issue; for Plato's logical power quenched his imagination, and he became incapable of understanding the purely imaginative element either in poetry or painting: he therefore somewhat overrates the pure discipline of passionate art in song and music, and misses that of meditative art' (xvii. 208). Plato questioned whether the imaginative truth of literature or painting could be of value in the establishment of a just society. Yet he did not reject all art; and Ruskin is at pains to emphasize the importance of music in the ideal scheme of

---

[24] The note was incorporated in the text in 1872 and has remained there in all subsequent editions.

education in the *Republic*. It is the representative aspect of literature and painting that Plato attacks. He argues that the painter or poet, producing images of objects that are in themselves no more than shadows of an essential reality, is at a third remove from truth. As such, the images he creates cannot safely be taken as a guide to life.[25] The paradox here is that Plato is himself pre-eminently a poet among philosophers, constantly turning to metaphor and myth to provide images for his exposition, as indeed did Ruskin. Yet Ruskin believed that Plato had good reason for his distrust of figurative art. Surprisingly, his sympathy is with the philosopher rather than with the poet:

We shall perhaps now every day discover more clearly how right Plato was in this, and feel ourselves more and more wonderstruck that men such as Homer and Dante (and, in an inferior sphere, Milton), not to speak of the great sculptors and painters of every age, have permitted themselves, though full of all nobleness and wisdom, to coin idle imaginations of the mysteries of eternity, and guide the faiths of the families of the earth by the courses of their own vague and visionary arts: while the indisputable truths of human life and duty, respecting which they all have but one voice, lie hidden behind these veils of phantasy, unsought, and often unsuspected. (xvii. 209)

Ruskin is in agreement with Plato in his regretting the inaccessibility of 'vague and visionary' arts. Unlike Plato, however, he feels that there is something valuable hidden behind their veils. Indeed, Ruskin named the Athenian among those thinkers of the past who require interpretation before their truths become accessible. What follows in Ruskin's analysis is often obscure, but its intended function is purely elucidatory. Beginning with Dante's description of the punishment of sins relating to wealth,[26] Ruskin goes on to compare Herbert's 'Take stars for money'[27] with Plato's image of the divine

---

[25] See Plato, *Republic*, x. 595 A–608 B.

[26] Dante, *Inferno*, vii; *Purgatorio*, xix; *Inferno*, xvii.

[27] 'What skills it, if a bag of stones or gold | About thy neck do drown thee? raise thy head; | Take starres for money; starres not to be told | By any art, yet to be purchased.' George Herbert, 'The Church Porch', in *The Works of George Herbert*, ed. F. E. Hutchinson (Oxford, 1941), xxix. 1–4. Ruskin misquotes, giving 'Lift up thy head' for 'raise thy head' (xvii. 211).

gold and silver in the souls of the guardians of the state.[28]
The disquisition ranges far beyond the bounds of economic
theory. The distress which Ruskin seeks to express through
the images of literature and myth is as much a personal as a
social malaise:

The Sirens are not pleasures, but *Desires*: in the *Odyssey* they are
the phantoms of vain desire; but in Plato's Vision of Destiny,
phantoms of divine desire; singing each a different note on the
circles of the distaff of Necessity, but forming one harmony, to
which the three great Fates put words. Dante, however, adopted
the Homeric conception of them, which was that they were demons
of the Imagination, not carnal; (desire of the eyes; not lust of the
flesh;) therefore said to be daughters of the Muses. Yet not of the
Muses, heavenly or historical, but of the Muse of pleasure; and
they are at first winged because even vain hope excites and helps
when first formed; but afterwards, contending for the possession
of the imagination with the Muses themselves, they are deprived of
their wings.[29] (xvii. 212)

The 'desire of the eyes' had indeed contended for the possession
of Ruskin's imagination; but the hope to which it led now
seemed vain. The note ends, evidently incomplete, with a
translation of Homer's description of the rocks of Scylla and
Charybdis, seen by Ruskin as images of labour and idleness,
or getting and spending.[30] 'The rock of gaining has its
summit in the clouds, invisible, and not to be climbed: that of
spending is low, but marked by the cursed fig-tree, which has
leaves, but no fruit' (xvii. 215). For Ruskin, Scylla and
Charybdis had a more than literary significance. They enabled
him to understand his own situation in terms of a wider and
more insidious mischief.

Ruskin believed this digression to be the most valuable part
of his essay. In 1872 he added a footnote to say so: 'What
follows, to the end of the chapter, was a note only in the first
printing: but for after service, it is of more value than any
other part of the book, so I have put it into the main text'

[28] Plato, *Republic*, iii. 416 E.
[29] See Homer, *Odyssey*, xii. 40–54, 153–200; Plato, *Republic*, x. 617 B–D; Dante,
Purgatorio, xix. 1–63.
[30] See Homer, *Odyssey*, xii. 59–64, 73–81, 85–110.

(xvii. 208 n.). Others have disagreed. E. T. Cook forgets his editorial discretion in his disapproval of such writing:

there is mixed with it so much of excursus into classical fields, so much of verbal and literary argument, that readers fail to keep hold of the main thread. Ruskin, as we have seen, was occupying himself at the time with a minute study of many Greek and Latin authors, and Dante was his constant companion. All of them were impressed into the service of his economic theories . . . Ruskin's reading of these 'enigmas' is full of flashes of insight and abounds in happy illustrations; but it sometimes led him into fanciful analogies, dubious etymologies, and strained interpretations. (vol. xvii, pp. lxiii–liv)

Certainly from the point of view of Ruskin's new career as political economist, already blighted by the curtailment of the series of essays in the *Cornhill* and soon to receive a further set-back in the discontinuation of publication in *Fraser's Magazine*, his extension of economic analysis into the field of literature and myth must be counted a mistake. Many commentators have agreed with Cook. The sharpest contemporary response may be seen in Arnold's 'The Literary Influence of Academies', which appeared in the *Cornhill* in August 1864.[31] Arnold singles out Ruskin's analysis of meaning in Shakespeare's names, included as a footnote in 'Commerce', the fourth of the essays in *Fraser's Magazine*, as an example of the provinciality in criticism:

Of Shakespeare's names I will afterwards speak at more length: they are curiously—often barbarously—much by Providence,—but assuredly not without Shakespeare's cunning purpose—mixed out of the various traditions he confusedly adopted, and languages which he imperfectly knew. Three of the clearest in meaning have already been noticed.[32] Desdemona, '$\delta\nu\sigma\delta\alpha\iota\mu\nu\nu\iota\alpha$', 'miserable

---

[31] Ruskin's editors refer to this article with implied approval. See vol. xvii, p. lxiv.

[32] In an earlier footnote for 'Commerce', Ruskin had remarked on the names Cordelia (heart-lady), Perdita (lost-lady), and Portia (fortune-lady). In 1872, perhaps with Arnold's attack in mind, Ruskin makes a defensive addition to his note: 'This note is literally a mere memorandum for the future work which I am now completing in *Fors Clavigera*; it was printed partly in vanity, but also with real desire to get people to share the interest I found in careful study of the leading words in noble languages' (xvii. 223 n). Nine years after the appearance of the essay in *Fraser's*, Ruskin recognizes that his etymological excursions were open to criticism —a 'mere memorandum' printed 'partly in vanity', but nevertheless continues to defend the value of such analysis.

fortune', is also plain enough. Othello is, I believe, 'the careful'; all the calamity of the tragedy arising from the single flaw and error in his magnificently collected strength. Ophelia, 'serviceableness', the true lost wife of Hamlet, is marked as having a Greek name by that of her brother, Laertes; and its signification is once exquisitely alluded to in that brother's last word of her, where her gentle preciousness is opposed to the uselessness of the churlish clergy:—'A *ministering* angel shall my sister be, when thou liest howling.'[33] (xvii. 257–8 n.)

Arnold's reaction is bad-tempered.

Now, really, what a piece of extravagance all that is! I will not say that the meaning of Shakespeare's names (I put aside the question as to the correctness of Mr. Ruskin's etymologies) has no effect at all, may be entirely lost sight of; but to give it that degree of prominence is to throw the reins to one's whim, to forget all moderation and proportion, to lose the balance of one's mind altogether. It is to show in one's criticism, to the highest excess, the note of provinciality.[34]

Seeking balance and rationality in criticism, Arnold bases his charge against Ruskin on inappropriate grounds. It was not the supposed 'note of provinciality' that alarmed him in Ruskin's work, but the note of individualism. He was disturbed by the scope which Ruskin claimed for the critical faculty. Arnold hoped to regulate a safer critical voice through the establishment of academies, external arbiters of taste. He rightly recognized Ruskin's 'extravagance' as a threat to any such plan. Here were accents that would not be harmonized into obedience.

Modern judgements have been equally unsympathetic. Joan Evans thought she had understood the work:

An ominous sign of psychological disturbance in his use of verbal jingles and such pseudo-philological argument as links Calypso and Apocalypse: most of his interpretation of Homer, for instance, are pure verbal phantasies. The reader who is familiar with Ruskin's earlier work will find in these essays—later reprinted under the Horatian title *Munera Pulveris*—the hall-marks of Ruskin's second literary phase: a phase marked by a decline in pure intellectual

[33] Ruskin derives 'Othello' from ὄθομαι to care for, take heed, regard, reck; and 'Ophelia' from ὄφελος meaning advantage or help.

[34] Arnold, *Works*, iii. 252.

power and a want of touch between himself and his imagined audience.[35]

John Rosenberg, too, saw *Munera Pulveris* as a work of madness: '*Munera Pulveris* is the first of Ruskin's books which clearly reveal his mental imbalance. . . . Unable to silence the echoes of the words he was writing, he divagated on their etymologies, as accidents of sound and chance associations led him from one word group to another, until both text and notes became incomprehensible.'[36] Ruskin's 'second literary phase' has, however, found defenders among more innovative critics. The most famous defence is to be found in the 'Polemical Introduction' of Northrop Frye's *Anatomy of Criticism* (1957):

Now whether Ruskin is right or wrong, he is attempting genuine criticism . . . Ruskin has learned his trade from the great iconological tradition which comes down through Classical and Biblical scholarship into Dante and Spenser, both of whom he had studied carefully, and which is incorporated into the medieval cathedrals he had pored over in such detail. Arnold is assuming, as a universal law of nature, certain 'plain sense' critical axioms which were hardly heard of before Dryden's time and which can assuredly not survive the age of Freud and Jung and Cassirer.[37]

Harold Bloom has made still larger claims for Ruskin: 'Ruskin is one of the first, if not the first, "myth" or "archetypal" critic, or more properly he is the linking and transitional figure between allegorical critics of the older, Renaissance kind, and those of the newer variety, like Northrop Frye, or like W. B. Yeats in his criticism.'[38] Bloom's understanding of myth is not Ruskin's. But the identification of myth as a means by which Ruskin was remaking criticism is accurate.

Munera Pulveris is not incomprehensible, though it is certainly odd. The originality of Ruskin's freely associative critical method lies in the confidence with which it can relate

[35] Joan Evans, *John Ruskin* (London, 1954), 154.

[36] John D. Rosenberg, *The Darkening Glass: A Portrait of Ruskin's Genius* (London, 1963), 153–4.

[37] Northrop Frye, *Anatomy of Criticism* (Princeton, 1957), 9–10.

[38] Harold Bloom, *The Ringers in the Tower: Studies in the Romantic Tradition* (Chicago and London, 1971), 174.

specifically economic, social, or even personal issues to a larger cultural context. In a more cautious and perhaps less interesting way this is what Ruskin had first attempted in *Unto This Last*. In *Munera Pulveris* he found a voice that enabled him to unite necessary public censure with compulsive private vision. The difficult years between 1860 and 1863 had changed his concept of criticism. He still felt the need to provide his writing with academic credentials, and the 1862 preface to *Unto This Last* shows that he found Greek authorities useful for this purpose. Yet his response to Aristophanes' *Plutus* shows the extent to which he saw their mythological culture in the light of his own convictions. Despite his insistence that his integration of economic theory with the concerns of literature and myth was no more than the continuance of an unchanging tradition, the syncretism of Ruskin's work in these years grows from a peculiarly personal creativity.

4
The Focus on Myth (1864–1866)

In the years immediately following his father's death in 1864, Ruskin began to find more urgently personal significance in mythology. A sense of religious perplexity lay behind this development. Having confessed his spiritual difficulties to Acland, Ruskin wrote to him of his attempt to find a solution through study: 'But you may suppose, from what we talked of then, that I was not likely to stay quiet in the mess I was in. So I am trying to understand what religions hitherto have been worth understanding, in some *impartial* manner—however little of each—and as I have strength and time, am endeavouring to make out how far Greeks and Egyptians knew God; or how far anybody ever may hope to know Him'[1] (vol. xviii, p. xxxiv). Half-serious references to Greek religion as an alternative to his own shaken faith had begun to occur in the difficult years following the completion of *Modern Painters*. In the winter of 1862 Ruskin had written to Charles Eliot Norton:

I've become a Pagan, too; and am trying hard to get some substantial hope of seeing Diana in the pure glades; or Mercury in the clouds (Hermes, I mean, not that rascally Jew-God of the Latins). Only I can't understand what they want one to sacrifice to them for. I can't kill one of my beasts for any God of them all—unless they'll come and dine with me, and I've such a bad cook that I'm afraid there's no chance of that. (xxxvi. 426)

Speaking of the Catholicism of Aubrey de Vere in a letter to Mrs Hewitt, Ruskin had claimed that 'if ever I get better, *I* mean to be religious again too, but my religion is to be old Greek. It will do quite as well as his, and is entirely "certain" also, which is an immense comfort'[2] (xxxviii. 384). A letter to

---

[1] The letter dates from 1864. It was probably written in Sept. when Ruskin was spending much time on the study of ancient religions, drawing particularly on the resources of the British Museum. See *Winnington Letters*, 514–16.

[2] The letter is dated 13 Sept.; internal evidence suggests that it was written in 1862 or 1863. Ruskin thought highly of the poet Aubrey Thomas de Vere (1814–1902).

Richard St John Tyrwhitt speaks of a wish for the comfort of Greek nature-religion and again strikes a characteristically defensive note of self-mockery:

my personal experience of spiritual treatment has been chiefly from sun, moon, wind, and water—when the sun's bright—I'm always pious: and always wicked in a windy day. And I've the greatest possible desire to 'believe' in Apollo and Diana —and in Nereus, and in water-symbols—and I do, *very* nearly; so that just a little touch or two of strong will will do it—quite: and what is more, it would make me quite comfortable and happy at once, and I don't see at all how I can possibly get on without it, for I'm very wretched just now: only I've a horrible habit of thinking, whenever I *want* to believe a thing, that it can't possibly be true, just because I want it to be; and I try it, and pinch it, and poke at it and plague it, till it all goes to pieces—if there's the least crack in it anywhere. So just because I wanted so much to believe in Diana, and dedicate a pine to her in my garden, I must needs, like a goose, go and watch which she seemed to like best; and all I could make out was that she shone on them all alike except one which she didn't shine on because there was a great high chimney and a chalet-roof in the way—and I couldn't somehow get to believe in a goddess who wouldn't or couldn't get round a corner: But if I could only cure myself of that nasty habit of measuring angles and things, I should be all right and comfortable—but it's too late, I'm afraid.[3]

The letter's flippancy covers painful need. It was 'that nasty habit of measuring angles and things', together with a real wish for belief, that led Ruskin to enquire into ancient religions. The private importance that such enquiry had for him was still very much in his mind when, in 1866, he wrote again to Mrs Simon: 'I am thinking of putting a patchwork faith together for myself out of any coloured rags I can pick up that look pretty—dropped by the dead nations—stitching them somehow into a pillowcase or a bed cover, and going to sleep with such warmth as I can get out of them and my poor

'Aubrey de Vere is one of the best and ablest men in England,' he wrote in 1871. See *Winnington Letters*, 672. Mrs Hewitt was a friend and protégée of both Ruskin and his father. See *Winnington Letters*, 191–2.

[3] Jay Wood Claiborne, 'Two Secretaries: The Letters of John Ruskin to Charles Augustus Howell and Rev. Richard St. John Tyrwhitt', unpubl. Ph.D. thesis (University of Texas, 1969), 207–8. The letter is dated 29 Aug. 1863. I am indebted to Claiborne's thesis for much valuable information. Tyrwhitt was later to become Ruskin's secretary in Oxford.

little life together—Poor Tom's a cold—at present—But the glitteringest rags tear so!'[4]

Religious uncertainty gave a special impetus to the study of ancient mythology. Yet, as the letter to Acland suggests, Ruskin intended the research to be impartial. It was related to themes that had long occupied him. He had written of an interpenetration of natural and moral truths in Greek myth in the third and fifth volumes of *Modern Painters*. The letter to Acland suggests Ruskin's continuing interest in this association. He goes on to assert that 'half the force and dignity of all Greek and Egyptian conception arise out of lower organism, and physical phenomena. The rising and setting of the sun—the Nile inundation and harvest—the sweep of sea in the Greek and Sicilian bays, are necessary swaddling clothes of all noble human conception and religion; that Church font by which I held Harry had Nile water in it, if we could have seen clearly'[5] (vol. xviii, p. xxxv). The connection between natural phenomena and mythology had attracted the attention of Max Müller, in particular, among contemporary scholars. In his letter to Acland, however, Ruskin refers to the earlier scholarship of Gibbon, Grote, and Bunsen.[6] The letter suggests that he had found little to help him:

If you know—and I think you know—much of Bunsen, you may guess how pleasant it is to me to have to wade and work through his masses of misarranged material; and if you know the state of Egyptian science in general—and contemplate a little the fact that the only two works of value on Rome and Greece are by a polished infidel, Gibbon, and a vulgar materialist, Grote—you may wonder that I have not had fever of the very scarletest, long ago.[7] (vol. xviii, p. xxxiv)

The reference to 'Egyptian science' is important, for Ruskin's study of Egypt was to influence his subsequent approach to Greek myth. His admiration for the ancient Egyptians was long-standing. Indeed, he had previously declared them a

[4] Unpubl. letter, Bodl. MS Eng. Lett. c. 36, fo. 88 (20 Oct. 1866).

[5] Ruskin was godfather to Acland's second son.

[6] The first volume of Bunsen's massive *Aegyptens Stelle in der Weltgeschichte* had appeared in 1844; the last in 1857. Cottrell's English translation appeared 1848–60. Gibbon's *Decline and Fall of the Roman Empire* was published 1776–88. Grote's *History of Greece* dates from 1846–56.

[7] Acland was recovering from an attack of scarlet fever.

greater people than the Greeks. His interest in Egypt at this point is, however, involved with the religious research described in the letter to Acland.[8] For Ruskin and his contemporaries, the new science of Egyptology seemed especially pertinent to the study of religion. Many looked to Egypt for evidence either to prove or disprove the historical authenticity of the Bible.[9] Bunsen, whose work was included in the notorious *Essays and Reviews* (1860), used Egyptological research to cast doubt on the chronology of the Old Testament. His reputation for religious free thinking gave him a wide readership: 'Bunsen wrote in such an incredibly dull style, and the complete set of his works on Egypt was so expensive, that had not the reviewers accused him of rampant heresy his books might have had only a very limited circulation. The attacks of the pious, however, succeeded in stimulating great interest in them.'[10] Though Ruskin may have turned to Bunsen as a source of information in matters of religious controversy, he found little pleasure in the work. The art of the Egyptians was of more interest to him. In his letter to Acland, Ruskin notes that 'of course *my* hold on all these races is through their art, and so I am cast perforce into figure work, and quite independent research' (vol. xviii, pp. xxxiv–v). Those works of Egyptology which enabled Ruskin to study Egyptian art had a more immediate appeal than the dry and factual text of Bunsen.

Ruskin's use of Egyptological work of this kind was not new. In 1851, expressing his admiration for decorated Egyptian columns in the first volume of *The Stones of Venice*, he had referred to David Roberts's weighty volumes of drawings made in Egypt: 'Of the ornamentation of colossal shafts, there are no examples so noble as the Egyptian; these the

[8] A manuscript book containing unpublished notes on Egyptian mythology is now preserved in the Ruskin Galleries at Bembridge, Isle of Wight. Ruskin embarks on his studies with a declaration of faith: 'Begin Myths with clear conviction that *all* Good and Truth is of God, in man. as in stones and animals' (Bem. MS 17, fo. 4).

[9] This was a question that had aroused intermittent interest throughout the nineteenth century. See, for instance, 'An Analysis of the Egyptian Mythology', *Monthly Review*, 92 (July 1820), 225–42; Isaac Cullimore, 'The Trinity of the Gentiles: Egyptian Mythology', *Fraser's Magazine*, 20 (July–Sept. 1859), 1–10, 200–11, 326–32; J. N. Hoare, 'The Religion of the Ancient Egyptians', *Nineteenth Century*, 4 (Dec. 1878), 1105–20.

[10] J. D. Wortham, *British Egyptology 1549–1906* (Norman, Okla., 1971), 101.

reader can study in Mr. Roberts' work on Egypt nearly as well, I imagine, as if he were beneath their shadow'[11] (ix. 355). Thirteen years later he gave unreserved praise to the monumental *Description de L'Égypte*, a work in nine folio volumes accompanied by 894 separately-bound plates published by the French government after the Napoleonic expedition in Egypt. In September 1864 Ruskin wrote to Margaret Bell: 'My delay in coming is mainly because this Egyptian work has led me into such an abyss of things I want to think over quietly. I have got the great Description de l'Egypte—which of all the things I've ever seen done by man is the most splendid monument of a dignified and useful industry. It is as wonderful as Egypt itself.'[12] Four days later he wrote to Georgiana Burne-Jones:

When Ned begins again to paint, he must do some Egyptian things. Fancy the corselet of the King fastened by two Golden Hawks across his breast, stretching each a wing up to his shoulder, and his quiver of gold inlaid with enamel; and his bow-gauntlet of gold, and his helmet twined round with a golden asp, and all his chariot of divers colours, and his sash of 'divers colours of needlework on both sides', and a leopard running beside him, and the Vulture of Victory over his head.[13] (vol. xviii, p. xxxiv)

Ruskin may have found the inspiration for this vision of an Egyptian king in the *Description de l'Égypte*. He was reading other works on Egypt at the time; these too provided material for his excited exploration of Egyptian art.[14] The images of

---

[11] See David Roberts, *Egypt and Nubia*, 3 vols. (London, 1846).

[12] *Winnington Letters*, 515. Margaret Alexis Bell (1818–1889) was the headmistress of the girls' school at Winnington Hall, Cheshire, which Ruskin often visited during these years and which was to provide the setting for *The Ethics of the Dust* (1866).

[13] See Judg. 5: 30. The letter is dated 13 Sept. 1864.

[14] These included Jean François Champollion's *Panthéon égyptien: collection des personnages mythologiques de l'ancienne Égypte* (Paris, 1823–5); Ippolito Rosellini's *I Monumenti dell'Egitto e della Nubia*, 11 vols. (Pisa, 1832–46); John Gardner Wilkinson's *Manners and Customs of the Ancient Egyptians*, 6 vols. (London, 1837–41); Francis Arundale and Joseph Bonomi's *The Gallery of Antiquities: Selected from the British Museum* (London, 1844); David Roberts's *Egypt and Nubia*, 3 vols. (London, 1846); Annie Kearie's *Early Egyptian History for the Young* (Cambridge, 1861). Ruskin had, however, some reservations about these works, for their illustrations seemed to him poor reflections of the statues he had seen in the British Museum. This was 'not owing to any wilful want of veracity: the plates in Arundale's book are laboriously faithful: but the expressions of both face

Egyptian religion had an impact which affected Ruskin's approach to mythology in *The Cestus of Aglaia* (1865–6) and *The Ethics of the Dust* (1866).

Ruskin had not written on art since the completion of *Modern Painters* in 1860. In January 1865 he broke his silence with the first of a series of papers for the *Art Journal*. Collectively known as *The Cestus of Aglaia*, these had the aim of determining 'some of the simplest laws which are indeed binding on Art practice and judgement'[15] (xix. 57–8). This first essay, 'The Black Outline', returns to a theme treated in *Munera Pulveris*—the enigmatic nature of the teaching of the great. The mythological artists of the ancient world shared in this mystery:

You never, I grieve to say, get from the great men a plain answer to a plain question; still less can you entangle them in any agreeable gossip, out of which something might unawares be picked up. But of enigmatical teaching, broken signs and sullen mutterings, of which you can understand nothing, and may make anything;—of confused discourse in the work itself, about the work, as in Dürer's 'Melancholia';—and of discourse not merely confused, but apparently unreasonable and ridiculous, about all manner of things *except* the work,—the great Egyptian and Greek artists give us much: from which, however, all that by utmost industry may be gathered comes briefly to this,—that they have no conception of what modern men of science call the 'Conservation of forces,' but deduce all the force they feel in themselves, and hope for in others, from certain fountains of perpetually supplied strength, to which they give various names. . . (xix. 63–4)

Here Ruskin touches on a theme that is to become central in his work: the opposition of ancient myth and modern science. These 'fountains or centres of perpetually supplied strength' are the gods and goddesses of mythology, embodying natural and moral insights lost in scientific thought. His list

and body in a figure depend merely on emphasis of touch; and, in barbaric art, most draughtsmen emphasize what they plainly see—the barbarism: and miss conditions of nobleness, which they must approach the monument in a different temper before they will discover, and draw with great subtlety before they can express' (xviii. 363).

[15] The essays were reprinted under the title *The Cestus of Aglaia* in *On the Old Road* (1885), without the passages used in *The Queen of the Air*. They were first reprinted in their complete and original form in the Library Edition.

of ancient deities includes Greek and Egyptian figures, [16] and his interpretation emphasizes both the ethical and physical aspects of their meaning. Athena is described as 'The Spirit of Wisdom in *Conduct*, bearing, in sign of conquest over troublous and disturbing evil, the skin of the wild goat, and the head of the slain Spirit of physical storm. In her hand, a weaver's shuttle, or a spear' (xix. 64). This recalls the storm mythology of the fifth volume of *Modern Painters*. The style of the description, however, is not that of *Modern Painters*. A calm and static image is evoked, its stillness suggesting the influence of the hieratic iconography of the Egyptian divinities Ruskin had been studying. In *The Cestus of Aglaia* the meaning of the gods is fixed and discoverable. Though the discourse of the Greek and Egyptian artists may have been confused, Ruskin believed that the deities of which they spoke had a clear and unchanging meaning. Indeed, their images reflect the same unalterable laws that Ruskin thought governed the proper function of art itself.

Ruskin chose a mythological title for his series of essays. Identifying Aglaia with Aphrodite, he explains that 'I have taken the two lines in which Homer describes her girdle, for the motto of these essays: partly in memory of these outcast fancies of the great masters: and partly for the sake of a meaning which we shall find as we go on' [17] (xix. 65). Aglaia, seen by Ruskin as a type of grace, is the 'true wife of Vulcan, or Labour'. [18] Homer relates how she gives her cestus, or girdle, in which 'all things are wrought' [19] to Hera. The girdle of grace, at once confining and enriching, provides an image for the necessary laws of art. Ruskin now sets the spiritual meaning in ancient mythologies directly against the materialism of modern science: 'From these ludicrous notions of motive force, inconsistent as they are with modern physiology and organic chemistry, we may, nevertheless, hereafter gather, in the details of their various expressions, something useful to us' (xix. 65). Here Ruskin makes sorrowful distinction between the eternal figures of the divine and the myths which represent

---

[16] Apollo, Hypnos, Athena, Pthah, Hephaestus, Aphrodite, and Dionysus.

[17] See Homer, *Iliad*, xiv. 220–1.

[18] She is so described in *Munera Pulveris*. See xvii. 226; also Hesiod, *Theogony*, 945.

[19] ᾧ ἔνι πάντα τετεύχαται (Homer, *Iliad*, xiv. 220).

man. Divine myths are helpful; myths concerning human affairs are perplexing and disheartening: 'But I grieve to say that when our provoking teachers descend from dreams about the doings of Gods to assertions respecting the deeds of Men, little beyond the blankest discouragement is to be had from them' (xix. 65). The gods, distant and invulnerable, provide paradigms for spiritual truth. But the myths of Daedalus and Icarus, of Prometheus, or of Orpheus, are 'anything rather than helpful or encouraging instruction for beginners' (xix. 66). Ruskin turns away from mythology, noting that 'we shall, for the present, I think, do well to desire these enigmatical teachers to put up their pipes and be gone; and betaking ourselves in the humblest manner to intelligible business, at least set down some definite matter for decision, to be made a first stepping-stone at the shore of this brook of despond and difficulty (xix. 66).

The essays which followed 'The Black Outline' in the *Art Journal* bear out Ruskin's sense of the hazardous enigmas of purely human art. He begins his third paper, 'Patience', with Chaucer's image of Patience sitting on a heap of sand:

> Dame Paciencë sitting there I fonde,
> With facë pale, upon an hill of sonde.[20]

Ruskin finds Chaucer's meaning impossible to fix. 'Not but that this is just one of those enigmatical pieces of teaching which we have made up our minds not to be troubled with, since it may evidently mean just what we like' (xix. 84). He is now uneasy about the freely associative style that he had first used in *Munera Pulveris*. 'I cannot get to my work in this paper, somehow; the web of these old enigmas entangles me again and again' (xix. 87). This complaint precedes a passage of formidable concentration and complexity. Ruskin's editors, perhaps wearied by the extensive annotation required by such writing, here reaffirm their disapproval.[21] The obscurity of

---

[20] Chaucer, *The Parliament of Fowls*, i. 242–3.

[21] 'Just as it is possible to understand the bewilderment of business men when invited to govern their commercial transactions by reference to Archytas and the Gran Nemico, so it is not difficult to believe that artists or students, into whose hands the *Art Journal* may have fallen, may have been put off from taking up the author's more practical points by some puzzlement over Homer's Aglaia and Chaucer's hill of sand and the Grison Grey' (vol. xix, p. lxiv). Joan Evans echoes the

the passage lies, however, in the personal nature of its allusions rather than the drift of its structure. Ruskin's love for Alpine scenery, his interest in Swiss history, his reading of Tennyson's poetry, his pleasure in Turner's water-colour sketches and his anger at their inaccessibility to the public: all figure in one paragraph—indeed, in one sentence. 'But it is a noble colour that Grison Grey;—dawn colour—graceful for a faded silk to ride in, and wonderful, in paper, for getting a glow upon, if you begin wisely, as you may perhaps see by those sketches at Kensington, if ever anybody can see them'[22] (xix. 88). A new paragraph begins with self-reproachful abruptness: 'But we *will* get to work now' (xix. 88). Ruskin's disquiet suggests a need for a frame of reference which might channel individual insight into communicable form. Mythology could fill this need. The static, benevolent images of the divine which Ruskin had seen in the course of his Egyptian studies, and which in *The Cestus of Aglaia* he associates with the Greek pantheon, offered a release from the confusion and difficulty encountered in his urge to make 'assertions respecting the deeds of Men' (xix. 65).

These images are fundamental to *The Ethics of the Dust*, which followed *The Cestus of Aglaia* in 1866. This book takes the form of a series of dialogues between a group of schoolgirls and Ruskin in the guise of an 'old Lecturer'. The ostensible aim is to teach the girls about crystals. In fact, as quickly becomes clear, Ruskin uses crystallography as a means of approaching a wide range of subjects;—ethics and education, art and botany, social responsibility and religion. The book has never enjoyed a high critical reputation. It received generally poor reviews,[23] and was not a selling success until the second edition appeared in 1877. What attention *The Ethics of the Dust* has received has focused on its biographical aspect. Critics have tended to follow

disapproval; and also, with no acknowledgement, the annotation. See Evans, *John Ruskin*, p. 286.

[22] Ruskin is thinking of the history of the Swiss Grison country; of the faded silk dress in which Enid rides in Tennyson's *Idylls of the King* ('The Marriage of Geraint', 762); and of Turner's water-colour sketches on grey paper, then shown at the South Kensington Museum. See xix. 87n.

[23] The *Saturday Review* was particularly harsh, dismissing it as 'whimsical and incongruous and silly beyond all measure'. See *Saturday Review*, 30 Dec. 1865, 819.

Wilenski's interpretation of the book as an expression of Ruskin's passion for Rose La Touche as it found vicarious fulfilment in his relationship with the schoolgirls at Winnington Hall. The school in Cheshire had, according to Wilenski, 'provided a refuge and at the same time substitute gratification of his obsessional desire to talk to Rosie, and touch her, and look upon her lips and eyes. And *The Ethics of the Dust*, in which all this is most charmingly sublimated, is thus a kind of thank-offering for the service which Winnington had rendered.'[24] The dismissive implications of 'charming' as a term of praise recur in Rosenberg's valuation of the book. He describes it as a 'charming if trivial dialogue' and goes on to claim that 'the essential subject of *The Ethics of the Dust* is not crystallography but Ruskin's heart'.[25] Whether or not Ruskin's heart may be considered trivial, it is certainly true that the apparently arbitrary diversity of subject in *The Ethics of the Dust* has discouraged popularity. Peter Quennell, who sees the chief value of the work as 'a sketch for a self-portrait', remarks that 'it serves to illustrate the increasingly capricious latitude that, as a result both of private distress and public disappointment, he was now prepared to permit his own creative impulses'.[26] Joan Evans is similarly disparaging: 'It is an extraordinary farrago of all his current interests—crystals, and Greek art, and Egyptian religion—dished up with a conscious childish quaintness.'[27]

The Ethics of the Dust is both eccentric and experimental. It is a preliminary attempt to define many of the preoccupations that were to find their full development in the years which followed. This is particularly true of the theory of mythology which, suggested in *Modern Painters* and *The Cestus of Aglaia*, was to receive its most complete expression in *The Queen of the Air* (1869). Ruskin himself, who thought well of *The Ethics of the Dust* and regretted its cold reception, describes the links between this book and his later writings on mythology in his preface to the edition of 1877:

---

[24] R. H. Wilenski, *John Ruskin: An Introduction to Further Study of his Life and Work* (London, 1933), 75.

[25] Rosenberg, *The Darkening Glass*, p. 153.

[26] Peter Quennell, *John Ruskin: The Portrait of a Prophet* (London, 1949), 187–9.

[27] Evans, *John Ruskin*, p. 285.

'The summary of the contents of the old book . . . is thus the clearest expression of the general conditions under which the Personal Creative Power manifests itself in the forms of matter; and the analysis of heathen conceptions of Deity . . . not only prefaces, but very nearly supersedes, all that in more lengthy terms I have since asserted, or pleaded for, in *Aratra Pentelici* and *The Queen of the Air*' (xviii. 203–4). The passages to which Ruskin refers are part of his tenth and last lecture to the girls, 'The Crystal Rest'. This lecture represents the most serious public affirmation of the importance of mythology that he had yet made.

'The Crystal Rest' is closely related to the statement of mythological theory in *The Cestus of Aglaia*. In 'The Black Outline' Ruskin had stressed the opposition between ancient myth and the investigations of contemporary science. He had used the topical phrase 'Conservation of forces' to suggest the character of modern thought (xix. 64). It recurs in 'The Crystal Rest'. Dora declares that 'we've been reading scientific books about the "conservation of forces", and it all seems so grand, and wonderful; and the experiments are so pretty: and I suppose it must be all right: but then the books never speak as if there were any such thing as "life"' (xviii. 341). In fact, the concept of 'conservation of force' is only modern in the sense that it is not ancient. As Ruskin's editors point out, the phrase originates with Leibniz, in the seventeenth century. Leibniz had argued that there exists a given amount of force in the universe and that its quantity never changes. This doctrine had been developed and modified in the nineteenth century. In referring to the theory here, however, Ruskin's purpose is not so much to question its validity as to deny its relevance. He had suggested in *The Cestus of Aglaia* that the mythological artists of ancient Egypt and Greece had expressed a better understanding of the world. In 'The Crystal Rest' he is more explicit. Art and mythology share a common vision. The artist's comprehension of truth, like that of myth, is based on form rather than force. It approaches the life of things in a way that the scientist cannot. Ruskin advises his pupils to 'hold fast to the form, and defend that first, as distinguished from the mere transition of forces. Discern the moulding hand of the potter commanding the clay, from his merely beating foot, as it turns the wheel'[28] (xix. 343). The artist's alliance with form enables him to understand what Ruskin sees as the distinction between the 'ideas of Life, as the power of putting things together, or "making" them; and of Death, as the power of pushing things separate, or "unmaking" them' (xviii. 344). The modern scientist, on the other hand, is in Ruskin's terms identified with the ideas of Death. 'Modern Philosophy is a great separator' (xviii. 344).

The confusion of subject matter in *The Ethics of the Dust* is not the result of Ruskin's incompetence, but of his considered refusal to 'separate'. The book endeavours to bring the vital understanding of art to the concerns of science. In this it is part of a central development in Ruskin's thought. For it was not his first attempt to define the 'ideas of life'. He had pondered the distinction between life and death in the fifth volume of *Modern Painters*, and in 'The Crystal Rest' he affirms the continuity of his teaching by quoting the earlier passage: 'The highest and first law of the universe, and the other name of life, is, therefore, "help". The other name of death is "separation". Government and co-operation are in all things and eternally the laws of life. Anarchy and competition, eternally, and in all things, the laws of death' (vii. 207). In one sense *The Ethics of the Dust* can be read as a gloss on the illustration which followed in *Modern Painters*. To conclude 'The Crystal Rest' Mary reads this passage aloud: 'Perhaps the best, though the most familiar, example we could take of the nature and power of consistence, will be that of the possible changes in the dust we tread on' (xviii. 359). Dust is capable of crystallization, and this is the theme of *The Ethics of the Dust*. 'Let us suppose that this ounce of mud is left in perfect rest, and that its elements gather

---

[28] The image of the potter may be an indirect reference to Egyptian mythology. In 'The Black Outline' Ruskin had identified 'The Spirit of Wisdom in *Arrangement*', as opposed to 'The Spirit of Wisdom in *Conduct*', who is Athena, with the Egyptian god Pthah: 'called the Lord or Father of Truth: throned on a four-square cubit, with a measuring rod in his hand, or a potter's wheel' (xix. 64–5). He refers again to Pthah as a potter in *The Ethics of the Dust*. See xviii. 227. The association between Pthah and the potter's wheel is made in Arundale and Bonomi's *Gallery of Antiquities*. 'In his second character, which is called Phtah Totonen, he is represented at Philae, holding on a potter's wheel an egg' (Arundale and Bonomi, p. 13); see xviii. 362.

together, like to like, so that their atoms may get into the closest relation possible' (xviii. 359). The result is a radiant image of Ruskin's ideal of social organization: 'And for the ounce of slime which we had by political economy of competition, we have, by political economy of co-operation, a sapphire, an opal, and a diamond, set in the midst of a star of snow' (xviii. 360).

In citing this passage from the fifth volume of *Modern Painters*, Ruskin calls attention to his view of the connection between political theory and physical science. This was essential to his aim in *The Ethics of the Dust*.[29] Crystallography provides natural images of political life: 'And sometimes you will see fat crystals eating up thin ones, like great capitalists and little labourers; and politico-economic crystals teaching the stupid ones how to eat each other, and cheat each other; and foolish crystals getting in the way of wise ones, and impatient crystals spoiling the plans of patient ones, irreparably; just as things go on in the world' (xviii. 335). In 'The Crystal Rest' Ruskin links these images with the 'ideas of life' expressed in the mythologies of the past:

You may at least earnestly believe, that the presence of the spirit which culminates in your own life, shows itself in dawning, wherever the dust of the earth begins to assume any orderly and lovely state. You will find it impossible to separate this idea of gradated manifestation from that of the vital power. Things are not wholly alive, or wholly dead. They are less or more alive . . . We know no higher or more energetic life than our own; but there

[29] Ruskin had first suggested the link between geology and political science in the fourth volume of *Modern Painters* (1856) in a passage which, in 1885, he describes as 'the germ, or rather bulb, of *Ethics of the Dust*' (vi. 132 n). 'It can hardly be necessary to point out how these natural ordinances seem intended to teach us the great truths which are the basis of all political science; how the polishing friction which separates, the affection that binds, and the affliction that fuses and confirms, are accurately symbolized by the processes to which the several ranks of hills appear to owe their present aspect; and how, even if the knowledge of those processes be denied to us, that present aspect may in itself seem no imperfect image of the various states of mankind: first, that which is powerless through total disorganization; secondly, that which, though united, and in some degree powerful, is yet incapable of great effort or result, owing to the too great similarity and confusion of offices, both in ranks and individuals; and finally, the perfect state of brotherhood and strength in which each character is clearly distinguished, separately perfected, and employed in its proper place and office' (vi. 132–3).

seems to me this great good in the idea of gradation of life—it admits the idea of a life above us, in other creatures, as much nobler than ours, as ours is nobler than that of the dust. (xviii. 346–7)

The acknowledgement of a 'nobler' life allows the growth of mythological belief. Ruskin now gives a clear and full statement of the tripartite nature of myth, which he had hinted at in earlier works and was to repeat with specific reference to Greek mythology in *The Queen of the Air*:

Every heathen conception of deity in which you are likely to be interested, has three distinct characters:—

I. It has a physical character. It represents some of the great powers or objects of nature—sun or moon, or heaven, or the winds, or the sea. And the fables first related about each deity represent, figuratively, the action of the natural power which it represents; such as the rising and setting of the sun, the tides of the sea, and so on.

II. It has an ethical character, and represents, in its history, the moral dealings of God with men. Thus Apollo is first, physically, the sun contending with darkness; but morally, the power of divine life contending with corruption. Athena is, physically, the air; morally, the breathing of the divine spirit of wisdom. Neptune is, physically, the sea; morally, the supreme power of agitating passion; and so on.

III. It has, at last, a personal character; and is realised in the minds of its worshippers as a living spirit, with whom men may speak face to face, as a man speaks to his friend. (xviii. 347–8)

He specifies the roots of his dissatisfaction with the mythological scholarship that his interest in Egyptology had led him to explore. Such research lacked the impartiality which, as he had indicated in his letter to Acland, had been the aspiration of his own studies. Ruskin explains that it is

impossible to define exactly how far, at any period of a national religion, these three ideas are mingled; or how far one prevails over the other. Each enquirer usually takes up one of these ideas, and pursues it, to the exclusion of the others; no impartial efforts seem to have been made to discern the real state of the heathen imagination in its successive phases. For the question is not at all what a mythological figure meant in its origin; but what it became in each subsequent mental development of the nation inheriting the thought. (xviii. 348)

As we have seen, Ruskin's emphasis on the objectivity proper to mythological research was in part prompted by his impulse to use such study as a means of freeing himself from private anxiety. Similarly, his dislike for a purely historical approach to the understanding of mythology is partly due to his feeling that such a method tended to disparage a phenomenon which had come to have a personal importance for him. Ruskin's remarks are particularly apposite to the work of Max Müller, who had explained the sources of mythology in the light of his own idiosyncratic linguistic theories. But developments in mythological scholarship had only a limited influence on Ruskin's thinking in the years between 1860 and 1866. His interpretation of Athena in 'The Crystal Rest' is close to that given in the fifth volume of *Modern Painters*. His exposition is, however, now prefaced by a reference to the Egyptian goddess Neith. He identifies her with the Greek Athena:[30]

The Neith, of Egypt, meant, physically, little more than the blue of the air; but the Greek, in a climate of alternate storm and calm, represented the wild fringes of the storm-cloud by the serpents of her aegis; and the lightning and cold of the highest thunder-clouds, by the Gorgon on her shield: while morally, the same types represented to him the mystery and changeful terror of knowledge, as her spear and helm its ruling and defensive power.[31] (xviii. 348–9)

[30] The association between Neith and Athena is made in Plato's *Timaeus*, a dialogue to which Ruskin makes indirect reference in 'The Crystal Rest'. See Plato, *Timaeus*, 21E; xviii. 344. It may be that Ruskin's identification of Athena with the air, a theory which is first made explicit in 'The Crystal Rest', was suggested by the connection between Neith and Athena. Diodorus Siculus makes a direct reference to the Egyptian Neith as the air: 'The air, . . . they called Athena, as the name is translated, and they considered her to be the daughter of Zeus and conceived of her as a virgin, because of the fact that the air is by its nature uncorrupted and occupies the highest part of the entire universe; for the latter reason also the myth arose that she was born from the head of Zeus. . . . They add that she is also called Glaucopis, (Blue-eyed), not because she has blue eyes as some Greeks have held—a silly explanation, indeed—but because the air has a bluish cast' (Diodorus Siculus, I. xii. 7–8). Ruskin, who knew the authority of Diodorus Siculus (see xix. 313, xx. 348), may have had this passage in mind in suggesting that the Egyptian Neith meant the 'blue of the air'.

[31] Ruskin's view of Athena in *The Ethics of the Dust* not only looks back to *Modern Painters*, but foreshadows many of the details of his interpretation in *The*

In 'The Crystal Rest', however, it is neither the physical nor even the moral meaning of myth that chiefly interests Ruskin. He turns to the third character of the gods' existence—their personal identity. His recent studies had confirmed his belief that all true religions express aspects of the same truth. He had come to feel that it was through the medium of personality that they did so. In the fifth volume of *Modern Painters* he had expressed the connection between the Bible and Greek mythology largely through their shared symbolic language. It is to the continuity of divine personality, rather than of symbolism, that he now gives his attention. This is one of the most unexpected aspects of *The Ethics of the Dust*. One wonders what the parents of the girls at Winnington Hall would have made of Ruskin's claim that his pupils' attitude to the 'pagan' gods would be formed by their approach to the spirits of the Bible. Belief in the gods of myth 'will much depend upon the clearness of your faith in the personality of the spirits which are described in the book of your own religion;—their personality, observe, as distinguished from merely symbolical visions' (xviii. 349). The personal agency represented by the spirits of the Bible seemed to Ruskin analogous with that to be seen in ancient mythology. Ruskin identifies the angel which appeared to David by the threshing floor of Araunah[32] with the 'angel standing in the sun' of Revelations[33] and suggests that this spirit may also be recognized in the primitive god at first called 'Destroyer' (Apollo), and later, 'as the light, or sun, of justice, was recognised in the chastisement, called also, "Physician" or "Healer"' (xviii. 350–1). It is the personal element in this spiritual ministry that links Christian faith with ancient legend:

I assure you, strange as it may seem, our scorn of Greek tradition depends, not on our belief, but our disbelief, of our own traditions. We have, as yet, no sufficient clue to the meaning of either; but you will always find that, in proportion to the earnestness of our own

Queen of the Air. See particularly the digression on Athena in his note on 'The Greater Pthah' (xviii. 362–5).

[32] 2 Sam. 24: 16.

[33] Rev. 18: 17–18. Ruskin may also have intended a reference to Turner's *The Angel Standing in the Sun*; though in 1856 he had referred to this picture among those 'painted in the period of decline' (xiii. 167).

faith, its own tendency to accept a spiritual personality increases: and that the most vital and beautiful Christian temper rests joyfully in its conviction of the multitudinous ministry of living angels, infinitely varied in rank and power. (xviii. 352)

Myth seemed to Ruskin both human and natural, while 'Modern Philosophy' (xviii. 344) was abstract and mechanistic. Yet, though mythological truth was in *The Ethics of the Dust* removed from the private, shifting enigmas of *Munera Pulveris* and *The Cestus of Aglaia*, it received treatment that was hardly less eccentric. Myth might be a universal dream. For Ruskin, it was also a personal vision. The intimate effect of the dialogue form in *The Ethics of the Dust* creates a curiously private tone. The book included its own audience, one that seemed pliant indeed after the intractable public that Ruskin had lately experienced through the reaction to his papers in the *Cornhill* and *Fraser's*:

ISABEL. But that was only a dream?
L. Some dreams are truer than some wakings, Isabel; but I won't tell you unless you like.
ISABEL. Oh, please, please.
L. You are all such wise children, there's no talking to you; you won't believe anything.
LILY. No, we are not wise, and we will believe anything, when you say we ought. (xviii. 224)

Ruskin was to speak of the relation between dream and myth in *The Queen of the Air* in a passage which provides a commentary on the mythological dreams of *The Ethics of the Dust*:

For all the greatest myths have been seen, by the men who tell them, involuntarily and passively—seen by them with as great distinctness (and in some respects, though not in all, under conditions as far beyond the control of their will) as a dream sent to any of us by night when we dream clearest; and it is this veracity of vision that could not be refused, and of moral that could not be foreseen, which in modern historical inquiry has been left wholly out of account: being indeed the thing which no merely historical investigator can understand, or even believe; for it belongs exclusively to the creative or artistic group of men, and can only be interpreted by those of their race, who themselves in some measure also see visions and dream dreams. (xix. 309)

Here Ruskin speaks of himself. He saw it as his own task to interpet the visionary or moral aspects of mythology which 'in modern historical inquiry has been left wholly out of account'. Most of the second lecture of *The Ethics of the Dust*, 'The Pyramid Builders', is taken up with the story of a supposed dream, or myth, of the Egyptian deities Pthah and Neith. Ruskin begins with a reference to Bunsen, as if to declare an intention of supplying what Bunsen lacks. He claims that 'from all that we had been reading in Bunsen about stones that couldn't be lifted with levers, I began to dream about stones that lifted themselves with wings'[34] (xviii. 225). Neith, or Athena, appears to the dreamer as the 'Lady of wisdom', in company with the god who is her brother in the Egyptian pantheon—Pthah, the 'Lord of Truth', identified with Hephaestus by the Greeks.[35] They converse with formality suggestive of the Bible. Neith accuses Pthah of condemning men to 'weary life and wasteful death' (xviii. 228) in denying them the opportunity to pay homage to the gods in art. 'Oh, Lord of Truth! is this then thy will, that men should mould only four-square pieces of clay: and the forms of the gods no more?' (xviii. 226–7). With the aid of Neith, Pthah's pyramid is instantly brought into being, and the gods depart. But Pthah returns in the form of a beetle—'lower Pthah' (xviii. 230) or rather 'Pthah in his lower office'[36] (xviii. 363). He reduces the pyramid to a tiny size. It becomes, of course, a crystal; the central image of *The Ethics of the Dust*.

To build with 'four-square pieces of clay', superintended by the 'Lord of Truth', who 'represents the formative power of order and measurement' (xviii. 362), is merely slavery without the intervention of the divine wisdom of Neith; and repetitive mechanical labour, represented by the deformed

---

[34] See Bunsen, *Egypt's Place*, ii. 147–50.

[35] 'By the Greeks he was paralleled to Hephaistos or Vulcan, and considered as the artisan who did all things with truth' (Arundale and Bonomi, p. 13). The *Gallery of Antiquities* (1844), a work which Ruskin sees as 'the book of best authority easily accessible', adding that its text is 'excellent' (xviii. 363) gives the supposed Greek equivalent to each of the Egyptian gods described.

[36] Ruskin notes here that 'the Egyptian symbolism of him by the beetle was not a scornful one; it expressed only the idea of his presence in the first elements of life. But it may not unjustly be used, in another sense, by us, who have seen his power in new development' (xviii. 363).

lower Pthah with his hammer, pincers, and eyeless helmet, has the power to degrade and diminish what divine wisdom has created. The meaning of Ruskin's dream is to be found in doctrines stated many times elsewhere in his writing. 'But you showed us this the other day', Sybil remarks of the crystal the lecturer gives to the girls. 'Yes, but you would not look at it the other day' (xviii. 231). The universal appeal of mythology communicates ideas otherwise inaccessible, for the constancy of Athena's significance transcends that of private enigma. Ruskin goes on to discount his own part in the 'dream': 'What *I* mean, is of little consequence. What the Egyptians meant, who called her "Neith,"—or Homer, who called her "Athena,"—or Solomon, who called her by a word which the Greeks render as "Sophia," you must judge for yourselves. But her testimony is always the same, and all nations have received it' (xviii. 231–2). 'The Pyramid Builders' ends with a reminder of the function of personality in such teaching. Mary, always the voice of prosaic common sense in *The Ethics of the Dust*, objects to Ruskin's allusion to the wisdom of Proverbs as a manifestation of Athena: 'But is not that only a personification?'[37] (xviii. 232). Ruskin replies with a direct appeal to the authority of the Bible: 'If it be, what will you gain by unpersonifying it, or what right have you to do so? Cannot you accept the image given you, in its life; and listen, like children, to the words which chiefly belong to you as children: "I love them that love me, and those that seek me early shall find me"?'[38] (xviii. 232). The personality of Athena and the personality of biblical wisdom are now of comparable weight and value in Ruskin's eyes.

Ruskin is yet bolder in his second dream-vision. Here he suggests that the traditions of the ancient world, older than those of the Christian faith, might also be wiser. The dream involves Neith and St Barbara, a mythic saint whom Ruskin sees as having special charge over Gothic architecture.[39] Far from being educated by the representative of a purer faith,

[37] 'Then I was by him, as one brought up with him: and I was daily his delight, rejoicing always before him; Rejoicing in the habitable part of his earth; and my delights were with the sons of men' (Prov. 8: 30–1).

[38] See Prov. 8: 17.

[39] Here Ruskin departs from tradition; though, as his editors point out, St Barbara is often portrayed with a Gothic tower in her hand (xviii. 316n).

Neith, seen as much the more important spirit, leads St Barbara to realize that her 'pinnacle and flame work . . . is all vanity' (xviii. 319). Here again, Ruskin's meaning is clear. He is repeating what he had often claimed elsewhere—that Gothic architecture, once corrupted by folly and pride, becomes worthless. That he should use Egyptian wisdom to chastise Gothic pretension is remarkable. The message is reinforced by a second dream, in which Gothic imps challenge 'Neith's old workpeople' (xviii. 321) to a contest in building. The result is disaster for Gothic ambition. The imps' tower is built on sand, and in falling breaks itself off short against Neith's pyramid. Once again the waking dreamer is left with a crystal to illustrate the meaning of the vision—a pyramid built of fluorspar with Gothic 'pinnacles of mischievous quartz' (xviii. 323). These extraordinary passages may be compared with nothing else in Ruskin's work. Under cover of his impersonal mask as dreamer, he now claims that the teachings of myth take precedence over the traditions of Christianity.

In the preface which he wrote for *The Ethics of the Dust* in 1877, Ruskin looks back on these dream-visions.

One licence taken in this book, however, though often permitted to essay-writers for the relief of their dulness, I never mean to take more,—the relation of composed metaphor as of actual dream . . . I assumed, it is true, that in these places the supposed dream would be easily seen to be an invention; but must not any more, even under so transparent disguise, pretend to any share in the real powers of Vision possessed by great poets and true painters. (xviii. 206)

The dreams in *The Ethics of the Dust* were intended as interpretations of mythology. They could also be understood as mythopoeic creations in their own right. It was a method of exposition to which Ruskin never returned, and in the 1877 preface we see why he discarded it. The supposedly interpretative dreams came close to the private fantasy that he had hoped myth would enable him to avoid. Ruskin's mythological writings are as much concerned with his own convictions as with the beliefs of the ancient world. He could never admit this, for his teaching depended on the premise that truth existed outside the perception of the individual and that he was doing no more than revealing a previously existing code of universal wisdom to his pupils and readers. After the publication of *The Ethics of the Dust* Ruskin abandoned the experiment of dialogue form. It seemed to admit too openly the presence of the author.

The more familiar subject matter of Greek rather than Egyptian mythology soon regained Ruskin's attention. There is no doubt that the abundant literary and artistic associations which enriched Greek mythology made it enduringly attractive to him in a way that the traditions of Egypt could not rival. The brief excursion into Egyptian myth does, however, have a lasting effect on Ruskin's thinking about the Greeks in the 1860s. *The Queen of the Air* grew out of the concerns of *The Ethics of the Dust*.

5
The Queen of the Air (1866–1869)

Images of Mortality

The Ethics of the Dust appeared in December 1865, in time
for the Christmas market. Shortly afterwards Ruskin wrote
to Charles Eliot Norton. He was in melancholy humour:

> But how can you expect a man living alone, and with everything
> gone cross to him, and not in any way having joy, even of the
> feeblest sort,—but at the best only relief from pain, and that only
> when he is at work,—to show anything but a cramped shadow of
> the little there is in him? Turner is dead—all his works are
> perishing, and I can't see those that exist. Every thirteenth-century
> cathedral in France, and every beautiful street in my favourite
> cities, has been destroyed. Chamouni is destroyed—Geneva—
> Lucerne—Zurich—Schaffhausen—Berne,—might just as well have
> been swallowed up by earth-quakes as be what they are now. There
> are no inns, no human beings any more anywhere; nothing but
> endless galleries of rooms, and Automata in millions. (xxxvi.
> 500–1)

Ruskin had long been angry, but it was only now that his
anger began to obsess him. These 'endless galleries of rooms',
the 'Automata in millions', have the quality of nightmare. In
1866 Ruskin's sense of isolation, and of the futility of his
work, became intense. Remarkably, he continued to look to
the ancient religion of the Greeks for support, rather than to
the Christianity of his youth. The letter to Norton continues:
'I could get, and do get, some help out of Greek myths—but
they are full of earth, and horror, in spite of their beauty.
Persephone is the sum of them, or worse than Persephone—
Comus' (xxxvi. 501). In *The Queen of the Air* Ruskin chose
to dwell on more ethereal aspects of Greek religion. Yet the
strength which he drew from its mythology was closely
connected with his sense of its darkness. The Greek concept
of death, with which the figure of Persephone is particularly
associated, now had a special importance for him.

Ruskin's concern with the sterner elements of Greek religion ran counter to the widely-held view of the Greeks as a light-hearted and beauty-loving people. Like many features of Hellenism in England, this had origins in German scholarship, particularly in the work of Winckelmann. Partly through Carlyle, who speaks in terms of the 'light gracefulness of the old Greek Paganism', the idea had become a commonplace.[1] Matthew Arnold wrote of the Greeks as a 'gay and pleasure-loving multitude. . . . The ideal, cheerful, sensuous, pagan life is not sick or sorry.'[2] In *Culture and Anarchy*, published in 1869, the year in which *The Queen of the Air* appeared, Arnold coined the phrase 'sweetness and light' to characterize the spirit of Hellenism. The expression came to epitomize the supposed serenity of the bright civilization of the Greeks. Walter Pater, who was aware of more clouded elements in Greek culture, was among the few who came to question this belief. In his influential essay on Winckelmann, first published in the *Westminster Review* in 1867, he writes that 'Cardinal Newman speaks of "the classical polytheism which was gay and graceful, as was natural in a civilized age". Yet such a view is only a partial one. In it the eye is fixed on the sharp, bright edge of high Hellenic culture, but loses sight of the sombre world across which it strikes.'[3] Nevertheless, it was this 'sharp, bright edge' which primarily interested Pater, and his approach is dominated by the ideas of Winckelmann. '*Heiterkeit*—blitheness or repose, and *Allgemeinheit*—generality or breadth, are, then, the supreme characteristics of the Hellenic ideal.'[4] Examples of this picture of the sunny Greek character, notably different from the emphasis of Ruskin's interpretation, could be multiplied indefinitely.[5]

---

[1] Carlyle, 'The Hero as Divinity' (1841), in *The Works of Thomas Carlyle*, 30 vols. (London, 1897–9), v. 19.

[2] Arnold, 'Pagan and Mediæval Religious Sentiment' (1865), *Works*, iii. 22.

[3] Pater, 'Winckelmann' (1867), in *Works of Walter Pater*, 10 vols. (London, 1910), i. 200.

[4] Ibid. 213.

[5] Such an interpretation of the Greek spirit is not peculiar to the Victorian age. It remained a common idea for many years. H. J. Rose's valuable and widely known *A Handbook of Greek Mythology* (London, 1928), for instance, notes that 'The Greeks at their best were sane, high-spirited, clear-headed, beauty-loving optimists, and not in the least other-worldly. Hence their legends are almost without exception free from the cloudiness, the wild grotesques, and the horrible features which beset the popular traditions of less gifted and happy peoples' (p. 14).

Such were the features that seemed to some contemporary writers to make Greek myths particularly suitable for the education of children. Charles Kingsley writes in the preface to his *The Heroes* (1855) that 'next to those old Romances, which were written in the Christian middle age, there are no fairy tales like these old Greek ones, for beauty, and wisdom, and truth, and for making children love noble deeds, and trust in God to help them through'.[6] Kingsley, however, in choosing Greek 'fairy tales' for the education of his child readers in *The Heroes* felt the need to expurgate his mythical material. Ruskin differed on both counts. He saw no justification for the bowdlerization of myth; nor did he believe Greek legends to be particularly fitted for children. The final lessons of Greek myth seemed to him for adult comprehension. In 1868 he wrote of the moral education of children in a preface for an edition of Grimms' fairy stories. Myth might contribute to such education, but the first source must be the wise teaching of parents:

Children so trained have no need of moral fairy tales; but they will find in the apparently vain and fitful courses of any tradition of old time, honestly delivered to them, a teaching for which no other can be substituted, and of which the power cannot be measured; animating for them the material world with inextinguishable life, fortifying them against the glacial cold of selfish science, and preparing them submissively, and with no bitterness of astonishment, to behold, in later years, the mystery—divinely appointed to remain such to all human thought—of the fates that happen alike to the evil and the good. (xix. 235–6)

In his own mythological work for the young, *The Ethics of the Dust*, Ruskin used the traditions of Egypt rather than Greece. The apparently forbidding Egyptian gods were for him less severe than those of the Greek pantheon and more appropriate for the teaching of children. The Egyptian Neith was a figure of benevolence and wisdom; the Greek Athena, though equally wise and benevolent, carried on her shield the Gorgon's head, with represents

that knowledge which separates, in bitterness, hardness, and sorrow, the heart of the full-grown man from the heart of the

---

6 Kingsley, *The Heroes: Or Greek Fairy Tales for my Children* (1855), in *The Life and Works of Charles Kingsley*, 19 vols. (London, 1903), xix. 212–13.

child. For out of imperfect knowledge spring terror, dissension, danger, and disdain; but from perfect knowledge, given by the full-revealed Athena, strength and peace, in sign of which she is crowned by the olive spray, and bears the resistless spear. (xviii. 445–5)

The bitter consequences of 'imperfect knowledge' seem to reflect the difficulty of Ruskin's own struggle for religious understanding. But 'full-revealed Athena' represents 'perfect knowledge', and with it a peace denied to the understanding of the child. It is a dark peace, for Ruskin's reference to the crown of wild olive as its sign indicates its association with the acceptance of human mortality. We have seen how he derived the title of the collection of essays in which this passage was published, *The Crown of Wild Olive*, from Aristophanes' *Plutus*, making the wild olive an image for the acknowledgement of death's finality. Ruskin had come to feel the lack of any comforting belief in eternal reward in Greek mythology as the most essential of the features which distinguished it from Christianity. In this respect the Greeks also differed from the Egyptians, whose religion was largely based on the concept of a life after death. The Egyptians were preoccupied with 'the perpetual contemplation of death, and of future judgement' (xviii. 461). This may partly account for the prominence of Greek rather than Egyptian mythology in works of this period other than *The Ethics of the Dust*. In turning from Christianity to a concept of religious faith in which ancient mythology could play a serious part, Ruskin was not moving towards a more liberal, or indeed more comfortable, spiritual position. His reverence for Greek myth was part of his need to come to terms with his changed belief. The Greek concept of human mortality, in which Ruskin hoped to find new strength, figures prominently in his work in the late 1860s.

Ruskin had been concerned with the question of eternal life since the religious crisis of the late 1850s. In 1861, at a time when religious issues were much on his mind, he had written to his father: 'It is a difficult thing, to live without hope of another world, when one has been used to it for forty years. But by how much the more difficult, by so much it makes one braver and stronger; it is a grand thing to feel what a lie that is of Young's, when he says that a man who has no eternal hopes must necessarily be a knave'[7] (vol. xvii, p. xxxviii). He returned to the theme in a letter of the following year claiming that

so far from its being difficult or strange for a man to hold his morality when he has lost what is called in modern language religion, I believe that all true nobleness and worthiness only comes out when people cease to think of another world. The relations of God to us have been entirely broken and obscured by human lies; it is impossible at present to recover or ascertain them, on *our* side, and we must walk in darkness, till better days come.[8] (vol. xvii, pp. xxxviii–xxxix)

The loss of faith increased, rather than lessened, the burden of moral responsibility. The concept of eternity has a temporal force. Either man is immortal or he is not. There could be no compromise. In 1867 Ruskin posed the dilemma in a lecture at Cambridge:

One of these alternatives must, I repeat, be true, and if you are men you cannot encounter either of them with a smile, nor steel yourself by mockery against the hour which must bring you either face to face with Death, or face to face with God. But this you know, that whether you have to prepare for inexorable judgement or for endless darkness, and for one you must, the deeds and methods of life which you will be able joyfully to look back upon must be the

---

[7] The letter is dated 29 Sept. 1861. Ruskin refers to Young's *Night Thoughts*, vii. 1179–80: 'Who tells me he denies his soul immortal, | Whate'er his boast, has told me he's a knave.' A subsequent letter to his father, written six days later, provides further evidence of Ruskin's association of the loss of faith with the loss of childhood: 'I have your kind note of the 2nd, saying you would give half of all you have if I were feeling like the Nun at Le Puy. Would you rather, then, have kept me in the ignorance necessary to produce that feeling? It might have been once. Never can be now—once emerged from it, it is gone for ever, like childhood. I know no example in history of men once breaking away from their early beliefs, and returning to them again' (xxxvi. 384). Ruskin recalls his encounter with the nun at Le Puy in *Praeterita* (1885–9). See xxxv. 478.

[8] The counsel which Ruskin received from his father may well have influenced the much more circumspect approach to these matters in his public writings. Writing to his son on Christmas Day 1862, John James Ruskin advised caution: 'There appears to me to be great Heartlessness in parading our Doubts if we can do no harm by being Quiet—& on the contrary risk great harm by spreading them—Think of all English Towns exhibiting Sabbath Scenes like the neighbourhood of Victoria Theatre—in place of the sweet Parish Churches & congregations approaching them in decency & order' (Unpubl. letter, Bem. MS C4).

same, and that of these glittering days of yours, numbered or numberless, no ray should fade that has not seen some strain to scatter the evil and confirm the good and grace in your souls; that so the light of them may at last endure either in the sight of angels, or memory-assisted strength of men. (xix. 189–90)

'The Mystery of Life and its Arts' (1868), one of the severest works of this troubled period in his life, echoes this solemn note:

Although your days are numbered, and the following darkness sure, is it necessary that you should share the degradation of the brute, because you are condemned to its mortality; or live the life of the moth, and of the worm, because you are to companion them in the dust? Not so; we may have but a few thousands of days to spend, perhaps hundreds only—perhaps tens; nay, the longest of our time and best, looked back on, will be but as a moment, as the twinkling of an eye; still we are men, not insects; we are living spirits, not passing clouds. (xviii. 179–80)

The supposedly 'heathen' position is given a dignity equal with that of Christianity.

The preface to *The Crown of Wild Olive* (1866) expresses the humanistic mood which characterizes Ruskin's middle years in terms of Greek religion. The 'heathen' creed seemed to offer no consoling prospect of heaven. Any afterlife which the Greeks envisaged was, at best, that of a grey world of melancholy shades. τεθνᾶσιν οἱ θανόντες, says Admetus in Euripides' *Alcestis*,[9] a play which Ruskin describes as 'perhaps the central example of the *idea* of all Greek drama' (vii. 273n.). Without the dubious solace of reparation or reward beyond the grave, the Greeks had no alternative but to concentrate their energies on the life of this world.[10] In this Ruskin felt they had something important to teach his Christian readers. For there were chastening implications in

---

[9] 'Dead are the dead' (Euripides, *Alcestis*, 541).

[10] The Greeks were not without a concept of immortality; nor was Ruskin unaware of this. The *Alcestis* turns on life restored from the grave. Ideas of eternal life appear in the writings of Plato and Pindar, two favourite authors for Ruskin. Redemption from death is not, however, a foundation of Greek religion in the same way that it can be said to form the basis of Christianity. In the closing pages of 'Athena Chalinitis', the first section of *The Queen of the Air*, Ruskin qualifies his emphasis on the absence of heaven in Greek faith by quoting the beautiful description of the Isles of the Blest from Pindar's second *Olympian Ode*.

the acceptance of the mortality of the individual. Ruskin's point is sharpened by irony: 'It made all the difference in addressing a body of men subject to considerable hardship, and having to find some way out of it—whether one could confidently say to them, "My friends,—you have only to die, and all will be right;" or whether one had any secret misgiving that such advice was more blessed to him that gave than to him that took it' (xviii. 393). The 'secret misgiving' was Ruskin's own, and it prompted the imperative tone of the preface to his volume.

'Traffic', the second of the lectures published in *The Crown of Wild Olive*, assigns a wider treatment to the concept of Greek religion introduced in the preface. In this justly famous lecture, Ruskin juxtaposes modern materialism with three great religions of the past—the Greek, the medieval, and that of the Renaissance. The Christian faith of the medieval age is described as the 'religion of Comfort. Its great doctrine is the remission of sins; for which cause, it happens, too often, in certain phases of Christianity, that sin and sickness themselves are partly glorified, as if, the more you had to be healed of, the more divine was the healing' (xviii. 446). The religion of the Renaissance is 'the religion of Pleasure, in which all Europe gave itself to luxury, ending in death' (xviii. 447). Only the Greek faith earns Ruskin's unmixed respect. Taking the religion of Athens to be representative of the religion of Greece, Ruskin defines it as the worship of 'the God of Wisdom' (xviii. 445). He begins his description with a reference to Max Müller's etymological theory of the origins of ancient myth: 'The first Greek idea of deity was that expressed in the word, of which we keep the remnant in our words "*Di*-urnal" and "*Di*-vine"—the god of *Day*, Jupiter the revealer. Athena is his daughter, but especially daughter of the Intellect, springing armed from the head'[11] (xviii. 445). Ruskin goes on to summarize the interpretation of Athena that he had built up in the fifth

[11] F. M. Müller's essay, 'Jupiter, the Supreme Aryan God', is the most likely source for Ruskin's etymology here. Müller's essay was published in the second series of his *Lectures on the Science of Language* in 1864. This would suggest that Ruskin included his reference after he had first delivered the lecture, for Müller's volume appeared after 21 Apr., the date of Ruskin's lecture. Müller dates his preface 11 June 1864.

volume of *Modern Painters*, *The Cestus of Aglaia*, and *The Ethics of the Dust*:

We are only with the help of recent investigation beginning to penetrate the depth of meaning couched under the Athenaic symbols: but I may note rapidly, that her aegis, the mantle with the serpent fringes, in which she often, in the best statues, is represented as folding up her left hand, for better guard; and the Gorgon, on her shield, are both representative mainly of the chilling horror and sadness (turning men to stone, as it were,) of the outmost and superficial spheres of knowledge—that knowledge which separates, in bitterness, hardness, and sorrow, the heart of the full-grown man from the heart of the child. For out of imperfect knowledge spring terror, dissension, danger, and disdain; but from perfect knowledge, given by the full-revealed Athena, strength and peace, in sign of which she is crowned with the olive spray, and bears the resistless spear. (xviii. 445–6)

We have seen that this interpretation had some degree of personal meaning for Ruskin. As if to conceal this implication, he prefaces his description of Athena with acknowledgement of a debt to contemporary research. The explicit reference previously made to the work of Max Müller might suggest this as the source that his readers are intended to recognize in his allusion to 'recent investigation' at this point. In fact, Ruskin's interpretation of Athena bears no resemblance to that of Müller, who, predictably, sees the goddess as a manifestation of the dawn.[12] Ruskin is not here concerned with the 'physical character' of Athena, but with her 'ethical character', an aspect of the goddess which held no interest for Max Müller. His aim is to show that this conception of deity is founded on the stern discipline that resulted from the lack of the 'comfort' that had defined the Christianity of the middle ages. For the Greek, as Ruskin now hoped for himself, 'every habit of life, and every form of his art developed themselves from the seeking this bright, serene, resistless wisdom; and setting himself, as a man, to do things evermore rightly and strongly; not with any ardent affection or ultimate hope; but with a resolute and continent energy of will as

---

[12] 'I believe that the root *ah*, which yielded in Sanskrit Ahanâ (Aghnyâ, i.e. Ahnyâ), the Dawn, *ahan* and *ahar*, day, supplied likewise the germ of Athênê' (F. M. Müller, *Lectures on the Science of Language*, 2nd Ser. (London, 1864), 502).

knowing that for failure there was no consolation and for sin there was no remission' (xviii. 446). A footnote to this passage asserts that the Greek faith was as far from the Renaissance devotion to beauty as from the medieval religion of comfort:

It is an error to suppose that the Greek worship, or seeking, was chiefly of Beauty. It was essentially of rightness and strength, founded on Forethought: the principal character of Greek art is not beauty, but design: and the Dorian Apollo-worship and Athenian Virgin-worship are both expressions of divine wisdom and purity. Next to these great deities, rank, in power over the national mind, Dionysus and Ceres, the givers of human strength and life; then, for heroic examples, Hercules. There is no Venus-worship among the Greeks in the great times: and the Muses are essentially teachers of Truth, and of its harmonies (xviii. 446)

Truth, rightness, and strength—moral rather than aesthetic qualities seemed to Ruskin the foundation of Greek worship. These are the qualities which fail in the European religion that Ruskin finally describes; the religion of the Bradford merchants to whom his address is directed.

Their goddess, 'Britannia Agoraia', the 'Goddess of Getting on', is an ugly parody of Athena. Ruskin mockingly points to the honoured place she should have in the new Bradford Exchange:

And in the innermost Chambers of it there might be a statue of Britannia of the Market, who may have, perhaps advisably, a partridge for her crest, typical at once of her courage in fighting for noble ideas, and of her interest in game; and round its neck, the inscription in golden letters, 'Perdix fovit quae non peperit'.[13] Then, for her spear, she might have a weaver's beam; and on her shield, instead of St. George's Cross, the Milanese boar, semi-fleeced, with the town of Gennesaret proper, in the field; and the legend, 'In the best market', and her corselet, of leather, folded over her heart in the shape of a purse, with thirty slits in it, for a piece of money to go in at, on each day of the month.[14] (xviii. 450–1)

---

[13] 'The partridge fosters what she has not brought forth.'

[14] Michael Simmonds has elucidated a reference to Shakespeare's *Timon of Athens* in Ruskin's denunciation of the 'Goddess of Getting on'. Like 'Traffic', *Timon of Athens* affirms the futility of owning gold for its own sake. Simmonds

This condemnation of modern paganism is weighted with a reference to the supposed paganism of the past. Ruskin translates the incisive closing words of Plato's fragmentary *Critias*, with its attack on materialism and greed, to confirm his own creed that there is 'no wealth but life'. Like the degenerate race that Plato describes, the merchants of Bradford have fallen into 'shapelessness of life, and baseness in the sight of him who could see, having lost everything that was fairest of their honour; while to the blind hearts which could not discern the true life, tending to happiness, it seemed that they were then chiefly noble and happy, being filled with all iniquity of inordinate possession and power'[15] (xviii. 457). The austerity of Plato's later philosophy did not exclude the promise of immortality. 'Traffic' ends with a severely qualified hope for eternal life; to be won, as Plato believed, through moral exertion and obedience to the law. 'You will know then how to build, well enough; you will build with stone well, but with flesh better; temples not made with hands, but riveted of hearts; and that kind of marble, crimson-veined, is indeed eternal' (xviii. 458).

In this carefully written public lecture, the mordant and passionate solemnity with which Ruskin uses Greek religion as a standard of faith with which to condemn modern materialism must have startled his first audience. The central part that Athena plays in his argument points to the fuller study of the goddess which was to appear, three years later, in *The Queen of the Air*.

Max Müller and The Queen of the Air

The ostensible subject of *The Queen of the Air* is the cycle of legends surrounding the Greek goddess Athena. An explanatory subtitle—'Being a Study of the Greek Myths of Cloud and

---

suggests that Ruskin derived the title of his lecture from Shakespeare's play:

APEMANTUS: Traffic confound thee, if the gods will not!
MERCHANT: If traffic do it, the gods do it.
APEMANTUS: Traffic's thy god, and thy god confound thee.
(*Timon of Athens*, I. i. 236–8)

See Michael Simmonds, 'Ruskin, Apemantus, and his Father', *Notes and Queries*, NS 26 (August 1979), 308–10.

[15] See Plato, *Critias*, 121 B.

Storm'—seems to suggest a scholarly direction for the book. In fact, like *The Ethics of the Dust*, *The Queen of the Air* is more eccentric, more ambitious, less coherent, and more interesting than its professed subject might lead its readers to imagine. Ruskin's research on Athena leads him into a disquisition on social, political, and ethical issues that had preoccupied him throughout the 1860s. For Ruskin, Athena is not simply a figure from the history of Greek religion. She is a living image of wisdom and of moral regeneration. To interpret the wisdom, and urge the regeneration, seemed to him a more appropriate purpose for his study than to give a substantially academic account of her mythology.

The emphases of *The Queen of the Air* are not separate from those of Ruskin's preceding works. During the 1860s his many themes and projects overlapped. It is difficult to look at any given book in isolation. They must be read in relation to each other, as parts of a continuous composite whole. *The Queen of the Air* is the least self-contained, and the least ordered, of Ruskin's works in these years. Robert Hewison has pointed out that the book suffers from a lack of editing.[16] Ruskin himself described it as 'desultory memoranda on a most noble subject' (xix. 291). He was in Italy and Switzerland while *The Queen of the Air* was going through the press and delegated his editorial duties to Charles Eliot Norton. Ruskin wrote to Norton from Verona:

The only excuse I made to myself for giving you the burden of seeing that book out, was that *no questions* might come to me—I intended *you* to decide. The moment I found questions sent I wrote home in a great passion, "Publish, anyhow". After that, they sent to ask me if I couldn't find a better word for "manifest", and nearly drove me crazy with the intense desire to knock them all down with the types. What they're about now I haven't the slightest idea. (xxxvi. 568)

Such a letter provides some explanation of the evident discontinuity in *The Queen of the Air*. The way in which the book depends on and refers to its immediate predecessors may be less obvious. For *The Queen of the Air* says surprisingly little that Ruskin had not said before. Passages are republished with

---

[16] Robert Hewison, *John Ruskin: The Argument of the Eye* (London, 1976), 154.

little alteration from previous writing—papers on 'Modesty' and 'Liberty' from the *Art Journal*; material from the pamphlet *Notes on the General Principles of Employment for the Destitute and Criminal Classes* (1868).[17] Less directly, Ruskin transferred material from other works to *The Queen of the Air* to a remarkable degree. The borrowed aspect of the book is particularly relevant to the mythological theory at its centre.

Here, Ruskin's readers have in part been misdirected by mistaken expectations. An apparently academic form invites the application of inappropriate criteria. Judged by the standards of scholarly research, *The Queen of the Air* displays the most alarming defects. A prefatory reference to 'the aspects of mythology, which only recent investigation has removed from the region of conjecture into that of rational inquiry' (xix. 291) has encouraged readers to see the work as a contribution to the school of comparative mythology. Few historians of the study of myth take account of *The Queen of the Air*: those who do usually condemn its eccentricity. Douglas Bush's influential survey of mythological influences on the literature of the nineteenth century assumes Max Müller to be a dominant presence in *The Queen of the Air*. He remarks on the book's 'scholarly moderation' as compared with the work of Müller and his followers, describing it as 'very sound ethically if not etymologically'.[18] This mildly dismissive note has proved persistent. More recently K. K. Ruthven writes that 'Norse mythology, with its storm-god Woden and its thunder-god Donar, encouraged late-Romantic thunder-mythologists like Adalbert Kuhn and Wilhelm Schwartz to reduce mythology to meteorology, as John Ruskin did while examining Greek myths of cloud and storm in *The Queen of the Air*.'[19] The work of German thunder-mythologists has only the remotest bearing on Ruskin's thinking in *The Queen of the Air*. He never, unlike Carlyle, took the slightest interest in Norse myths. Nor is it

---

[17] For an account of the complicated bibliographical history of *The Queen of the Air*, see xix. 283.

[18] Douglas Bush, *Mythology and the Romantic Tradition in English Poetry* (Cambridge, Mass., 1937), 399.

[19] K. K. Ruthven, *Myth* (London, 1976), 13.

fair to claim that Ruskin reduced mythology to meteorology. Ruskin's particular dislike for German scholarship makes it ironic that he should be associated with a German tradition so different from his own line of thought.

Far from assuming that *The Queen of the Air* owed its inspiration to the school of comparative mythology, the first critics of the book took Ruskin to task for not following the precedent of Max Müller more closely. Reviews were not sympathetic. The *Spectator* rebukes Ruskin for taking 'no notice whatever of the happy suggestion put forward by Max Müller, who identifies Athena with the dawn springing from the East, the forehead of the sky, and thus both explains her name and makes the strange legend of her birth significant and beautiful. This would have been a field eminently suitable to the display of Mr. Ruskin's peculiar mastery of language, and it is strange that he has altogether missed it.'[20] Ruskin must have been enraged by this complacent assumption that his proper function was the discovery of subjects suitable for the display of his 'peculiar mastery of language'. The *Saturday Review* was both tarter and more perceptive. Ruskin's method is shrewdly criticized as being 'not more scientific than that of Lord Bacon':[21]

Mr. Ruskin is not careful to reproduce the myths accurately, nor does he appear to be conscious that no explanation can be received as accurate in the case of any one myth which fails at the same time to explain all other cognate myths. Still less does he seem to see that the names in one language cannot be safely interpreted until we have compared them with names belonging to similar legends in other dialects; that Athene and Achilleus, Erinys, Helen, Paris, and Briseis cannot be explained except by a comparison with Ahana, Aharyu, Saramâ, Saranya, Paru, and Brisaya.[22]

Such strictures demonstrate a contemporary recognition that Müller's theories were not synonymous with those of Ruskin. Historical accuracy was never allowed to claim priority in Ruskin's methods of mythological analysis; nor were Indian myths of any more interest to him than those of the North.

---

[20] *Spectator*, 17 July 1869, 852.
[21] See below, pp. 123–4.
[22] *Saturday Review*, 21 Aug. 1869, 258.

The idea that Müller was the primary influence on Ruskin's analysis of myth in *The Queen of the Air* came later and owes much to the way in which the work was presented in the Library Edition. The editorial introduction to the volume places it in a particular setting:

In considering *The Queen of the Air* as a contribution to the study of Greek mythology, the reader should remember the date at which it was written. The views of the philological school, headed by Max Müller, were then in the ascendant. 'Comparative mythology', as the philological school understand the term, consisted of a comparison of the roots of words; mythology was 'a disease of language', and the common origin of all the myths was to be found in natural, and especially in solar, phenomena. This is the doctrine to which, by implication, Ruskin assented; indeed, he expressly refers . . . to 'the splendid investigation of recent philologists', he says . . . 'to account for the errors of antiquity'. (vol. xix. p. lxvii)

A quotation without its context here creates a peculiarly misleading effect. For Ruskin's use of the phrase 'the errors of antiquity' is partly ironical. His most deeply felt objection to contemporary mythological research lay in his conviction that it was all too certain of the 'errors of antiquity', while it remained blind to its wisdom. Ruskin begins his work with a plea for such recognition:

I will not ask your pardon for endeavouring to interest you in the subject of Greek Mythology; but I must ask your permission to approach it in a temper different from that in which it is frequently treated. We cannot justly interpret the religion of any people, unless we are prepared to admit that we ourselves, as well as they, are liable to error in matters of faith; and that the convictions of others, however singular, may in some points have been well founded, while our own, however reasonable, may in some particulars be mistaken. You must forgive me, therefore, for not always distinctively calling the creeds of the past, 'superstition', and the creeds of the present day, 'religion'; as well as for assuming that a faith long forgotten may once have been sincere. It is the task of the Divine to condemn the errors of antiquity, and of the Philologist to account for them: I will only pray you to read, with patience and human sympathy, the thoughts of men who lived without blame in a darkness they could not dispel; and to remember that, whatever charge of folly may justly attach to the saying,—'There is no God', the folly is prouder, deeper, and less pardonable, in saying 'There is no God but for me'. (xix. 295–6)

Ruskin was in accord with Müller's belief that mythology had an intimate connection with natural phenomena, though he had not been persuaded of the predominant influence of the sun in Greek myth. Yet the idea that the gods of Greece might represent forces in nature had been common long before German scholarship developed it into scientific theory. In *The Queen of the Air* Ruskin refers to poets, rather than scholars, as guides in these matters: 'So that you may obtain a more truthful idea of the nature of Greek religion and legend from the poems of Keats, and, in general grasp of subject, far more powerful, recent work of Morris, than from frigid scholarship, however extensive' (xix. 309). Keats, Morris, and countless others had used the natural scheme of reference in Greek religion for purposes quite other than the investigative ends of scholarship. There is no reason to suppose that this widely attractive concept had been suggested to Ruskin by the researches of Max Müller.

Ruskin's debt to the school of comparative mythology in *The Queen of the Air* may be seen in his thinking on language, rather than on myth. His occasional references to Müller are made in the context of etymological research. It is in this direction that his respect for Müller's work chiefly lay. His most substantial and public acknowledgement of a debt appears in the lecture 'Of Kings' Treasuries' (1865). Ruskin recommends that his audience should study the histories of words: 'Read Max Müller's lectures thoroughly, to begin with; and, after that, never let a word escape you that looks suspicious. It is severe work; but you will find it, even at first, interesting, and at last endlessly amusing. And the general gain to your character, in power and precision, will be quite incalculable' (xviii. 69). Other references confirm the nature of his debt. In *The Ethics of the Dust* Ruskin alludes to Müller's analysis of the word 'virtue': 'The very word "virtue" means, not "conduct", but "strength", vital energy in the heart. Were you not reading about that group of words beginning with V,—vital, virtuous, vigorous, and so on,—in

Max Müller, the other day Sibyl?' (xviii. 288). Ruskin returns to the question in the following lecture:

L. You know I was to tell you about the words that began with V. Sibyl, what does 'virtue' mean, literally?

SIBYL. Does it mean courage?

L. Yes; but a particular kind of courage. It means courage of the nerve; vital courage. That first syllable of it, if you look in Max Müller, you will find really means 'nerve', and from it comes 'vis', and 'vir', and 'virgin' (through vireo), and the connected word 'virga'—a 'rod';—the green rod, or springing bough of a tree, being the type of perfect human strength, both in the use of it in the Mosaic story, when it becomes a serpent, or strikes the rock; or when Aaron's bears its almonds; and in the metaphorical expressions, the 'Rod out of the stem of Jesse', and the 'Man whose name is the Branch', and so on. And the essential idea of real virtue is that of a vital human strength, which instinctively, constantly, and without motive, does what is right. (xviii. 301)

The etymology may have been inspired by Müller; the moral emphasis is entirely Ruskin's own. Max Müller's *Lectures on the Science of Language* do not in fact provide the direct reference to the root of the word 'virtue' that Ruskin's allusion implies;[23] though Müller does suggest the vegetative associations of the word: 'Navigation in the Greek water was considered safe after the return of the Pleiades; and it closed after they disappeared. The Latin name for the *Pleiades* is *Vergiliae*, from *virga*, a sprout or twig.'[24] Müller had referred to the word 'virtue' in his famous essay on 'Comparative Mythology' (1856), but again without Ruskin's specific interpretation. Müller uses the word as an example of the way in which language struggles to express abstract concepts:

As far as language is concerned, an abstract word is nothing but an adjective raised into a substantive; but in thought the conception of a quality as a subject, is a matter of extreme difficulty, and, in strict logical parlance, impossible. If we say, 'I love virtue', we seldom connect any definite notion with virtue. Virtue is not a being, however insubstantial; it is nothing individual, personal, active; nothing that could by itself produce an expressible impression on

---

[23] Writing to Constance Oldham in a letter of 7 Nov. 1866, Ruskin confesses 'I cannot find this passage about nerves in Muller myself now, but I am still almost sure it is there' (*Winnington Letters*, p. 594).

[24] F. M. Müller, *Lectures on the Science of Language*, 1st Ser. (London, 1861), 7.

our mind. The word virtue is only a short-hand expression, and
when men said for the first time 'I love virtue', what they meant by
it originally was 'I love all things that are virtuous'.[25]

From this position Müller moves, in the second series of his
Lectures on the Science of Language, to use the word 'virtue'
to illustrate the linguistic basis of his theory of myth. His
dismissive attitude towards mythology here underlines the
divergence between his approach and that of Ruskin:

A name like the Latin *virtus* was originally intended to express a
quality, manliness, the quality of a man, or rather every good
quality peculiar to a man. As long as this noun was used merely as a
noun of quality, as an adjective changed into a substantive, no
mischief could arise. . . . But when the mind, led away by the
outward semblance of the word *virtus*, conceived what was
intended merely as a collective predicate, as a personal subjective
essence, then the mischief was done: an adjective had become a
substantive, a predicate had been turned into a subject; and as there
could not be any real and natural basis on which the spurious being
could rest, it was placed, almost involuntarily, on the same pedestal
on which the statues of the so-called divine powers had been
erected; it was spoken of as a supernatural or a divine being.
Virtus, manliness, instead of being possessed by man, was herself
spoken of as possessing, as ruling, as inciting man. She became a
power, a divine power, and she soon received temples, altars, and
sacrifices, like other more ancient gods.[26]

For Müller, mythology was idolatry. Ruskin must have
known this passage. He may have had it in mind when he
returned to the word 'virtue' in *The Queen of the Air*: 'But
the first syllable of the name of Virgil has relation also to
another group of words, of which the English ones, virtue,
and virgin, bring down the force to modern days. It is a group
containing mainly the idea of "spring", or increase of life in
vegetation—the rising of the new branch of the tree out of the
bud, and of the new leaf out of the ground' (xix. 336). Müller
is the likely source for this etymological analysis of 'virtue',
which is close to that previously given in *The Ethics of the
Dust*. But Ruskin makes no reference to Müller's use of the
word as an illustration of the origins of myth. It is not likely

25 F. M. Müller 'Comparative Mythology', p. 34.
26 F. M. Müller, *Lectures* (2nd Ser.), pp. 560–4.

that he responded sympathetically to this aspect of Müller's argument.

Ruskin was attracted by the idea that words conceal a veri-fiable meaning which is unchanging, a core of moral truth such as he discerned in Greek mythology. The study of words could, like the study of myth, provide a counterbalance for the false ideal of 'progress' in modern thought. In suggesting that etymology might have an important contemporary applica-tion, he is in agreement with Max Müller. Müller had pointed to such a possibility in his *Lectures on the Science of Language*:

Men would often see what a small pittance of reason and truth, or possibly none at all, is mixed with those huffing opinions they are swelled with, if they would but look beyond fashionable sounds, and observe what ideas are, or are not, comprehended under those words with which they so confidently lay about them. I shall imagine I have done some service to the truth, peace, and learning, if, by an enlargement on this subject, I can make men reflect on their own use of language, and given them reason to suspect, that since it is frequent for others, it may also be possible for them, to have sometimes very good and approved words in their mouths and writings, with very uncertain, little, or no signification.[27]

Müller's disquiet arises from a conviction that certain emo-tive words lack the significance claimed for them. In 'Of Kings' Treasuries' Ruskin suggests that they may assume false meaning. He claims that words may

wear chameleon cloaks—"ground-lion" cloaks, of the colour of the ground of any man's fancy: on that ground they lie in wait, and rend them with a spring from it. There never were creatures of prey so mischievous, never diplomatists so cunning, never poisoners so deadly, as these masked words; they are the unjust stewards of all men's ideas: whatever fancy or favourite instinct a man most cherishes, he gives to his favourite masked word to take care of for him; the word at last comes to have an infinite power over him,—you cannot get at him but by its ministry. (xviii. 66)

Again, this is a theme to which Ruskin returns in *The Queen of the Air*. It is now chiefly religious controversy that he has in mind. He suggests a linguistic connection between

---

[27] Müller, op. cit., 335.

Athena's function as goddess of the air and her spiritual power, noting that the word 'spirit' came to be associated with the Greek word for 'breathing'[28] (xix. 351). He asserts that the meaning of the word 'spirit' is 'certain and practical' (xix. 351) as a shaping force in human life and that a proper understanding of this word protects against the materialism of science on the one side and religious fanaticism on the other:

You need not fear, on the one hand, that either the sculpturing or the loving power can ever be beaten down by the philosophers into a metal or evolved by them into a gas: but, on the other hand, take care that you yourselves, in trying to elevate your conception of it, do not lose its truth in a dream, or even in a word. Beware always of contending for words: you will not find them easy to grasp, if you know them in several languages. (xix. 351–2)

Ruskin is in agreement with Müller in stressing the elusiveness of words: unlike Müller, however, he claimed that their shifting forms concealed an underlying certainty of meaning.

Müller had focused public attention on the study of etymology. But the discipline has a long history, and Plato's *Cratylus* reminds us that it was not unknown to the Greeks.[29] This dialogue, concerned with the origins and nature of language, includes much etymological speculation. The *Cratylus* suggests the fascination of such research, while it doubts its ultimate value. The etymologies proposed by Socrates grow wilder and wilder, and hint at some scepticism on the part of Plato. Nevertheless, Ruskin would have been interested by the insistent focus on words in the *Cratylus*. The dialogue may be read as a refutation of the Heraclitean

[28] The idea of πνεῦμα as 'breath-soul' is an old one. According to Aristotle it originated with the Pythagoreans: ἔοικε δὲ καὶ τὸ παρὰ τῶν Πυθαγορείων λεγόμενον τὴν αὐτὴν ἔχειν διάνοιαν· ἔφασαν γάρ τινες αὐτῶν ψυχὴν εἶναι τὰ ἐν τῷ ἀέρι ξύσματα, οἱ δὲ τὸ ταῦτα κινοῦν. 'The theory handed down from the Pythagoreans seems to mean the same thing; for some of them have declared that the soul is identical with the particles of the air, and others with what makes these particles move' (Aristotle, *De Anima*, 404a17–19). W. Guthrie notes that 'The first form of the Pythagorean view mentioned by Aristotle sounds the more primitive, and the second a refinement on it in a spiritual direction, though "what moved them" was no doubt still thought of in what we should call material terms as the air (which indeed it is), identified with *pneuma* or the breath-soul' (W. Guthrie, *A History of Greek Philosophy* (Cambridge, 1962), i. 307).

[29] Ruskin had referred to the *Cratylus* in *Time and Tide* (1867).

doctrine of flux, to which Cratylus subscribes. The concept
of eternal change, made topical by the Darwinian revolution
in thought, was one which Ruskin found repellent. Like
Plato in the *Cratylus*, he uses etymology as a means of
opposing the idea. Ruskin is closer to Plato than Max Müller
in using etymology to demonstrate a spiritual meaning in the
myth of Athena. For the idea is not one which would have
found favour with Müller. We have seen how the linguistic
theory of myth denied its religious status. Müller begins his
lecture on 'Jupiter, the supreme Aryan God', the likely
source for Ruskin's etymological analysis of the words
'diurnal' and 'divine' in 'Traffic', by making his position on
this issue unequivocally clear:

There are few mistakes so widely spread and so firmly established
as that which makes us confound the religion and the mythology of
the ancient nations of the world. How mythology arises, necessarily
and naturally, I tried to explain in my former Lectures, and we saw
that, as an affection or disorder of language, mythology may infect
every part of the intellectual life of man. True it is that no ideas are
more liable to mythological disease than religious ideas, because
they transcend those regions of our experience within which
language has its natural origin, and must therefore, according to
their very nature, be satisfied with metaphorical expressions. Eye
hath not seen, nor ear heard, neither hath it entered into the heart
of man. Yet even the religions of the ancient nations are by no
means inevitably and altogether mythological. On the contrary, as
a diseased frame presupposes a healthy frame, so a mythological
religion presupposes, I believe, a healthy religion. Before the
Greeks could call the sky, or the sun, or the moon *gods*, it was
absolutely necessary that they should have framed to themselves
some idea of the godhead.[30]

Müller finds evidence for his belief that the Greeks had some
conception of a single godhead in Homer, quoting a passage
from the *Odyssey*, in which the swine-herd Eumaios offers

[30] F. M. Müller, *Lectures* (2nd Ser.), p. 413. The Greeks themselves had of course
questioned the truth of polytheism long before Plato's attack on the religious status
of mythology. Müller might, for instance, have found support from his theory that
the religion of the ancient world was not wholly mythological in the work of the pre-
Socratic philosopher Xenophanes, who argued against the existence of an
anthropomorphic hierarchy of divinities: 'God is one, greatest among gods and
men, in no way like mortals either in body or in mind' (Xenophanes, Fr. 23, trans.
Guthrie, *History of Greek Philosophy*, i. 374).

his hospitality to the disguised Odysseus. '"Eat", says the swineherd to Ulysses, "and enjoy what is here, for God will grant one thing, but another he will refuse, whatever he will in his mind, for he can do all things."'[31] Müller's use of Homer as a source of evidence for his conviction that Greek mythology was the corruption of an originally true religion is a reminder of Gladstone's Homeric studies. Gladstone, however, manifests none of the distaste for the supposed corruption that we find in Max Müller, who is vehement on this point:

Mythology has encroached on ancient religion, it has at some times well nigh choked its very life; yet through the rank and poisonous vegetation of mythic phraseology we may always catch a glimpse of that original stem round which it creeps and winds itself, and without which it could not enjoy even that parasitical existence which has been mistaken for independent vitality.[32]

Nothing could be further from Ruskin's claim that mythology was the expression of an intensely religious view of the world.

The Goddess of Wisdom

Since his earliest years, Ruskin had concerned himself with the attempt to interpret the 'inner language' of nature. Human myths—the 'dark sayings of men'—dismayed him. 'Natural myths', in contrast, enabled him to synthesize perceptions of the physical world with moral convictions, while preserving his image of himself as interpreter rather than creator.

For it seems to me that the scholars who are at present occupied in interpretation of human myths have most of them forgotten that there are any such things as natural myths; and that the dark sayings of men may be both difficult to read, and not always worth reading; but the dark sayings of nature will probably become clearer for the looking into, and will very certainly be worth reading. And, indeed, all guidance to the right sense of the human and variable myths will probably depend on our first getting at the sense of the natural and invariable ones. The dead hieroglyph may have meant this or that—the living hieroglyph means always the

---

[31] F. M. Müller, *Lectures* (2nd Ser.), p. 415. See Homer, *Odyssey*, xiv. 444.
[32] F. M. Müller, *Lectures* (2nd Ser.), p. 414.

same; but remember, it is just as much a hieroglyph as the other; nay, more,—a 'sacred or reserved sculpture', a thing with an inner language. (xix. 361)

In fact, Ruskin recreates rather than interprets myth in *The Queen of the Air*. Yet he was able to preserve his belief that his analysis was dependent on the separate and fixed body of meaning hidden in the forms of myth. This was an essential part of their attraction for him.

The uncompromisingly moral focus in Ruskin's study of myths led to a consideration of their developed forms, rather than the process of their origins and development. He repeats the analogy of the plant that he had introduced in speaking of the 'root and two branches' of a myth to indicate that it is the flower rather than the seed which interests him:

And the real meaning of any myth is that which it has at the noblest age of the nation among whom it is current. The farther back you pierce, the less significance you will find, until you come to the first narrow thought, which, indeed, contains the germ of the accomplished tradition, but only as the seed contains the flower. As the intelligence and passion of the race develop, they cling to and nourish their beloved and sacred legend; leaf by leaf, it expands, under the touch of more pure affections, and more delicate imagination, until at last the perfect fable burgeons out into symmetry of milky stem, and honeyed bell. (xix. 301)

The 'perfect fable' was that expressed in what Ruskin believed to be the greatest literature of the greatest period of Greek history. He names Pindar and Aeschylus as representatives of this perfection; while Homer expresses as much of the 'less developed thought of the preceding epoch' (xix. 303) as Ruskin feels to be his concern. The contrast between his 'milky stem, and honeyed bell' and the 'rank and poisonous vegetation' that Müller saw in Greek myth needs no pointing.

Though Ruskin differs from the comparative mythologists in his emphasis on the meaning of myths in their fully-developed state, he was not alone in his approach among those whose interest was founded in literature rather than science. In his *Studies of the Greek Poets* (1873-6) John Addington Symonds looked at myth as a form of art. 'The raw material of silk may interest the merchant or the man of science; the artist cares for the manufactured fabric, with its curious patterns and refulgent hues.'[33] Symonds, though he acknowledges a debt to Müller, is firm in his rejection of the 'disease of language' theory. Like both Ruskin and Müller, he suggests an organic concept of myth, comparing its growth with that of a plant:

Antiquarian theorists may persuade us that Myths are decayed, disintegrated, dilapidated phrases, the meaning of which had been lost to the first mythopœists. But they cannot tell us how these splendid flowers, springing upon the rich soil of rotting language, expressed in form and colour to the mental eye the thoughts and aspirations of whole races, presented a measure of the faculties to be developed during long ages of expanding civilization.[34]

Symonds develops an open opposition to Müller in the second series of his *Studies of the Greek Poets*. In his essay on 'Mythology', he refers to those who have 'taken refuge in the extraordinary paradox that myths are a disease of language'.[35] He rejects Müller's ideas largely because myth seemed to him the foundation of supreme art:

Seriously to entertain this view is tantamount to maintaining that corruption and disease may be the direct efficient causes of the highest art on which humanity can pride itself, since it is indisputable that the poems of Homer and the sculptures of Pheidias are the direct outgrowth of that 'bane of the ancient world', which, to quote another pithy saying of Max Müller, converted 'nomina' into 'numina'.[36]

Symonds did not wholly share Ruskin's veneration for mythology as a phenomenon valuable in itself. For him myth was to be esteemed because it led to art.

---

[33] John Addington Symonds, *Studies of the Greek Poets*, 2nd Ser. (London, 1876), 6.

[34] Symonds, *Studies of the Greek Poets*, 1st Ser. (London, 1873), 2.

[35] Symonds, *Studies* (2nd Ser.), p. 3.

[36] Ibid. 18–19. Symonds saw Ruskin's studies of mythology as part of the school inspired by Müller. In a letter dated 10 July 1881, he refers to 'people like Coxe and Ruskin, investigators mainly fanciful into Greek stories of a prehistoric period, who by Greeks of the age of Sophocles would have been held harmful as impious or harmless as crazy' (*The Letters of John Addington Symonds*, ed. H. M. Schueller and R. L. Peters, 3 vols. (Detroit, Mich., 1968), ii. 683). G. W. Cox (1827–1902) was a follower of Max Müller who had carried his master's theories to extraordinary lengths. But Ruskin, as we have seen, disclaimed any interest in the 'Greek stories of a prehistoric period'.

Though the mythological scholarship which Ruskin respected was characteristically that of an earlier generation, he was not wholly isolated from contemporary work. Edward Burnett Tylor (1832–1917) propounded an evolutionary theory of myth that was influential in the 1870s and 1880s; and in 1876 Ruskin described his *Researches into the Early History of Mankind and the Development of Civilization* (1865) as a book of 'rare value and research' (xxviii. 614). Ruskin knew Edward Tylor's brother, the geologist Alfred Tylor (1824–84), and this may have led to his interest in such a work. Edward Tylor was, like his brother, a rationalist. Yet his view of mythology stresses the role of poetic intuition. 'Fully to understand an old-world myth needs not evidence and argument alone, but deep poetic feeling.'[37] Like Ruskin, Tylor saw myth as an imaginative language rather than a scientific or purely historical phenomenon. Sensitive interpretation could reveal its meaning to the modern student:

> The poet contemplates the same natural world as the man of science, but in his so different craft strives to render difficult thought easy by making it visible and tangible, above all by referring the being and movement of the world to such personal life as his hearers feel within themselves, and thus working out in far-stretched fancy the maxim that 'Man is the measure of all things.' Let but the key be recovered to this mythic dialect, and its complex and shifting terms will translate themselves into reality, and show how far legend, in its sympathetic fictions of war, love, crime, adventure, fate, is only telling the perennial story of the world's daily life.[38]

Tylor, Ruskin, and Müller agree in seeing man's experience of the natural world as the basis of mythology. Tylor, however, has misgivings about Müller's all-embracing theories. 'Rash inferences which on the strength of mere resemblance derive episodes of myth from episodes of nature must be regarded with utter mistrust, for the student who has no more stringent criterion than this for his myths of sun and sky and dawn, will find them wherever it pleases him to seek them.'[39] Tylor skittishly illustrates his point with an exposition of the

---

[37] E. B Tylor, *Primitive Culture: Researches into the Development of Mythology, Philosophy, Religion, Art, and Custom*, 2 vols. (London, 1871), i. 276.

[38] Ibid. 285–6.

[39] Ibid. 287.

nursery 'Song of Sixpence' as a solar myth, which Ruskin might have enjoyed.

Ruskin was, however, quite at variance with Tylor's evolutionary theory of myth. Tylor was solidly convinced of the 'Rise and Progress of Human Civilization', which meant that he saw ancient mythology as necessarily savage and crude in relation to modern culture. Though Ruskin had praised Tylor, he also included a disparaging reference to the myth of Apollo in Tylor's *Researches into the Early History of Mankind* among a catalogue of modern follies[40] (xxviii. 613–14). The assumption of superiority in contemporary study of mythology was, for him, a pernicious result of the belief that the mythopoeic age marked a primitive stage of man's development. No amount of historical research could provide the scholar with a substitute for an

understanding of the nature of all true vision by noble persons; namely, that it is founded on constant laws common to all human nature; that it perceives, however darkly, things which are for all ages true;—that we can only understand it so far as we have some perception of the same truth;—and that its fulness is developed and manifested more and more by the reverberation of it from minds of the same mirror-temper, in succeeding ages. (xix. 310)

Ruskin had found stronger support for his veneration of Greek mythology in the work of Carl Otfried Müller. C. O. Müller, the most sensitive and intelligent of the pre-anthropological theorists in Germany, based his mythological studies entirely on the evidence of Greece. An ardent enthusiasm for Greek mythology is evident throughout his books. It is hardly an exaggeration to say that Müller's work, soon translated, introduced into England the concept of a scientific study of mythology in the modern sense. The tentative terminology of the translator's preface to the *History and Antiquities of the Doric Race* (1830) suggests the novelty of mythological studies:

As a considerable part of the following pages is dedicated to an examination of the early history and religion, and therefore the

---

[40] Tylor had noted that 'if the sun travels along its course like a glittering chariot, forthwith the wheels and the driver and the horses are there' (*Researches into the Early History of Mankind and the Development of Civilization* (London, 1865), 370).

mythology of the Doric race, we have had frequent occasion for a word which should express that subject of which mythology treats. Now, as mythology is a λόγος περὶ μύθων, nothing could be more precise or convenient than the term *mythus*, and its derivative *mythical*, which have been naturalized by the German writers, and which it has been lately attempted to introduce into our language.[41]

In 1864 Ruskin included an extensive quotation from C. O. Müller's *Doric Race* in his lecture on 'War', where he describes the book as one which 'probably most of you know well, and all ought to know' (xviii. 472). *The Doric Race*, together with Müller's *Ancient Art and its Remains*, provides important points of comparison with Ruskin's approach to the interpretation of myth. Particularly striking is Müller's decisively moral view of Greek mythology. For the Dorians, Apollo was the primary god, while Athena was chiefly worshipped by the Ionians. The analysis of religion in Müller's *Doric Race* focuses on Apollo. Müller sees Apollo as an expression of the Doric concept of a stern code of morality, asserting that 'the religion of the northern races . . . had in early times taken a more moral turn . . . Hence the Jupiter Hellanius of Aeacus, the Jupiter Laphystius of Athamas, and finally, the Doric Jupiter, whose son is Apollo, the prophet and warrior, are rather representatives of the moral order and harmony of the universe, after the ancient method, than of the creative powers of nature.'[42] Apollo is 'the far-darting god; his divine vengeance never misses its aim'.[43] His retribution is, however, 'only to inflict deserved punishment'.[44]

Ruskin contemplated writing a study of Apollo after the completion of *The Queen of the Air*.[45] He too saw Apollo as a god of moral order and shared C. O. Müller's view that this moral significance lay behind the god's association with music. In *Time and Tide* (1867) Ruskin claimed that 'music was, among the Greeks, quite the first means of education; that it

[41] Carl Otfried Müller, *The History and Antiquities of the Doric Race*, trans. H. Tufnell and G. C. Lewis, 2 vols. (London, 1830), vol. i, pp. iv–v.

[42] Ibid. 16–17.

[43] Ibid. 315.

[44] Ibid. 317.

[45] See vol. xix, pp. lxi, lxvi, 346. Ruskin wrote of *The Queen of the Air* that 'I should have had another such out by this time on the Apolline myths, and, perhaps, one of the Earth-Gods, but for my Oxford work' (xxxiv. 504). The letter is dated 18 May 1871.

was so connected with their system of ethics and of intellectual training, that the God of Music is with them also the God of Righteousness;—the God who purges and avenges iniquity, and contends with their Satan as represented under the form of Python, "the corrupter". And the Greeks were incontrovertibly right in this' (xvii. 368). Ruskin believed the Apollonian music of stringed instruments, rather than the wilder, more emotional music of wind instruments, to be the expression of order in its opposition to chaos. This seemed to him the meaning of Apollo's musical contest with Marsyas. 'Then, the strife of Apollo and Marsyas represents the enduring contest between music in which the words and thought lead, and the lyre measures or melodizes them, (which Pindar means when he calls his hymns "kings over the lyre,") and music in which the words are lost, and the wind or impulse leads,—generally, therefore, between intellectual, and brutal, or meaningless, music'[46] (xix. 343). Carl Müller, like Ruskin, saw Apollo's music as representative of an ordered harmony in the universe;[47] and, though Ruskin's interpretation clearly owes something to his dread of uncontrolled emotion and his instinct for verbal expression, he may have had Müller's precedent in mind here.

A wider parallel between C. O. Müller and Ruskin lies in their common belief that Greek mythology expresses a system of opposition, as the music of Apollo opposes the music of Marsyas. Müller notes that Apollo was

always considered as attended with certain beings whose nature was contrary to his own; his character could only be shewn in opposition with a system of hostile attributes and powers. As the *warring* and *victorious* god, he required enemies to combat and conquer: as the *pure* and *bright* god, he implies the existence of a dark and impure side of nature. In this manner the worship of Apollo resembled those religions, such as the ancient Persian, which were founded on the doctrine of *two principles*, one of good, the other of evil.[48]

This concept is to be found in Ruskin's view of myth. A Greek deity is marked by its opposite, by the enemy to be

---

[46] See Pindar, *Olympian Odes*, ii. 1. This is a point which Ruskin had previously made in his 1867 lecture on 'The Relation of National Ethics to National Arts'. See xix. 177.

[47] See C. O. Müller, *Doric Race*, i. 362–73.   [48] Ibid. 329.

overcome, 'as Hercules wears for his chief armour the skin of the Nemean lion, his chief enemy, whom he slew; and Apollo has for his highest name "the Pythian", from his chief enemy, the Python, slain; so Athena bears always on her breast, the deadly face of her chief enemy slain; the Gorgonian cold, and venomous agony, that turns living men to stone' (xix. 352-3). Greek mythology seemed to Ruskin as to Müller to express a fundamental morality: the contention between good and evil.

In 1869, however, the advent of comparative mythology made the moral bias of Carl Otfried Müller, and the limited field from which he drew his evidence, seem old-fashioned. We have seen that Max Müller, then at the zenith of his reputation, had suggested a view of mythology quite separate from religion or ethics. Ruskin's echoes of C. O. Müller are a reminder of his detachment from any scholarly vanguard. Ruskin is not unaware of the possibility of comparing the myths of the Greeks with those of supposedly more primitive races. He names, for instance, Fergusson's *Tree and Serpent Worship* (1866) as 'a work of very great value' (xix. 364) and refers those interested in the influence of the serpent 'over degraded races' (xix. 364) to its pages. He firmly declines, however, to investigate such an influence himself:

I cannot touch upon any of them here, except only to point out that, though the doctrine of the so-called 'corruption of human nature', asserting that there is nothing but evil in humanity, is just as blasphemous and false as a doctrine of the corruption of physical nature would be, asserting that there was nothing but evil in the earth,—there is yet the clearest evidence of a disease, plague, or cretinous imperfection of development, hitherto allowed to prevail against the greater part of the races of men; and this in monstrous ways, more full of mystery than the serpent-being itself. (xix. 364-5)

Ruskin never concerned himself with myths that could not be seen as religious or moral phenomena. 'You must remember, however, that in this, as in every other instance, I take the myth at its central time. This is only the meaning of the serpent to the Greek mind which could conceive an Athena' (xix. 364). The inclusive comparative approach was of no real interest to him.

In a guarded acknowledgement of the help he had received from Richard Payne Knight's *An Inquiry into the Symbolical Language of Ancient Art and Mythology* (1818),[49] Ruskin returns to an older tradition of scholarship. Knight's work showed more of the dash of the eighteenth-century dilettante and man of letters than the meticulous diligence of the generation that had succeeded him. He was not an orthodox authority for a student of mythology in the 1860s. Knight was, however, one of the first to be interested in the idea of a comparative mythology. His *An Account of the Remains of the Worship of Priapus* (1786) had suggested that pagan cults could be seen to share a common basis of religious symbolism, often grounded in fertility worship. The argument was seriously developed; but the illustrative evidence in *The Worship of Priapus* is gleefully obscene. The *Symbolical Language of Ancient Art* is more decorous. Knight's views, however, are unchanged.[50] Speaking of the religion of the Chaldeans, Knight remarks that

Like the Greeks, they personified these subordinate emanations, and gave them names expressing their different offices and attributes; such as Michael, Raphael, Uriel, Gabriel, & c.; which the Jews having adopted during the captivity, and afterwards engrafted upon the Mosaic system, they have still retained their primitive sanctity, and are solemnly invoked in many parts of Europe by persons, who would think themselves guilty of the most flagitious impiety, if they invoked the same personifications by the Greek or Latin titles of Mars, Mercury, Hermes or Apollo.[51]

Ruskin had only limited sympathy with Knight's belief in a universal worship of a generative principle. Yet, though he was not in any sense a comparative mythologist, the idea that the religion of the Jews and the religion of the Greeks concealed the same central truths was of great significance to

[49] Ruskin describes the work as 'not trustworthy, being little more than a mass of conjectural memoranda, but the heap is suggestive, if well sifted' (xix. 381 n.).

[50] See Frank J. Messmann, *Richard Payne Knight: The Twilight of Virtuosity* (The Hague and Paris, 1974): 'Analyzing Christianity's relationship to pagan religious ideas and practices, he showed himself a harbinger of radical theories that were to challenge old complacencies and to beget the nineteenth-century discipline of comparative religion' (p. 10).

[51] Richard Payne Knight, *An Inquiry into the Symbolical Language of Ancient Art and Mythology* (London, 1818), 61.

him. 'You would, perhaps, hardly bear with me if I endeavoured farther to show you—what is nevertheless perfectly true—the analogy between the spiritual power of Athena in her gentle ministry, yet irresistible anger, with the ministry of another Spirit whom we also, believing in as the universal power of life, are forbidden, at our worst peril, to quench or grieve'[52] (xix. 346). The circumspection with which Ruskin identifies Athena with the Holy Ghost only serves to highlight the fixity of his conviction.

Ruskin would also have found confirmation of his own beliefs in Knight's theory of a symbolic language in ancient religion. In *The Worship of Priapus*, Knight claimed that the 'forms and ceremonials of a religion are not always to be understood in their direct and obvious sense: but are to be considered as symbolical representatives of some hidden meaning, which may be extremely wise and just, though the symbols themselves, to those who know not their true signification, may appear in the highest degree absurd and extravagant.'[53] Thirty-two years later, Knight repeats his argument in *The Symbolical Language of Ancient Art*. Knight defends his allegorical method of interpreting mythology: 'Such refinement may, perhaps, seem inconsistent with the simplicity of the early ages: but we shall find, by tracing them to their source, that many of the gross fictions, which exercised the credulity of the vulgar Heathens, sprang from abstruse philosophy conveyed in figurative and mysterious expression.'[54] The description of myth with which Ruskin opens *The Queen of the Air* shows the extent to which he shares Knight's views: 'A myth, in its simplest definition, is a story with a meaning attached to it, other than it seems to have at first; and the fact that it has such a meaning is generally marked by some of its circumstances being extraordinary, or, in the common use of the word, unnatural' (xix. 296). It is noteworthy that the

[52] The first edition gave 'holding for' rather than 'believing in as'. The amendment, made in 1883, suggests the more positive Christianity to which Ruskin returned in his later years.

[53] Richard Payne Knight, *An Account of the Remains of the Worship of Priapus* (London, 1786), 24.

[54] Knight, *Symbolical Language*, 28–9. George P. Landow notes that Knight may have influenced Ruskin in this respect. See his *The Aesthetic and Critical Theories of John Ruskin* (Princeton, 1971), 401–3.

example with which Ruskin chooses to develop his theme—the myth of Hercules killing the water-serpent in the Lake of Lerna—is one which Knight treats in his *Symbolical Language of Ancient Art*.[55] Ruskin and Knight have more in common than the single cautious reference in *The Queen of the Air* would imply.[56]

The idea that myth might conceal a spiritual meaning beneath a marvellous story has a long history. One of the more important of Ruskin's encounters with this belief is to be seen in his study of Francis Bacon. In *The Wisdom of the Ancients* (1609)[57] Bacon, like Knight, suggests that 'when a story is told which could never have entered any man's head to conceive or relate on its own account, we must presume that it had some further reach.'[58] Ruskin, too, claims that the myth-maker, in order to point to the meaning which his story conceals, is careful to 'surprise your attention by adding some singular circumstance' (xix. 296). Tentative suggestions of correspondence between the religion of the ancient Greek and that of the Christian is also to be found in Bacon. In describing the story of Prometheus, a 'common and hacknied fable'[59] in his view, Bacon notes that it

is true that there are not a few things beneath which have a wonderful correspondency with the mysteries of the Christian faith. The voyage of Hercules especially, sailing in a pitcher to set Prometheus free, seems to present an image of God the Word hastening in the frail vessel of the flesh to redeem the human race. But I purposely refrain myself from all licence of speculation in this kind, lest peradventure I bring strange fire to the altar of the Lord.[60]

Bacon did not, however, ordinarily refrain himself from licence of speculation; his exegesis in *The Wisdom of the*

[55] Knight, *Symbolical Language*, pp. 100–1.

[56] This is suggested by the large number of references to Knight in Ruskin's 'Myth Book' (Bem. MS 45). Knight's discussion of the myth of Hercules and the Hydra and his association of this myth with that of the Python and Apollo is noted there.

[57] Ruskin had referred twice to *The Wisdom of the Ancients* in *Munera Pulveris*. See xvii. 208, 212.

[58] *The Works of Francis Bacon*, ed. J. Spedding, R. L. Ellis, and D. D. Heath, 7 vols. (London, 1858–61), vi. 697. Quoted by Landow, *Aesthetic and Critical Theories*, pp. 400–1.

[59] Bacon, *Works*, vi. 753.

[60] Ibid.

Ancients often owes more to ingenuity than to research. The haphazard quality of such an approach had been discredited by the more scientific procedures of Ruskin's contemporaries. Yet the method of *The Queen of the Air* often suggests a parallel with that of Bacon.

This is partly due to the fact that the investigation of myth in the work of both Bacon and Ruskin owes a substantial debt to the allegorical tradition of scriptural interpretation. Much of Ruskin's mythological analysis has a pervasively biblical and hortatory tone; for myths, like the Bible, seemed to him to have an ethical rather than a historical significance. He intended his readers to respond to *The Queen of the Air* as a religious work before they studied it as a scholarly text. Throughout the 1860s Ruskin had developed the concept of Greek religion as a standard of faith with which to measure and condemn the modern spirit. *The Queen of the Air* is the culmination of this development. 'Athena Chalinitis' approaches a conclusion with reference to the Greek concept of mortality that had haunted him since the loss of his faith. Ruskin asks his readers to remember that

what of good or right the heathens did, they did looking for no reward. The purest forms of our own religion have always consisted in sacrificing less things to win greater;—time, to win eternity,—the world, to win the skies. The order, 'sell that thou hast' is not given without the promise,—'thou shalt have treasure in heaven;' and well for the modern reader if he accepts the alternative as his Master left it—and does not practically read the command and promise thus: 'Sell that thou hast in the best market, and thou shalt have treasure in heaven also.' But the poor Greeks of the great ages expected no reward from heaven but honour, and no reward from earth but rest. (xix. 349–50)

As 'Traffic' had finally admitted a qualified hope for immortality, so 'Athena Chalinitis' ends with a balancing note of optimism. Ruskin translates the lyrical evocation of the Isles of the Blest from Pindar's second *Olympian Ode*, 'where there is sun alike by day, and alike by night—where they shall need no more to trouble the earth by strength of hands for daily bread—but the ocean breezes blow around

the blessed islands, and golden flowers burn on their bright
trees for evermore'[61] (xix. 350).

Ruskin's editors note that this passage is here 'rendered
freely' (xix 350 n.). In fact, it is very much condensed. The
Library Edition is provided with a number of dry notes to
warn the reader of what might be described as Ruskin's
departures from the conventions of classical scholarship in
The Queen of the Air. Ruskin remarks on an association
between the cloud and the Greek god Hermes: 'Now, it will
be wholly impossible, at present, to trace for you any of the
minor Greek expressions of this thought, except only that
Mercury, as the cloud shepherd, is especially called Eriophoros,
the wool-bearer' (xix. 322). Ruskin's editors note that this 'is
a puzzling statement, for no instance can be found of the
application of this rare epithet to Hermes' (xix. 322 n.).
Hermes is, however, sometimes called 'criophorus', which
means 'ram-bearing'. Ruskin's editors plausibly suggest that
Ruskin had mistaken either the English 'c' for an 'e' or the
Greek 'κ' for 'ε' in a manuscript note. This would seem to be
an error of the kind which the scanty editing that *The Queen
of the Air* received might explain. However, Ruskin repeats
his attribution of the epithet 'eriophorus' to Hermes in
Ariadne Florentina (1872), having had three years in which to
discover his mistake. It was not, for him, a matter of priority.

Though Ruskin did not consider scholarly accuracy to be
of primary importance, he did not deviate from its standards
without reason. Considerations other than those of the scholar
often lay behind his interpretations. Most would agree, for
instance, that his translation of Homer's description in the
Odyssey of the house of Aeolus is inexact. Ruskin gives:

Then we came to the Aeolian island, and there dwelt Aeolus
Hippotades, dear to the deathless gods: there he dwelt in a floating
island, and round it was a wall of brass that could not be broken;
and the smooth rock of it ran up sheer. To whom twelve children
were born in the sacred chamber—six daughters and six strong

---

[61] See Pindar, *Olympian Odes*, ii. 60–73. This ode was evidently to the forefront
of Ruskin's mind at this time. He had already referred, as we have seen, to its
opening line; and in 'Athena Chalinitis' he refers also to Pindar's epithet for Semele
in this ode—ταννέθειρα—Semele 'with the stretched-out hair' (xix. 327); see
Olympian Odes, ii. 26.

sons; and they dwell for ever with their beloved father, and their mother strict in duty; and with them are laid up a thousand benefits; and the misty house around them rings with fluting all the day long.[62]

There are two difficulties here. The first lies in Ruskin's rendering of the word κνισῆεν as 'misty', rather than 'steaming', which would be a more usual choice in association with the word ὀνείατα. Similarly, 'food' rather than 'benefits' would ordinarily translate ὀνείατα.[63] Writing censoriously to Ruskin about his version of this passage, Charles Eliot Norton was quick to note these unorthodox points. Norton did not, however, remark on the second difficulty in Ruskin's version; the silent omission, one must assume for modesty's sake, of Homer's reference to Aeolus giving his six daughters as wives to his sons.[64] In replying to Norton's protest at the idea of the house being misty, rather than full of the steam of cooking, Ruskin reveals the role he saw for himself as interpreter of myths. He was no whit abashed by Norton's strictures:

That use of κνισῆεν is precisely the most delicious thing in the myth —it is that which makes it an enigma. Had Homer used any other word than that he would have shown his cards in a moment—which he never does, nor any other of the big fellows. Yet it ought at once to lead you to the mythic meaning when you remember that meat smoke is precisely what winds would carry away—that the house being full of the smell of dinner is precisely the *Unwindiest* character you could have given it. Well, that ought to have set you considering: and then you will see that while the *Calm* cloud is high in heaven, the Wind cloud rises up from the earth and is actually the steam of it, under the beneficent Cookery of the winds, which make it good

---

[62] Homer, *Odyssey*, x. 1–11. See xix. 311.

[63] Ruskin defended this translation in a letter to Charles Eliot Norton: 'ὀνείατα is a perfectly heavenly word—it means the benefit of *well digested* anything; all my books are ὀνείατα—it means a dinner ate imaginatively—"ὅσον ἐν ἀσφοδέλῳ" —(xxxvii. 20). The letter is not precisely dated, but its place in a sequence of letters to Norton suggests that it was written between 17 and 26 Aug. 1870. See Hesiod, *Works and Days*, 40–1: 'Fools! They know not how much more the half is than the whole, nor what great advantage there is in mallow and asphodel.' Ruskin had quoted from these lines in the closing pages of *Unto This Last* to illustrate his point that the sum of enjoyment depends 'not on the quantity of things tasted, but on the vivacity and patience of taste' (xvii. 114).

[64] 'ἔνθ' ὅ γε θυγατέρας πόρεν υἱάσιν εἶναι ἀκοίτις: and he gave his daughters to his sons to wife' (Homer, *Odyssey*, x. 7).

for food. 'Thy Dwelling shall be of the Dew of Heaven, and of the fatness of the Earth.'

My long training in Hebrew myths had at least the advantage of giving this habit of always looking for the under-thought, and then my work on physical phenomena just gave me what other commentators, scholars only, can never have, the sight of what Homer saw.

I bought a picture by Holman Hunt this year, of a Greek sunset, with all the Homeric colours in the sky—and the κνισῆεν cloud just steaming up from the hills, so *exactly* true that everybody disbelieves it being true at all.[65] (xxxvii. 19–20)

Ruskin here makes startling claims with disarming confidence. Other commentators, 'scholars only' as they are patronizingly termed, seemed to him ill-equipped to penetrate the enigma of myth. For learning is no guarantee of access to the complex of truths on which myth was founded. Myths, as they appear in great literature, are concealed in mystery which only a creative insight can penetrate. Ruskin's quotation from Genesis and his reference to 'Hebrew myths' remind us of his belief that this mythological body of truth expressed itself equally in Hebraic and Hellenic tradition. It is as difficult of access in both: a difficulty which Ruskin saw as essential to its nature. Rejecting the concept of a popular origin for mythology and associating the truths of myth with those of art, Ruskin believed that the Greek myth-maker deliberately veiled the truth he expressed. He refers again to Pindar's second *Olympian Ode*: 'And this withholding of their meaning is continual, and confessed, in the great poets. Thus Pindar says of himself: "There is many an arrow in my quiver, full of speech to the wise, but for the many, they need interpreters" '[66] (xix. 309). Ruskin believed himself to be such an interpreter; this gave him confidence to assert his views in the face of scholarly precedent. Occasionally, however, he did regret the confusions to which such confidence led him. His exposition of the Homeric myth of Aeolus and the winds continues with the remark that 'Aeolus gives them to Ulysses, all but one, bound in a leathern bag' (xix. 312). It is, however, only the blustering winds that Aeolus gives to

[65] Quoted in part at xix. 311 n. The biblical reference is to Gen. 27:39.
[66] See Pindar, *Olympian Odes*, ii. 83–6.

Ulysses.[67] Ruskin confessed his error to the reproving Charles Eliot Norton: 'That is indeed an important mistake about the bag.' Uncharacteristically chastened, he goes on to lament that 'it is strange that I hardly ever get anything stated without some grave mistake, however true in my main discoveries' (xxxvii. 19).

That he was true in his main discoveries in *The Queen of the Air* Ruskin never doubted. It remained for years a favourite book with him. The major 'discovery' of the book, so far as mythological interpretation went, was the association of Athena with the air. In 1871 Ruskin wrote to the editor of the *Asiatic*:

The Queen of the Air was written to show, not what could be fancied, but what was felt and meant, in the myth of Athena. Every British sailor knows that Neptune is the god of the sea. He does *not* know that Athena is the goddess of the air; I doubt if many of our school-boys know it—I doubt even if many of our school-masters know it; and I believe the evidence of it given in the 'Queen of the Air' to be the first clear and connected approximate proof of it which has yet been rendered by scientific mythology, properly so called. (xxxiv. 504)

Ten years later Ruskin's pride in this discovery was undiminished. In 1881 he wrote of *The Queen of the Air* to the Reverend J. P. Faunthorpe:

It is a great joy to me that you like *The Queen of the Air*. I shall be so thankful for your revise of it. In the point of original power of thought it leads all my books. My political economy is all in Xenophon and Marmontel; my principles of art were the boy's alphabet in Florence; but the Greeks themselves scarcely knew all that their imagination taught them of eternal truth, and the discovery of the function of Athena as the Goddess of the Air is, among moderns, absolutely I believe my own.[68] (xxxvii. 380–1)

Ruskin's claim of priority here seems to be justified. As he suggests, such elemental associations as that between Poseidon

---

[67] βυκτάων ἀνέμων κατέδηοε: 'he bound the paths of the blustering winds' (Homer, *Odyssey*, x. 20).

[68] The letter is dated 6 Dec. 1881. The Revd John Pincher Faunthorpe (1839–1924) was principal of Whitelands College, a teacher's training college. Ruskin had made his acquaintance through the *Fors Clavigera* correspondence and affectionately referred to him as 'chaplain' of the Guild of St George. Faunthorpe helped to revise a new edition of *The Queen of the Air* in 1883. See vol. xix, p. lxxi.

and the sea or Apollo and the sun were commonplace; but if any deity were assigned to the air, it was usually either Zeus or his consort Hera.[69] We have seen that Ruskin's first source for this idea may have been the theory that the Egyptian goddess Neith, whom he identified with Athena, was associated with the air. This has been suggested as a likely source for his connecting the air with the Greek goddess. One of Athena's epithets is Amaria, the counterpart of Zeus' Amarios, which may mean the luminous atmosphere.[70] Amaria, however, is not to be found in Ruskin's extensive list of Athena's epithets.[71]

Reference to an association between Athena and the air is made in Lenormant and De Witte's *Élite de monuments céramographiques*, Ruskin's favourite source of reference for information about Greek vase-painting. Among its reproductions is a red-figure showing Athena in pursuit of a daughter of Cecrops. She is holding the carved stem of a ship, decorated with a face, in her left hand. The accompanying text describes the picture:

Minerve venant à travers les airs, ayant jeté le mont Lycabattus qu'elle portait et poursuivant une des filles de Cécrops qui a violé le dépôt confié à ses soins par la déesse. On apprend par Ciceron que les aplustres placés à la poupe des vaisseaux indiquaient la présence et la direction du vent; c'étaient des espèces de girouettes garnies de lames qui paraissent de métal, minces et tres-sensibles à l'influence de l'air. On pourrait donc croire, jusqu'à un certain point, que l'aplustre n'a été mis aux mains de Minerve que pour designer l'air. Mais l'idée de la navigation s'attache trop naturellement à cet attribut, pour qu'il nous soit permis de nous arrêter à cette conjecture.[72]

[69] Athena 'seems to have been a divinity of a purely ethical character, and not the representative of any particular physical power manifested in nature', Dr William Smith notes in his *Dictionary of Biography and Mythology*, a standard work of reference owned and occasionally cited by Ruskin (Smith, *Dictionary of Greek and Roman Biography and Mythology*, 3 vols. (London, 1844–9), i. 398). See xxv. 311–12, xxvii. 357. Smith notes that Hera was anciently seen as 'the personification of the atmosphere' (Smith, *Dictionary*, ii. 386).

[70] See G. G. Drake, 'Ruskin's Athena, Queen of the Air', *Classical Bulletin*, 51 (Dec. 1974), 18–19.

[71] Such a list is to be found in the 'Myth Book'. Ruskin does, however, note the association between Zeus and Athena in the 'Myth Book'. He writes: 'As daughter of Jove. she has *his* aegis. metaphorically. storm or air. daughter of sky. and wisdom. daughter of God' (Bem. MS 45).

[72] C. Lenormant and J. De Witte, *Élite des monuments céramographiques*, 4 vols. (Paris, 1844–61), i. 248; see Plate LXXV.

Ruskin scored this passage in his copy of the work,[73] and it may have reinforced the idea of the special association between Athena and the air in his mind.

But it is not likely that any particular source for this connection can be traced, and there is no reason to deny Ruskin the originality on which he prided himself here. The sympathy with which he presents the idea counts for more than its possible origins. Ruskin quotes, for instance, Pope's translation of the passage in which Athena deflects the spear that Ares had thrown at Diomed:

> Pallas opposed her hand, and caused to glance,
> Far from the car, the strong immortal lance.[74] (xix. 332)

Ruskin notes that 'She does not *oppose* her hand in the Greek, for the wind could not meet the lance straight. She catches it in her hand, and throws it off. There is no instance in which a lance is so parried by a mortal hand in all the *Iliad*; and it is exactly the way the wind would parry it, catching it and turning it aside' (xix. 333). This is a telling point, for λαμβάνω would accurately be translated as 'to catch, seize, or grasp'; there is no sense of opposition in the verb.

In the first lecture of *The Queen of the Air*, Athena is evoked as an ideal inspiration. She becomes an informing presence in the two very much more discursive sections which follow. Here, the ancient meaning of the goddess carries less weight than Ruskin's vision of the significance she might have in a modern world. 'Athena Keramitis' is concerned with the 'supposed, and actual, relations of Athena to the vital force in material organism' (xix. 351). Athena, goddess of breath, is for Ruskin the goddess of life itself. 'Athena Keramitis' is simply a discourse on life, and it aspires to the range of reference that such a subject might imply. Ruskin's views on botany, on birds, on snakes, or on colour, have unexpected but not incongruous place in his study. The final section of the book, 'Athena Ergane' or 'Athena in the Heart: Various Notes Relating to the Conception of Athena as the Directress of the Imagination and Will' (xix. 388), seems to have still remoter bearing on a study of the ancient

---

[73] This is now preserved in the Ruskin Galleries at Bembridge, Isle of Wight.
[74] See Pope, *Poems*, vii. 316; Homer, *Iliad*, v. 853–4.

goddess who is ostensibly Ruskin's subject. His fiercest and most dislocated invective is to be found in this part of the book. For it is concerned with moral action over which Athena might preside: 'Her word to us all is:—"Be well exercised, and rightly clothed. Clothed, and in your right minds; not insane and in rags, nor in soiled fine clothes clutched from each other's shoulders. Fight and weave. Then I myself will answer for the course of the lance, and the colours of the loom"' (xix. 400).

The *Spectator* testily remarked that this section might more appropriately have been called 'Various Notes Relating to the Conceptions of Mr. Ruskin as a Director of Imagination and Will'.[75] There is, of course, truth in this charge. It is one which Ruskin would have utterly rejected. The intended function of Greek myths, and particularly of Athena in *The Queen of the Air*, is to establish and demonstrate an order of truth existing outside the limited authority of any individual insight. Creative interpretation, always Ruskin's medium, is in *The Queen of the Air* recognized and defined as part of what Ruskin hoped would be 'one continual and omnipotent presence of help, and of peace, for all men who know that they Live, and remember that they Die' (xix. 387). On 5 June 1869, seventeen days before the issue of *The Queen of the Air*, Ruskin heard that he had been called to a more public platform for the profession of Athena's wisdom.

[75] *Spectator*, 17 July 1869, 852.

6
The Return to Oxford (1870–1878)

The Election

Ruskin's first acquaintance with Oxford had not been wholly propitious. 'If I ever wished to see the towers of Oxford again, the wish is found only in conjunction with another—Rosalind's—that I had "a thunderbolt in mine eye" '[1] (i. 383), he had written to his old tutor, Thomas Dale, on leaving the university in 1840. Yet in 1870 he did return to fill the newly-created post of Slade Professor of Fine Art.[2] He still felt some of the mingled reverence and nervousness which the university had first inspired in him. Stronger yet was the revulsion from the academic competitiveness that he had seen and deplored at Oxford.[3] Greek history, literature, and philosophy had been the basis of his study at Christ Church. The Greeks continued to be important to Ruskin. But it was the symbolic language provided by their mythology that now chiefly attracted him. Ruskin's aims in returning to Oxford were in many ways opposed to the spirit of his earlier studies there. In order to understand the work that Ruskin did at Oxford, it is important to recognize the peculiarities of his position as professor.

He was not at first eager to return. The possibility of his doing so had arisen twice before his election in 1869, and on

[1] See Chap. 1, n. 3.

[2] In 1868 Felix Slade had bequeathed £35,000 for the foundation of Professorships of Fine Art in Oxford, Cambridge, and University College, London. The professors were to be elected for a term of three years. Ruskin was elected in 1869 and re-elected in 1873 and 1876. Sir William Richmond was chosen for the post after Ruskin's resignation in 1878, and Ruskin returned as professor for a final three-year period in 1882.

[3] Ruskin's feelings are typically expressed in a letter to his cousin George Richardson: 'I can only tell you that I myself look upon the years I spent at Oxford as among the most disagreeable of my life: and in many respects the least profitable. I am certain that in any position admitting intellectual exertion, a man in these pushing modern days can win for himself a respect and influence, by his own native sense and hard industry a thousandfold greater than any that depend on conferred degrees' (Unpubl. letter, Bodl. MS Eng. Misc. e. 182, fo. 6). The letter is dated 13 Jan. 1860.

both occasions he had decided not to go back. In 1866 the Professorship of Poetry had fallen vacant. Ruskin was then living in Switzerland, where he received a request that he should allow his name to be put forward for the position. His old college friends Henry Acland and Richard St John Tyrwhitt[4] were among the signatories. Ruskin agreed to the plan, but not whole-heartedly. He wrote to Tyrwhitt from Denmark Hill:

I am anxious to know the complete extent of the required duties, and their nature, for I fear there are some absolutely involving the need of better scholarship than mine. Not that I should under ordinary circumstances, give a gravely wrong opinion of any Latin or Greek writing which I had full time to examine. If once I make out a sentence at all, I make it out—(forgive the self assertion)—very *well*: and I should think few readers, even among accomplished scholars, had better notion than I of the power—to its last particle—of any sentence I have once well examined. But it sometimes takes me an hour to do it! and—though I can understand other writing, after that effort—by *no* effort could I write any endurable Latin or Greek myself.[5]

The letter suggests that Ruskin was hardly more confident of his powers as a classical scholar in 1866 than he had been in 1840. Eventually he withdrew his candidature. He wrote again to Tyrwhitt: 'Poetry is connected so vitally in my mind with religion and mythology that I cannot at present think one thought about it which I dare—or perhaps would be able to—put into words.'[6] The position seemed to Ruskin to require an orthodoxy, in both religion and scholarship, which he did not possess. The Professorship of Poetry was, however, an old-established chair, and quite a different matter from the brand-new Slade Professorship of Fine Art.

---

[4] Tyrwhitt was later to become Ruskin's secretary in Oxford. In June 1876 Ruskin acknowledged his help in the 'Notes and Correspondence' of *Fors Clavigera*, writing that 'my Oxford secretary, who has £200 a year, does such work for me connected with my Professorship as only a trained scholar could do, leaving me free to study hyacinths. I wish I could give him the Professorship itself, but must do as I am bid by Oxford' (xxviii, 632–3). Tyrwhitt had originally considered standing for the Slade Professorship himself. Ruskin wrote in support: 'I most sincerely trust that things may go on as they have begun, and that you may get the professorship' (Claiborne, *Letters*, p. 238 (8 June 1868)).

[5] Ibid. 224–5 (25 Oct. 1866).

[6] Ibid. 231 (12 Jan. 1867).

Ruskin was better suited to this new position and more confident of his capacity for it. Yet it was clear that he would not
limit his work to the field of art. Like poetry, art had become
so vitally connected in his mind with religion and mythology,
and with associated moral issues, that he could not speak of it
in isolation. Indeed, he was not certain that art could be
taught at all. Acland and Tyrwhitt, disappointed by Ruskin's
withdrawal from the election for the Professorship of Poetry,
but still eager to find a place for him at Oxford, had in 1867
suggested that he might become a curator of the Oxford
University Galleries. Ruskin wrote to Acland in reply to the
proposition: 'I sorrowfully assure you of one of the few
things which I myself know assuredly—that all art what-
soever rises spontaneously out of the heart and hands of any
nation honestly occupied with graven human and divine
interests. It cannot be taught from without; and you and
Tyrwhitt are merely directing artificial inspiration in a dead
body' (xxxvi. 542–3).

The Slade Professorship seemed to offer more attractive
possibilities than either the Poetry Professorship or an
appointment as Curator of the University Galleries. To
Acland, in particular, the creation of the post seemed the
opportunity to fulfil a long-cherished dream. Since his
undergraduate days, he had wanted to extend the field of
study at Oxford. He had written to his father from
Edinburgh in 1845:

You ask me why I am so energetic. Because I have been a year *here*,
and because I see the pious foundations of Oxford *could* do more
to regulate knowledge and to advance it in the right directions by
their wealth and their theological character than all Great Britain
besides. But how is it now? Every reading man reads for honours,
and his private tutor, if he has tastes for anything but his classics or
his mathematics, says 'You will lose your class.'[7]

Acland had gone on to promote the study of natural history in
Oxford and had involved Ruskin, who felt with him in these
matters, in the foundation of a new science museum.[8] He

[7] J. B. Atlay, *Henry Acland: A Memoir* (London, 1903), 132. Acland may have
been influenced by the ideas of John Stuart Blackie during his time in Edinburgh.
See above, pp. 34–6.

[8] In later life, as Ruskin's own approach to the study of natural history departed
from that of conventional science, he came to have mixed feelings about the part he

believed, however, that Ruskin had a more active part to play. Writing to his father, he described his wish to 'get Ruskin down; get him made Professor of Art; and invite Severn and some other enthusiasts. I think it is passing strange if with H. G. L. we cannot get up some life—and yet why did not Dr. Buckland? He did for awhile.'[9]

H. G. L.—Henry George Liddell (1811–98), who, like Ruskin and Acland was a Christ Church man, shared these ambitions. Liddell believed that the professors of the university could play a special role. He had written to Acland:

What we want is something at once permanent and intelligent. The Heads of Houses are permanent but not intelligent. Tutors may be intelligent, but are certainly not permanent. As I have heard a friend say, they seldom stay long enough at Oxford to see the effect of their own Legislation. Real Professors, *qualis sentio tantum*, would afford the double qualification required in one. They would be permanent and intelligent—a true Aristocracy,—not a jealous oligarchy, like the Heads, not a fleeting democracy, like the Tutors. *Voilà tout.*[10]

Liddell did not, however, think highly of Ruskin. He seems to have disapproved of the idea of his appointment as Curator of the University Galleries and had written sourly to Acland: 'Are you positively certain that Ruskin would like to be Curator of the Galleries? Have you it in writing? And can his inclination or wish in August be depended upon in November?' (vol. p. xxxv). The hostility between the two men is revealed in a passage, unpublished in Ruskin's lifetime, which had been intended for *Praeterita*:

had played in the establishment of scientific studies in Oxford. He wrote of the Oxford Museum to Tyrwhitt in 1877: 'But Acland and I were responsible for more than the architecture. He chiefly, I according to my power, were among the chief promoters of the Natural Science schools—Do the Natural History gentlemen think *they* were results of Evolution? They may thank us they are in Oxford at all—and Oxford,—has little reason to thank us,—but I suppose that is not the ground of attack' (Claiborne, *Letters*, p. 346 (3 Mar. 1877)). Ruskin's anger over the university's decision to allow vivisection in its laboratories was to precipitate his final resignation from the Slade Professorship in 1885. See vol. xxxiii, pp. liv–vi.

[9] Atlay, *Henry Acland*, p. 131. The letter is dated Easter Day 1845. William Buckland (1784–1856), geologist and canon of Christ Church, was a pioneer in the introduction of natural science into Oxford. See xxxv. 204–5.

[10] Unpubl. letter, Bodl. MS Acland d. 69, fo. 32 (23 Feb. 1854). See Juvenal, *Sat.*, vii. 56.

In his undergraduate days he had laid the foundation of his dictionary, and afterwards had slowly contracted all the faculties of his nature into the focus of his scrutiny of Greek. He had no imagination to disturb the patience of his philology,—but had taste, memory and judgement enough to make his philology faultless. He knew, and felt, just so much of the external world as enabled him to discriminate the sense of words properly,—but not enough to enable, or induce, him to pursue any object in the world itself with fruitful success, unless, it may be, forms of selfish happiness, and the poor ambition, or lowly duty, of dictionary making. So far as he perceived the right in any of his public functions, he has assuredly always done it, unflinchingly; but the ἀνάγκη[11] of his fate placed him in a position in which there was little to flinch from, and much to fail in . . . At Oxford, he had patiently corrected the proofs of the successively developed editions of a dictionary which in ten years more, it seems nobody will want, done an enormous quantity of University business, which might just as well have been done by the clerk of the Waterworks, and become in the University atmosphere a force of enduring frost of the sort which, I was going to have said, rather disintegrates rock than snow-crests it; but it will be a nearer image of the present dignity of the University if I say, rather bursts the pipes in the larder than saves the meat in it.[12]

The antipathy was long-standing. Acland had evidently tried and failed to change Liddell's mind about Ruskin's suitability as a professorial candidate. Liddell wrote in reply:

I enclose Ruskin's letter. It *is* written in a somewhat better temper; but there is the same presumptuous dogmatism that characterises all he writes; & it is impossible to say how long this phase of dogmatism may last, without giving way to some other. If he really takes to the study of the figure, it *may* engage his mind & time completely for a while. But I doubt his having the faculty to appreciate the special beauties of the animal form. He neither reverences the calm sublimity of the old religious face nor the perfect beauty of the Greek types. He will seek satisfaction in subtle effects of colour & play of light & shade, as he indicates in his *exaggerated* comparison of a pine forest & an eye-lash. He will *never* make a Professor. He may be a great Drawing-Master, or a

---

[11] 'Constraint, or necessity'.

[12] Samuel E. Brown, 'The Unpublished Passages in the Manuscript of Ruskin's Autobiography', *Victorian Newsletter*, 16 (Autumn 1959), 12–13.

great artistic Poet,—as he is & has been,—never anything more.—*Voilà mon avis*—.[13]

Both men were wrong—Ruskin in thinking that Liddell had wasted his life on a dictionary that would soon be superseded, Liddell in thinking that Ruskin would never be more than a 'Drawing-Master'. Liddell relented sufficiently to lend his support to Ruskin's candidature in 1869. The campaign was conducted without mishap. Ruskin, the 'Graduate of Oxford' who had written *Modern Painters*, must have seemed the obvious candidate and was duly elected.

The Lectures: The Greek School of Light

Though now little known and rarely read, Ruskin's lectures at Oxford are a central statement of his thought. They were considered and composed with meticulous care, particularly in the early days of the professorship, and almost all were published soon after delivery. This was partly because Ruskin was nervous about his academic position in Oxford and was anxious to conform to the pattern of professorial behaviour that the world expected. Soon after his election, he wrote to Acland to thank him for his and Liddell's support: 'I believe you will both be greatly surprised for one thing at the caution with which I shall avoid saying anything with the University authority which may be either questionable by, or offensive to, even persons who know little of my subject, and at the generally quiet tone to which I shall reduce myself in all public duty' (vol. xx, pp. xix–xx). Ruskin also wrote to the Dean, but here his reassurance was tinged with threat: 'I shall scrupulously avoid the expression of my own peculiar opinions when I speak by permission of the University, and I shall endeavour to bring whatever I teach into closer harmony with the system of University as it *used* to be, than its Conservative members would I think at present hope from

[13] Unpubl. letter, Bodl. MS Acland d. 69, fo. 56 (10 Oct. 1864). Ruskin had compared an eyelash with a pine forest in a letter which Acland had evidently forwarded to Liddell: 'The great error of modern figure work in sculpture no less than painting has been the want of understanding that chiaroscuro, and mystery, as elements of visible expression, have inseparable functions and dignity in an eyelash as much as in a pine forest' (vol. xviii, p. xxxv). See above, pp. 72–4, where other passages from this letter are quoted.

me' (vol. xx, p. xx). Christ Church, the college of Acland, Liddell, and Ruskin, was a stronghold of conservatism in the university. Ruskin, however, was to urge a concept of educational conservatism which found little favour in Christ Church. Even the most carefully composed of Ruskin's lectures at Oxford were not cautious. He could not conciliate the Dean for long,[14] for all the decorous attention he paid to the details of Greek scholarship. Five days before his inaugural lecture on 8 February 1870, he wrote to Tyrwhitt: 'The nuisance of the "professorship"—is the appalling necessity of Accentuation.'[15] Correct accents do not guarantee conventional opinions, however, as Ruskin was soon to show. The published version of Ruskin's first course of lectures at Oxford is exceptional among his writings for the guarded formality of its language. But he used the platform provided by the professorship in a way that must have surprised his audiences. This is especially true of his exposition of Greek culture. Ruskin's theory of Greek art and mythology lay at the very heart of the scheme of the history and practice of art described in these lectures and reflects the personal importance that the mythological symbolism of the Greeks now had for him. It was far from the cautious approach that he had promised his sponsors in Christ Church.

Ruskin sent the scheme of his first course of lectures to Liddell and Acland. He may have been hoping for an official stamp of approval. If so, he was not to receive it from the Dean. The second lecture, 'The Relation of Art to Religion', caused a particular problem. Liddell wrote to Acland:

Inclosed is Ruskin's programme of Lectures. Very interesting. But the second is startling. It is difficult to believe that the coarse creed

---

[14] 'I begin greatly to repent of having furthered his Election,' Liddell remarked coldly in a letter to Acland written on 15 Jan. 1871, only a year after Ruskin had taken up his duties (Unpubl. letter, Bodl. MS Acland d. 69, fo. 94).

[15] Claiborne, *Letters*, p. 257 (3 Feb. 1870). The technicalities of the Greek language continued to plague Ruskin, particularly when he came to publish his lectures. On 13 Nov. 1871 he wrote to Tyrwhitt about the lectures on sculpture delivered in Michaelmas term 1870, which he was preparing for the press under the title *Aratra Pentelici* (1872): 'I will send you a fair revise in which you must finally look for me at the Latin and Greek. How anybody ever gets a Greek book printed—it passes every effort of my poor imagination to conceive' (Claiborne, *Letters*, p. 281).

of Greek religion as we have it in Homer was debased by the ideal representations of the Gods by Phidias, though (doubtless) the works of Praxiteles and later sculptors had the effect of making the religion more earthy and sensuous. So, it is difficult to believe that the religious paintings of Orcagna & Fra Angelico, or even of Raffaelle, had the effect of debasing Xty., though no doubt the works of later Painters may have had this effect. Perhaps the worship of the Virgin was encouraged by it. But the human character of the Saviour as represented in the Gospels seems to invite representation by Art. However, he says his statement will be 'careful and guarded'. *Ainsi soit.*[16]

The Dean had previously criticized Ruskin on the grounds that he did not venerate either the beauty of 'Greek types' or the sublimity of 'the old religious face'. Liddell was a minister of the Church of England who had devoted his life to the study of the classics, and who had always loved the arts. The idea that a mutually beneficial relation between religion and art could be said to exist in both Greek and Christian ages was important to him. Yet Ruskin claimed no such relation. Liddell had picked on one of the central points of Ruskin's lectures in Oxford. Though the moral bias of his teaching is consistent, Ruskin never suggested that art could or should strengthen religious faith, or indeed that it had ever done so. It was his unexpected contention that pictures could and often did debase religion.

Small wonder that Liddell was taken aback by the second of Ruskin's lectures, 'The Relation of Art to Religion':

Our duty is to believe in the existence of Divine, or any other, persons, only upon rational proofs of their existence; and not because we have seen pictures of them. And since the real relations between us and higher spirits are, of all facts concerning our being, those which it is most important to know accurately, if we know at all, it is a folly so great as to amount to real, though most unintentional, sin, to allow our conceptions of those relations to be modified by our own undisciplined fancy.[17] (xx. 60)

---

[16] Unpubl. letter, Bodl. MS Acland d. 69, fo. 95 (16 Jan. 1870).
[17] In the fourth (1887) edition of *Lectures on Art*, Ruskin omitted the second sentence from this passage. He noted: 'I have expunged a sentence insisting further on this point, having come to reverence more, as I grow older, every simple means of stimulating all religious belief and affection. It is the lower and realistic world which is fullest of false belief and vain loves' (xx. 60 n.).

This iconoclasm seems to recall Ruskin's Evangelical heritage. But his position is as far from a traditionally pietistic distrust of images in 1870 as it had been in 1843. If the image is taken as symbolically representative of an imaginative truth, then it is of value; but not if it is taken as the specific expression of any particular religious creed. For Ruskin, this is as true of Greek as of Christian art. His lecture on 'The Relation of Art to Religion' continues:

For instance, the Greek design of Apollo crossing the sea to Delphi, which is one of the most interesting of Lenormant's series, so far as it is only an expression, under the symbol of a human form, of what may be rightly imagined respecting the solar power, is right and ennobling; but so far as it conveyed to the Greek the idea of there being a real Apollo, it was mischievous, whether there be, or be not, a real Apollo. If there is no real Apollo, then the art was mischievous because it deceived; but if there is a real Apollo, then it was still more mischievous, for it not only began the degradation of the image of that true god into a decoration for niches, and a device for seals; but prevented any true witness being borne to his existence. (xx. 61)

If art had not benefited religion, neither had religion, particularly Christianity, been of use to art.[18] An early draft of 'The Relation of Art to Religion' is forthright on this point, claiming that

the successes, of whatever positive value they may be, reached under the orders of Christianity have been dearly bought by the destruction of the best treasures of heathen art, by the loss of the records of what was most interesting in passing history, by the aversion of all eyes from what was lovely in present nature, and by the birth, in the chasm left by the contracted energies of healthful art, of a sensual art fed by infernal fire. (xx. 57n)

As part of the second lecture of Oxford's first Professor of Fine Art, this would have been startling indeed. It may have

[18] Ruskin took pleasure in his heretical second lecture. He wrote to Mrs Cowper Temple in Jan. 1870: 'What do you think is to be the gist of my second lecture at Oxford—on the relation of Art to Religion? That—on the whole—Art has always suffered for helping Religion—and Religion for being helped by art! . . . But won't the high church people be nicely taken in? I won't let the low-church people have any the better of them however—you may be sure of that!' (*The Letters of John Ruskin to Lord and Lady Mount-Temple*, ed. John Lewis Bradley (Columbus, Ohio, 1964), 252).

been at Liddell's suggestion that the passage was removed from the text.

The clear distinction that Ruskin drew between religion and morality is important. Though Christianity may have been of no benefit to art, moral insight is in Ruskin's view essential to art as to all else. Art, on the other hand is very much less necessary to morality. Ruskin's third lecture was entitled 'The Relation of Art to Morals': 'You must have the right moral state first, or you cannot have the art. But when the art is once obtained, its reflected action enhances and completes the moral state out of which it arose, and above all, communicates the exultation to other minds which are already capable of the like' (xx. 73). Ruskin's appointment as Slade Professor focused the implications of a dilemma which had long shadowed him. He had stated the problem succinctly five years before, in *The Cestus of Aglaia* (1865–66): 'Good pictures do not teach a nation; they are the signs of its having been taught' (xix. 57). If this is so, how could he fulfil his duties as professor in terms of art alone? J. R. Green, the historian, recalls that Ruskin's opening course of lectures caused some stir: 'he electrified the Dons by telling them that a chalk-stream did more for the education of the people than their prim "national school with its well-taught doctrine of Baptism and gabbled Catechism."' [19] Ruskin wanted to use his professorship to convey a vision of life to his audiences. He often treats art as a source of illustrative examples, rather than the central subject of his discourse. Art is only one among many urgent topics for Ruskin in the 1870s. He had told Acland three years before his inaugural lecture as Slade Professor that he believed it had come to be impossible to speak of art in the England of his time. Though he accepted the post at Oxford, he had not changed his mind. From the first, he interpreted his brief as professor in the widest possible sense. His view of the mythological art of the

---

[19] *Letters of John Richard Green*, ed. Leslie Stephen (London, 1901), 246. Quoted by Cook; vol. xx, p. xxviii. The letter is dated 5 Mar. 1870. No mention of chalk-streams is to be found in the published version of Ruskin's *Lectures on Art*. The published text of these lectures, as indeed all of the lectures that Ruskin delivered in Oxford, may be substantially different from the now irrecoverable version that Ruskin's audiences first heard.

Greeks, in particular, combines the concerns of scholarship with intensely personal preoccupations.

Ruskin argues that Greek art expresses a concern with light, while Gothic art represents the opposing school of colour. In his Oxford lectures, he claims that these two disciplines had defined the character of art from ancient times up to the days of Turner. The sixth lecture was entitled simply 'Light'. His definition of these two fundamental schools of Western art implies that the Greek school was more important and more interesting than its Gothic counter-part. His characterization of the school of colour is condescending:

The way by colour is taken by men of cheerful, natural, and entirely sane disposition in body and mind, much resembling, even at its strongest, the temper of well-brought-up children:—too happy to think deeply, yet with powers of imagination by which they can live other lives than their actual ones: make-believe lives, while yet they remain conscious all the while that they *are* making believe—therefore entirely sane. They are also absolutely contented; they ask for no more light than is immediately around them, and cannot see anything like darkness, but only green and blue, in the earth and sea. (xx. 139)

In describing the painters who belong to the Greek chiaroscurist school, Ruskin again suggests that the Greek character is marked by sadness rather than the optimism more usually associated with it:

The way by light and shade is, on the contrary, taken by men of the highest powers of thought, and most earnest desire for truth; they long for light, and for knowledge of all that light can show. But seeking for light, they perceive also darkness; seeking for truth and substance, they find vanity. They look for form in the earth,—for dawn in the sky; and seeking these, they find formlessness in the earth, and night in the sky. (xx. 139–40)

Ruskin had, in the 1860s, valued the mythology of the Greeks as a response to human mortality. Their art now seemed a reflection of this response. Greek art, like Greek myth, confronts death: 'I tell you only what I know—this vital distinction between them: the Gothic or colour school is always cheerful, the Greek always oppressed by the shadow of death; and the stronger its masters are, the closer that body of death grips them' (xx. 140). In speaking of Greek artists and their concern with mortality, Ruskin speaks of himself. He confesses his allegiance openly in 'Colour', his seventh lecture:

But for my own part, with what poor gift and skill is in me, I belong wholly to the chiaroscurist school; and shall teach you therefore chiefly that which I am best able to teach: and the rather, that it is only in this school that you can follow out the study either of natural history or landscape. The form of a wild animal, or the wrath of a mountain torrent, would both be revolting (or in a certain sense invisible) to the calm fantasy of a painter in the schools of crystal. (xx. 175)

The Greek school as Ruskin defines it is vital to his scheme of education, for it leads to the investigation of natural history and landscape. It also implies an active search for wisdom more in keeping with his temper than the static and passive spirit of the Gothic school of colour. Again, his description of the Greek school has a personal meaning:

And you cannot but wonder why, this being the melancholy temper of the great Greek or naturalistic school, I should have called it the school of light. I call it so because it is through its intense love of light that the darkness becomes apparent to it, and through its intense love of truth and form that all mystery becomes attractive to it. And when, having learned these things, it is joined to the school of colour, you have the perfect, though always, as I will show you, pensive, art of Titian and his followers.

But remember its first development, and all its final power, depend on Greek sorrow, and Greek religion. (xx. 142)

Here Ruskin develops the connection between his theory of Greek art and the study of Greek religion that had occupied his attention during the 1860s. Though chiefly interested in gods of air, cloud, wind, and light, he had pointed to the darkness in Greek myths. Athena, the goddess of the air, and Apollo, the god of light, are the deities presiding over the Greek chiaroscurist school. Yet they share dominion with more sinister powers:

But underlying both these, and far more mysterious, dreadful, and yet beautiful, there is the Greek conception of *spiritual* darkness; of the anger of fate, whether foredoomed or avenging; the root and theme of all Greek tragedy; the anger of the Erinnyes, and Demeter Erinnys, compared to which the anger either of Apollo or Athena is temporary and partial:—and, also, while Apollo and Athena only slay, the power of Demeter and the Eumenides is over the whole life; so that in the stories of Bellerophon, of Hippolytus, of Orestes, of Oedipus, you have an incomparably deeper shadow than any that was possible to the thought of later ages, when the hope of the Resurrection had become definite. (xx. 142–3)

In Ruskin's view, it is this unrelenting ethos that strengthens Greek art. 'Light' contains a discussion of vase-paintings depicting Apollo, Athena, and Artemis—the 'deities of light'[20] (xx. 145). His analysis is expressed in moral rather than aesthetic terms. Ruskin explains his approach to his audience: 'For nothing is more wonderful than the depth of meaning which nations in their first days of thought, like children, can attach to the rudest symbols; and what to us is grotesque or ugly, like a little child's doll, can speak to them the loveliest things' (xx. 144). In associating the opposing Gothic school of colour with the condition of childhood, Ruskin had hinted at immaturity; while the Greeks are childlike only in the vigour of their imaginative life.

It is for the sake of such symbolic meanings that Ruskin urges his pupils to study the vases and coins of ancient Greece. 'I have not loved the arts of Greece as others have' (xx. 103), he confessed in his seventh lecture, 'Colour'. Liddell had been right to suspect that Ruskin cared little for the ideal beauty often supposed to be the essence of Greek art. The classic Greek countenance, especially, hardly pleased him. In 'The School of Athens', sixth of the lectures which comprise *Aratra Pentelici*, he considers the faces represented on a series of Greek coins:

Are any of these goddesses and nymphs very beautiful? Certainly the Junos are not. Certainly the Demeters are not. The Sirens, and Arethusa, have well-formed and regular features: but I am quite sure that if you look at them without prejudice, you will think neither reaches even the average standard of pretty English girls. . . . You need only look at two or three vases of the best time to

---

[20] Here, as in *The Queen of the Air*, Ruskin drew his examples from Lenormant and de Witte's classic work on Greek vases. See above, p. 129.

assure yourselves that beauty of features was, in popular art, not only unattained, but unattempted. (xx. 342)

In 1879 he wrote in *St. Mark's Rest* that the function of the Greek image 'is not beauty, but instruction' (xxiv. 281). Instruction, rather than beauty, was his own first concern; this led to his study of Greek art at Oxford.

Ruskin did not believe that Christianity was more spiritual than Greek religion. But he felt that it had added a dimension of experience that gave Christian art a wider scope than that of the Greeks. In a lecture first delivered to the Art School of South Lambeth in March 1869, and later published in *The Queen of the Air*, Ruskin tells the students that

your own art is a better and brighter one than ever this Greek art was. Many motives, powers, and insights have been added to those elder ones. The very corruptions into which we have fallen are signs of a subtle life, higher than theirs was, and therefore more fearful in its faults and death. Christianity has neither superseded, nor, by itself, excelled heathenism; but it has added its own good, won also by many a Nemean contest in dark valleys, to all that was good and noble in heathenism: and our present thoughts and work, when they are right, are nobler than the heathen's. (xix. 418)

For this reason, Ruskin considered the art of the ancient Greeks an inadequate model for his students. 'The first series of my lectures on sculpture[21] must have proved to you that I do not despise either the workmanship or the mythology of Greece; but I must assert with more distinctness than even in my earliest works, the absolute unfitness of all its results to be made the guides of English students or artists' (xxii. 191), Ruskin remarked in the fifth of the lectures which comprise *The Eagle's Nest* (1872). Yet he claimed in his first course of lectures that most of his students ought to follow the pattern of the Greek chiaroscurist school: 'A certain number of you, by faculty and natural disposition,—and all, so far as you are interested in modern art,—will necessarily have to put yourself under the discipline of the Greek or chiaroscuro school' (xx. 154).

[21] Ruskin refers to his second course of lectures, delivered in 1870 and published under the title *Aratra Pentelici* (1872).

In speaking of Greek art, Ruskin speaks not only, nor even primarily, of the vases, coins, and sculptures of classical Greece. He is interested in a larger tradition. Ancient Greek art seemed to Ruskin of limited though genuine value. But later manifestations of the Greek school included nearly all that he admired or had ever admired, for this was the art that expressed his own moral concerns. In 1874 Ruskin suggested an extraordinarily inclusive definition of Greek work:

And here I get at a result concerning Greek art, which is very sweeping and wide indeed. That it is all parable, but Gothic, as distinct from it, literal. So absolutely does this hold, that it reaches down to our modern school of landscape. You know I have always told you Turner belonged to the Greek school. Precisely as the stream of blood coming from under the throne of judgement in the Byzantine mosaic or Torcello is a sign of condemnation, his scarlet clouds are used by Turner as a sign of death, and just as on an Egyptian tomb the genius of death lays the sun down behind the horizon, so in his Cephalus and Procris, the last rays of the sun withdraw from the forest as the nymph expires. (xxiii. 124)

Turner, supreme among modern painters, shared an ancient vision. His art was morally symbolic: it was therefore Greek. More surprisingly still, what Ruskin chiefly valued in architecture also came to be included in this concept of Greek art. He wrote of St Mark's in *St. Mark's Rest* (1877–84). Describing the bas-reliefs between the arches of the vaults, he notes that there 'is but one Greek school, from Homer's day down to the Doge Selvo's; and these St. Mark's mosaics are as truly wrought in the power of Daedalus, within the Greek constructive instinct, and in the power of Athena, with the Greek religious soul, as ever chest of Cypselus or shaft of Erechtheum. And therefore, whatever is represented here, be it flower or rock, animal or man, means more than it is itself' (xxiv. 281). The decoration of St Mark's showed the influence of Greek workmen and of the Eastern Byzantine empire. It now seemed to Ruskin that the greatest qualities of the building depended on its Greek character. Yet he is scarcely more enthusiastic about the vases, coins, or sculptures of classical Greek civilization than had been the case when he wrote *The Stones of Venice*.

Ruskin's double response to the Greeks in the 1870s, valuing them above all else on the one hand, yet questioning their traditional standing on the other, must be seen in relation to his position as Slade Professor at Oxford. We have seen how he insisted upon the moral basis of good art in his lectures. But the Greeks could be seen to have failed in moral strength. Though their religion was not inferior to Christianity in Ruskin's eyes, he felt their codes of social morality to be defective. In the third of his lectures at Oxford, 'The Relation of Art to Morals', he explained why:

Unhappily, the subordinate position of their most revered women, and the partial corruption of feeling towards them by the presence of certain other singular states of inferior passion which it is as difficult as grievous to analyse, arrested the ethical as well as the formative progress of the Greek mind; and it was not until after an interval of nearly two thousand years of various error and pain, that, partly as the true reward of Christian warfare nobly sustained through centuries of trial, and partly as the visionary culmination of the faith which saw in a maiden's purity the link between God and her race, the highest and holiest strength of mortal love was reached . . . (xx. 91).

Ruskin is speaking of homosexuality. In a lecture on 'The Sciences of Organic Form', delivered in 1872 as part of *The Eagle's Nest*, he returned to this trying question:

How far the study of the seldom-seen nude leads to perversion of morals, I will not, to-day, inquire; but I beg you to observe that even among the people where it was most frank and pure, it unquestionably led to evil far greater than any good which demonstrably can be traced to it. Scarcely any of the moral power of Greece depended upon her admiration of beauty, or strength in the body. The power of Greece depended on practice in military exercise, involving severe and continual ascetic discipline of the senses; on a perfect code of military heroism and patriotic honour; on the desire to live by the laws of an admittedly divine justice; and on the vivid conception of the presence of spiritual beings. The mere admiration of physical beauty in the body, and the arts which sought its expression, not only conduced greatly to the fall of Greece, but were the cause of errors and crimes in her greatest time, which must for ever sadden our happiest thoughts of her, and have rendered her example almost useless to the future. (xxii. 235–6)

This public statement of disapprobation reflects the topicality of such questions in Oxford during the 1870s. Walter Pater was among those who had, circumspectly, made the Greeks an emblem of liberation from restrictive codes of sexual behaviour. He was not alone. John Addington Symonds had also helped to make the Greeks representative of a more liberal morality. In 1877 Symonds stood for the Professorship of Poetry in Oxford. Tyrwhitt, Ruskin's secretary, responded to his candidature with an article in the *Contemporary Review*, attacking Symond's concept of Hellenism on the grounds of its 'total denial of any moral restraint'.[22] The article was one of the reasons for Symonds's failure in the election. Though Ruskin seems not to have been directly involved in the attack on Symonds, it is likely that he would have approved of the action of his secretary. Perhaps the rebuff that Symonds received discouraged Pater from standing in the election.[23] The incident reminds us that Ruskin was not what would have been considered a 'Hellenist' during his years as Slade Professor. He was less than whole-hearted in his praise for classical Greek art, and he had serious reservations about Greek culture.

Yet Greek myths had become essential to Ruskin's thought. Mythological symbolism lay behind his interpretation of the 'school of light'. Such symbolism had more than a historical significance for him. In the Michaelmas term of 1872, Ruskin delivered the fifth of his courses of lectures in Oxford. They were published under the title *Ariadne Florentina: Six Lectures on Wood and Metal Engraving* (1873–6): 'I am not fantastic in these titles, as is often said; but try shortly to mark my chief purpose in them', Ruskin remarked in the first of these lectures (xxii. 315). Why, then, had he chosen to name his course on engraving after the Greek heroine Ariadne? The published version of the lectures seems to give no clue. But in the October of 1872, Ruskin spoke of the legend of Theseus and his labyrinth in *Fors Clavigera*. He

[22] R. St John Tyrwhitt, 'The Greek Spirit in Modern Literature', *Contemporary Review*, 29 (Mar. 1877), 585.

[23] Accounts of the election are given in *Academy*, 11 Feb. 1877, 160, and *Oxford and Cambridge Undergraduate's Journal*, 15 Mar. 1877, 305.

discusses the quality of true leadership, embodied in 'squires', or law-givers, and tells his readers that

you will find all these squires essentially 'captaines', head, or chief persons, occupied in maintaining good order, and putting things to rights, so that they naturally become chief Lawyers without Wigs (otherwise called Kings) in the districts accessible to them. Of whom I have named first, the Athenian Theseus, 'setter to rights', or 'settler', his name means; he being both the founder of the first city whose history you are to know, and the first true Ruler of Beasts: for this mystic contest with the Minotaur is the fable through which the Greeks taught what they know of the more terrible and mysterious relations between the lower creatures and man; and the desertion of him by Ariadne (for indeed he never deserted her, but she him,—involuntarily, poor sweet maid,—Death calling her in Diana's name) is the conclusive stroke against him by the Third Fors.[24] (xxvii. 386–7)

The idea that there have existed, and should still exist, squires, kings, captains, lawyers—spiritual and moral authorities—was of great importance to Ruskin. There is no doubt that he considered himself in some sense a 'lawyer without wig'. Theseus, the first mythical lawyer in Ruskin's scheme, had acquired a particularly personal meaning. In September 1872, two months before the lectures comprising *Ariadne Florentina* were delivered, and a month before he discussed Theseus in *Fors*, Ruskin wrote to his secretary. Tyrwhitt, like many others, had been told of the unhappy suit for Rose La Touche. Ruskin wrote of her:

She seems appointed to break me down by the vision of her always when I'm coming to a leap anywhere—and *yet* has been at the root of all that I best know and ought to know—for my work. She sent me back last month from Cheshire so miserable that I couldn't speak to any one—but went to the Euston Hotel, and worked at British museum. In *consequence of which* I came on Sandro's engravings,[25] just when I wanted them—and found out a lot of

[24] The 'third Fors' is Ruskin's name for chance, or fortune. It may be that Ruskin read this passage during his lecture, for he often included *Fors* in the material of his Oxford teaching. See James Manning Bruce, 'Ruskin as an Oxford Lecturer', *Century Magazine*, 33 (Feb. 1898), 590–4.

[25] i.e. Sandro Botticelli. See xxvii. 410, 510–13. Ruskin reproduced a Florentine engraving of Theseus, Ariadne, and the labyrinth, attributed to Botticelli, as the frontispiece for his issue of *Fors Clavigera* for Apr. 1873. See plate opposite 511,

other things in the very nick of time for next lectures; Well,—in next Fors as I told you, I've got to do Theseus; and I've always hated and disbelieved the vulgar Ariadne story. Now I got at Lucca duomo[26] the *deliciousest* medieval labyrinth[27]—and its to go in next Fors with the coins of Cnossus and the Minotaur and I've got all Minos and Aeacus and Rhadamanthus as smooth and nice as can be—but Ariadne wouldn't work in, no how. Well—in thinking over her again, to-day, I came on the Odyssey bit;[28]—and there it is all at once—as right as right can be. My poor little Rose is dying, or like to die, at this moment, having been to me truly κουρην Μίνωος ὀλοόφρονος[29]—dying 'in the power of Diana', madly *pure*; Διονύσου μαρτυρίησιν[30] all the energies of her animal and passionate life becoming mortal to her. Now I knew that the Labyrinth meant the entanglement of the animal nature—and Theseus is the divine law giver conquering Minos and fate—but here is Ariadne crushed in another lovely rosey—filling up the fable on this beautiful side.—and I've actually *seen* it. It makes one think one must be worth something after all, to be plagued, in one's poor small way, like an Elgin marble—But did you ever hear—even in a novel—of a sensitive man's—meaning on the whole the best he can do for everybody—having two such things done to him as *that* girl has done—first—after holding fast to me against every human creature in her family for three years—and just at the end of them—suddenly believing herself deceived in me and cutting me dead when we met by chance.—that for Number one—and then,

vol. xxvii. He noted of it: 'Well, such as it is, that is "fine art" (if you will take my opinion in my own business); and even this poor photograph of it is simply worth all the illustrations in your *Illustrated News* or *Illustrated Times* from one year's end to another' (xxvii. 512).

[26] Ruskin had been at Lucca from 30 Apr. to 8 May 1872. See *Diaries*, ii. 724.

[27] See xxvii. 400–2, where this labyrinth, a sculpture from the southern wall of the porch, is reproduced and discussed.

[28] Ruskin refers to Odysseus' description of having seen Ariadne in the under-world: 'And Phaedra and Procris I saw, and fair Ariadne, the daughter of Minos of baneful mind, whom once Theseus was fain to bear from Crete to the hill of sacred Athens; but he had no joy of her, for ere that Artemis slew her in sea-girt Dia because of the witness of Dionysus' (Homer, *Odyssey*, xi. 321–5). The 'vulgar Ariadne story' is that Ariadne, having helped Theseus conquer the Minotaur by providing him with thread to enable him to retrace his steps through the maze in which the monster was kept, had fled from Crete with Theseus and was abandoned by him on the island of Naxos. Later, she was discovered and successfully wooed there by Dionysus. See Plutarch, *Theseus*, 20–1; Catullus, 64, 52–253; Ovid, *Heroid.*, x. Homer is alone in accounting for the separation of the lovers by the death of Ariadne rather than her abandonment.

[29] 'daughter of Minos of baneful mind'. Parental opposition had been an obstacle to marriage between Ruskin and Rose.

[30] 'because of the witness of Dionysus'.

unable to bear the pain of thinking me wicked—sending for me—repenting—making me as happy as it is possible for woman to make man for three days—and then darting away again into darkness and forbidding me to write a word to her till I have ceased to hope! That for Number Two—I suppose she'll die, for Number three,[31] at the end of the seventh year since she bid me wait, and I shall have to go down and try to drag up Persephone.[32] I've had the ἦγε μέν, οὐδ' ἀπόνητο with a vengeance.[33] There really never was a Greek story much sadder.

I'm not going mad though—nor thinking myself Theseus. Still,—I have certainly now more power and purpose of defining law than any man that I know among modern workers,—and surely—the pain is great enough for *anybody*.[34]

In naming his course of lectures on engraving after Ariadne Ruskin had named them after a Greek image of Rose. Certain emphases in *Ariadne Florentina* have a directly personal reference. In his first lecture, the 'Definition of the Art of Engraving', Ruskin digresses into an admonishment of his own Irish Ariadne, Rose La Touche: 'And I can assure my fair little lady friends,—if I still have any,—that whatever a young girl's ordinary troubles or annoyances may be, her true virtue is in shaking them off, as a rose-leaf shakes off rain, and remaining debonnaire and bright in spirits, or even, as the rose would be, the brighter for the troubles; and not at all in allowing herself to be either drifted or depressed to the point of requiring religious consolation' (xxiii. 316–17). More important, however, is the way in which the mythology of ancient Greece had provided Ruskin with an imaginative language adequate to express the issues that were closest to him. Theseus, the fabled lawgiver of the Greeks, seemed to reflect Ruskin's hopes for his own work.

The published lectures comprising *Ariadne Florentina* represent the first departure from the rigorously formal mode

[31] Rose survived her illness in 1872, but died in May 1875. See below, pp. 177–8.

[32] Ruskin's association of Ariadne with Persephone is not wholly fanciful. Both may be seen as goddesses of the underworld. See C. Kerenyi, *Dionysus*, trans. Ralph Mannheim (London, 1976). Kerenyi notes that "in one aspect of her being Ariadne was a dark goddess. Among the Greeks the epithet "utterly pure" was attached pre-eminently to Persephone, the queen of the underworld, although other goddesses also were termed *hagne*' (pp. 103–4). For Ruskin's identification of Persephone with Rose, see below, pp. 175–6.

[33] 'he was fain to bear, but he had no joy of her'.

[34] Claiborne, *Letters*, pp. 311–14 (29 Sept. 1872).

of writing which Ruskin had adopted for his earlier teaching in Oxford, and it is at this point that the material of *Fors* begins to fuse with that of the lectures. This may have been yet more apparent to his first audience, for they were the first that he trusted to extempore delivery. Ruskin takes Botticelli as representative of the art of engraving in Florence. Botticelli seemed to Ruskin a 'reanimate Greek' (xxii. 400) expressing graphically the lessons which are to be found in the mythology of the Greeks, different only in his Christian hope for immortality. Herein lay the special importance of Botticelli for Ruskin: 'I have told you that the first Greeks were distinguished from the barbarians by their simple humanity; the second Greeks—these Florentine Greeks reanimate—are human more strongly, more deeply, leaping from the Byzantine death at the call of Christ, "Loose him, and let him go". And there is upon them at once the joy of resurrection, and the solemnity of the grave'[35] (xxii. 405–6). Ruskin's eccentric view of Botticelli is consistent with the wider concerns of his teaching. 'The learned men of his age in general brought back the Greek mythology as anti-Christian. But Botticelli and Perugino, as pre-Christian; nor only as pre-Christian, but as the foundation of Christianity. But chiefly Botticelli, with perfect grasp of the Mosaic and classic theology, thought over and seized the harmonies of both' (xxii. 440–1). The odd mention of 'Mosaic' theology here is a reminder of Botticelli's 'Life of Moses'. In the spring of 1874, shortly before the published version of this lecture appeared, Ruskin had made a detailed study of this fresco. He had made a careful and lovely copy of Zipporah, Moses' wife.[36] In a lecture on Botticelli delivered in the Michaelmas term of 1874, Ruskin sees in Botticelli's Zipporah an image of the Greek goddess Athena as he had written of her in *The Queen of the Air* five years previously:

The Florentine Christian is, however, a Greek; and to him quite one of the first conditions of his [Moses'] perfectness was in the being bred by the Princess of Egypt, learned in all wisdom, even of the

---

[35] This is likely to be among the passages that Ruskin added in preparing the lectures for publication in 1874, for it was in that year that he had, after 'sixteen full years with "the religion of Humanity" for rough and strong and sure foundation of everything', begun to move closer to a renewed belief in immortality. See xxix. 90.

[36] See xxiii, frontispiece.

world he had to leave. His Zipporah is simply the Etruscan Athena, becoming queen of a household in Christian humility. Her spear is changed to a reed and becomes then her sceptre, cloven at the top into the outline of Florentine Fleur-de-Lys, and in the cleft she fastens her spindle. Her χιτών falls short of her feet, that it may not check her motion, and is lightly embroidered; above, the πέπλος unites with its own character that of the aegis. Where Athena's had the wars of the giants, it is embroidered with mystic letters, golden on blue, but it becomes the αἰγὶς θυσσανόεσσα at its edge, where what are only light tassels in the πέπλος become this waving fringe, typical of sacrifical fire, for you know she is a priest's daughter; but when the peplus falls in Greek statues into its κόλπος, sinus, gulph, or lap, the aegis is here replaced by a goatskin satchel, in which the maiden holds lightly with her left hand apples, here taking the character of the Etruscan Pomona, and oak for the strength of life. Her hair is precisely that of the Phidian Athena, only unhelmed, and with three leaves of myrtle in its wreaths. (xxiii. 275–6)

Athena had continued to be a transforming image in Ruskin's work after 1869. In his lecture on 'Imagination' Ruskin had shown Athena in her special function as the 'goddess of Art-Wisdom' (xx. 245). She is concerned with 'the giving of Form' (xx. 265), but her rule is moral rather than aesthetic:

the power of Athena, first physically put forth in the sculpturing of these ζῷα and ἑρπετά, these living and reptile things, is put forth, finally, in enabling the hearts of men to discern the one from the other; to know the unquenchable fires of the Spirit from the unquenchable fires of Death; and to choose, not unaided, between submission to the Love that cannot end, or to the Worm that cannot die. (xx. 266–7)

Ruskin believed that Botticelli shared in his own associative vision. This inspired much of the excitement with which he turns to the art of Florence in the early 1870s.

Ruskin's encounter with the Florentine engraving of Ariadne, Theseus, and the labyrinth in September 1872 may have initiated his comparison of Greek and Florentine art. It was at this point that Ruskin's enthusiasm for Botticelli began to gather momentum. Later he was to claim to have 'discovered' Botticelli. In 1883 he wrote:

But I say with pride, which it has become my duty to express openly, that it was left to me, and to me alone, first to discern, and then to teach, so far as in this hurried century any such thing *can* be taught, the excellency and supremacy of five great painters, despised until I spoke of them,—Turner, Tintoret, Luini, Botticelli, and Carpaccio. Despised,—nay, scarcely in any true sense of the word, known. (iv. 355–6)

This is not quite the case, for Rossetti, other Pre-Raphaelites, and Walter Pater, had previously spoken of Botticelli in England. Pater had written of Botticelli in August 1870, while Ruskin's first allusion to Botticelli seems to have occurred in his lectures on 'Landscape', delivered in the Lent term of 1871[37] (xxii. 18–19). Ruskin was, however, aware of Pater's precedence in 1872, though he may have forgotten it in 1883. In mid-September 1872, shortly before he wrote to Tyrwhitt about the Florentine engraving of Theseus and Ariadne, he had written to his secretary about Botticelli: 'I have your nice abstracts from Crowe & C. and the fortnightly with Pater's article—in looking over which I am surprised to find how much I have changed in my own estimation of Sandro in my last Italian journies—for I recollect thinking Pater's article did him full justice—and now—though quite *right*—it reads lukewarm to me.'[38] According to Collingwood, Ruskin had in his lectures of Michaelmas term 1872 quoted 'with appreciation the passage of the Venus Anadyomene from Mr. Pater's *Studies in the Renaissance* just published'.[39]

[37] See Walter Pater, 'A Fragment on Sandro Botticelli', *Fortnightly Review*, 14 (Aug. 1870), 155–60. See Herbert P. Horne, *Alessandro Filipepi Commonly Called Sandro Botticelli: Painter of Florence* (London, 1908), xii–xiii; and Michael Levey, 'Botticelli and Nineteenth Century England', *Journal of the Warburg and Courtauld Institutes*, 23 (1960), 291–306.

[38] Claiborne, *Letters*, pp. 307–8. Claiborne suggests the letter may be dated between 15 and 18 Sept. 1872. 'Crowe & C.' are Crowe and Cavalcaselle. Their *A New History of Painting in Italy from the Second to the Sixteenth Century* had been published in three volumes in London in 1864, and was followed in 1871 by a two-volume *History of Painting in North Italy*. See xxii. 337–9, xxv. 171.

[39] W. G. Collingwood, *The Life and Work of John Ruskin*, 2 vols. (London, 1893), ii. 137. The quotation appears in none of the published versions of the lectures and could not in any case have been to *Studies in the Renaissance*, which appeared after Ruskin's lectures were given. But it is perfectly possible that Ruskin may have referred to Pater's original article in the *Fortnightly Review*. Collingwood's word carried weight in that he may well have attended the lecture himself. He had entered Oxford in 1872 and had quickly established friendship with Ruskin. See *The Brantwood Diary*, ed. Helen Gill Viljoen (New Haven and London, 1971), 571.

Ruskin's belief in a close relation between the arts of Greece and Florence was confirmed by his journey to the Continent of 1874. He stayed in Florence from 19 August to 20 September.[40] From there he wrote to Carlyle: 'My chief discovery here is that the old Etruscan race has never failed and that Florentine art is all Etrurian—Greek—down to the 15th century—when it expires in modern confusion.'[41] Ruskin was occupied with Greek mythology as well as Florentine art during his month in Florence. On 14 September, the day after his letter to Carlyle, he recorded in his diary: 'Plan little preface for *Queen of Air*. The discovery of it. I knew ten times less Latin and Greek than the philologists; a thousand-fold more about the morning and its breeze. Also, I knew something of Greek art, and had a little, in my own mind, of actual Greek Faith.'[42] This renewed interest in Greek religion is expressed in his mythological interpretation of Botticelli's Zipporah and his claim of a Greek identity for the Florentine art which Botticelli represented.[43]

Ruskin claimed that Greek mythology lay behind Turner's painting and formed the architecture of St Mark's; so too it coloured fifteenth-century Florentine art. Its importance in his work at Oxford did not stop there. For it is in the years of the professorship that the study of natural history which was to preoccupy his thought during much of the final phase of his creative life took shape, and this too was closely connected with Greek mythology. Early in 1872 Ruskin delivered a series of ten lectures on the relation of natural science to art, later published as *The Eagle's Nest* (1872). Athena governs the proper function of both art and science. She represents the 'faculty called by the Greeks σοφία' (xxii. 119), or wisdom. Ruskin illustrates the wisdom embodied in the Greek goddess with an image of two girls watching the stars:

Supposing the one versed somewhat in abstract Science, and more or less acquainted with the laws by which what she now sees may be

[40] See *Diaries*, iii. 805–11.

[41] Unpubl. letter, Bodl. MS Eng. Lett. c. 40, fo. 28 (13 Sept. 1874).

[42] *Diaries*, iii. 810.

[43] It should be noted that Ruskin, like many others, attributed to Botticelli pictures and engravings not now considered to be his. The series of Florentine engravings of the sibyls, for instance, discussed in *Ariadne Florentina*, are unlikely to be the work of Botticelli. See Horne, *Alessandro Filipepi*, pp. xii–xiii.

explained; she will probably take interest chiefly in questions of distance and magnitude, in varieties of orbit, and proportions of light. Supposing the other not versed in any science of this kind, but acquainted with the traditions attached by the religions of dead nations to the figures they discerned in the sky: she will care little for arithmetical or geometrical matters, but will probably receive a much deeper emotion, for witnessing in clearness what has been the amazement of so many eyes long closed; and recognizing the same lights, through the same darkness, with innocent shepherds and herdsmen, who knew only the risings and settings of the immeasurable vault, as its lights shone on their own fields or mountains; yet saw the true miracle in them, thankful that none but the Supreme Ruler could bind the sweet influences of the Pleiades, or loose the bands of Orion. I need not surely tell you, that in this exertion of the intellect and the heart, there would be a far nobler sophia than any concerned with the analysis of matter, or the measurement of space. (xxii. 143)

This second kind of 'sophia' is Ruskin's aim in his investigation of natural history. The ninth lecture in *The Eagle's Nest*, 'The Story of the Halcyon', is a pattern for his subsequent scientific study. He choose the halcyon, or kingfisher, as the subject of his lecture because of its importance in Greek mythology. He describes what he sees as the three leading branches of natural history:

We have first to collect and examine the traditions respecting the thing, so that we may know what the effects of its existence has hitherto been on the minds of men, and may have at our command what data exist to help us in our inquiries about it, or to guide us in our own thoughts of it.

We have secondly to examine and describe the thing, or creature, in its actual state, with utmost attainable veracity of observation.

Lastly, we have to examine under what laws of chemistry and physics the matter of which the thing is made has been collected and constructed. (xxii. 245)

It is the first, mythological branch of natural history which interests Ruskin. 'I do not care what we call the first branch; but, in the accounts of animals that I prepare for my schools at Oxford, the main point with me will be the mythology of them' (xxii. 245). He illustrates the mythical associations which the 'lovely colour and fitful appearance of the bird'

(xxii. 256) have inspired from characteristically eclectic and diverse classical sources.[44] Theseus-like, Ruskin draws social and moral lessons from the myth of the kingfisher's nesting on a calm sea. 'If, indeed, the squire would make his seat worth painting, and would stay there, and would make the seats, or, shall we call them, forms, of his peasantry, worth painting too, he would be interpreting the fable of the Halcyon to purpose' (xxii. 259). Ruskin continued to explore the possibilities of mythological ornithology in a series of lectures delivered in Hilary term 1873. 'Three Lectures on English and Greek Birds as the Subjects of Fine Art', later published in parts as *Love's Meinie* (1873–81), began a new enterprise in Ruskin's career. The first part of *Proserpina*, his most serious attempt to establish a new mode of natural science, followed in 1875. Like the Oxford lectures, it is profoundly influenced by the complex significance that Greek myths had come to have in his life and work.

[44] Apollodorus, Hyginus, Virgil, Aristotle, Plutarch, and a dialogue which Ruskin attributes to Lucian, all contribute to the mythology of the halcyon.

7

Final Years in Oxford (1883–1885)

Ruskin's madness in the spring of 1878 brought his first term of office at Oxford to an end. This caused him little regret. The professorship had not provided the platform that he had hoped for, and his interest had faded. Between 1874 and 1878, Ruskin had given only two courses of lectures as Slade Professor and had published only one lecture.[1] He wrote to Liddell towards the end of 1878: 'It has long been my feeling that nobody really cared for anything that I *knew*; but only for more or less lively talk from me—or else drawing-master's work—and neither of these were my proper business'[2] (vol. xxix, p. xxv). There may be a personal reproach here, for Liddell himself had thought that Ruskin could never be anything more than a 'great Drawing-Master'. The Dean, now Vice-Chancellor of the University, represented forces that Ruskin felt had stifled the development of his Oxford school. Other projects gave him a freer hand. The Master of the Guild of St George could create his own vehicles for writing and teaching; the Slade Professor at Oxford could not. The interrupted sequence of *Fors Clavigera* was resumed in 1880. *Proserpina* (1875–86) and *Deucalion* (1875–83), books which had close links with the work at Oxford, claimed attention. Ruskin planned works on history and wrote *The Bible of Amiens* (1880–5). But the recovery from insanity was precarious. A further bout of illness struck in the early spring of 1881 and again in the following year. Sir William Gull, who attended Ruskin in 1882, recommended travel.[3] In August

[1] Ruskin gave 'Twelve Studies in the *Discourses* of Sir Joshua Reynolds' in Michaelmas term 1875, and 'Twelve Readings in *Modern Painters*' in Michaelmas term 1877. See xxii. 493–538. For the final lecture in the *Modern Painters* series, see 'An Oxford Lecture', *Nineteenth Century*, 3 (Jan. 1878), 136–45.

[2] The letter is not dated, but internal evidence suggests that it was written in Nov. or Dec. 1878.

[3] Sir William Withey Gull (1816–90), one of the most eminent doctors in England, had cemented his reputation by successfully treating the Prince of Wales's typhoid fever in 1871.

1882 Ruskin set out on what was to be his last successful continental journey.

W. G. Collingwood, secretary and disciple, accompanied him. We have his account of an energetic progress through familiar scenes and new acquaintance. In Florence, Ruskin met Francesca Alexander.[4] Collingwood describes his response: 'He had always called out for human interest, the evidence of sympathy, the poetry of feeling, in art: and he found this in Miss Alexander,—not professionally learned, but full of observation and the tokens of affectionate interest in her subject.'[5] Ruskin's excited admiration may in part be explained by the nature of her subject. Collingwood recalls: 'One evening before dinner he brought back to the hotel at Florence a drawing of a lovely girl lying dead in the sunset; and a little notebook. "I want you to look over this", he said, in the way, but not quite in the tone, with which the usual MS. "submitted for criticism" was tossed to a secretary to taste.'[6] The obsessive memory of Rose persisted. But it was not a melancholy shade that haunted Ruskin in Florence. He had found new energy and confidence away from the sedating influence of Brantwood. Joan Severn was constantly concerned to calm and restrain; Collingwood, without the domestic authority of Ruskin's cousin, could not effectively take over her function as custodian and nurse. Ruskin began to wish for the resumption of his post at Oxford and had no hesitation in communicating his feelings.[7] William Blake Richmond (1842–1921), son of Ruskin's old friend George Richmond (1809–96), had held the professorship since 1878.

[4] Francesca Alexander (1837–1917) was an American artist who had been brought up in Florence, and whose illustrated collection of songs and ballads Ruskin was to publish as *Roadside Songs of Tuscany* (1885).

[5] Collingwood, *Life*, ii. 219.

[6] Ibid. 218. The MS, recounting the illness and death of an Italian friend of Francesca Alexander, was edited and published by Ruskin as *The Story of Ida: Epitaph on an Etrurian Tomb* (1883).

[7] Ruskin wrote to Alexander Macdonald (1839–1921), who had remained in charge of the Drawing School during his absence from Oxford: 'It is curious I can't think its only three years since Richmond took the Professorship. I believe I'm quite able now to take it again myself, if they'd like me to. I shouldn't give exciting lectures any more—but sufficient ones on practical matters, and I should like to finish the arrangement of the schools as I meant them to be. You might say this to Acland when you see him' (Unpubl. letter, Bodl. MS Eng. Lett. c. 45, fo. 191 (22 Oct. 1882)).

Hearing of Ruskin's wish to return, he retired with loyal alacrity. On 16 January 1883 the *Oxford University Gazette* announced Ruskin's re-election to the post.

To Collingwood, Ruskin's companion for the past year, this was natural. 'He seemed now to have quite recovered his health, and to be ready for re-entry into public life. What was more, he had many new things to say.'[8] In fact, Ruskin had nothing new to say. He wanted the professorship again because he thought it necessary to repeat what he had often said before. The modern world filled him with increasing dismay, and what he had seen on the continent in 1882 had done nothing to mollify him. The success of the Grosvenor Gallery, in particular, suggested the defeat of all that he had stood for. He wrote to Alexander Macdonald: '*Modern Painters* itself left half that I had to say of landscape in the merest embryo—and the recent errors of the French schools have made it desirable that I should re-state many of the principles for which I have so long contended' (xxxvii. 421). Ruskin entered his second tenure of the Slade Professorship with few ambitions. He was fighting a rearguard action, defending rather than attacking. During the week of his re-election, he wrote rather hopelessly to F. A. Malleson: 'I am not stronger myself, but think it right to keep hold of the Oxford helm, as long as they care to trust it to me'[9] (xxxvii. 433). Two days later he wrote to Faunthorpe: 'I have only taken the Professorship again in order to keep my hand on the helm, not to talk. They will be quite content to hear me read Proserpina or anything else I am doing' (xxxvii. 434). Ruskin was not himself finally content with this and wrote two new courses of lectures in the two years of his second term at Oxford. Both were published—*The Art of England* in 1884, *The Pleasures of England* in 1884-5.

In these lectures new material demonstrates old precepts. The drawings of Francesca Alexander and Kate Greenaway were among his topics, as were the illustrations of John

---

[8] Collingwood, *Life*, ii. 219.

[9] The Revd F. A. Malleson (1819-97), vicar of Broughton-in-Furness, was the recipient of the letters published in *Letters to the Clergy on the Lord's Prayer and the Church* (1879-80).

Tenniel, or the early religious history of England.[10] But Ruskin often turned to the insistent recapitulation of private conviction only intermittently apposite to his supposed subject. Ruskin's second tenure of the chair at Oxford was sadly different from his first term of office. An eminent man in 1870, in 1883 he must have seemed almost an institution to the undergraduates. They listened to him as a performer rather than as a teacher. Yet he was still a commanding presence. It was during these years that Edward Tyas Cook, later Ruskin's editor and rival biographer to Collingwood, first came to meet him. Cook's account of the lectures comprising *The Pleasures of England* betray a curious mixture of reverence and disapproval: 'There was nothing here to check the range of his discursiveness, or restrain the violence of his feelings, and he let himself go freely. . . . The digressions and interpolations sometimes contained passages of serious and telling eloquence. . . . But at other times there was a lack of restraint' (vol. xxxiii, pp. lii–liii). Ruskin saw no need for restraint. He was not dependent on the university, either financially or intellectually, and he had less respect for its authority with every passing year. His final resignation came in March 1885. The immediate cause was the 'vote endowing vivisection'[11] (vol. xxxiii, p. lvi). But Ruskin had also been angered by the university's refusal to provide more convenient accommodation for his school and to buy two further Turner drawings. The uneasy relationship between Oxford University and its first Professor of Fine Art was broken with considerable mutual relief. Ruskin never visited Oxford again.

Ruskin's late lectures at Oxford show the extent to which self-consistency in his thought was now moving towards self-enclosure. Speaking of the art of England, or the pleasures of England, provided another mode of autobiography. This is obtrusive in those passages where Ruskin ponders the

---

[10] Ruskin had met Kate Greenaway (1846–1901) for the first time on 29 Dec. 1882; she soon became a disciple and friend. Sir John Tenniel (1820–1914), artist and cartoonist, worked for *Punch* over a period of fifty years.

[11] So called in a letter to the *Pall Mall Gazette*, explaining his resignation, of 24 Apr. 1885.

etymology of the word 'rose' or refers to his copy of the saint's head in Carpaccio's *Dream of St. Ursula*:

You will never see such hair, nor such peace beneath it on the brow—*Pax Vobiscum*—the peace of heaven, of infancy, and of death. No one knows who she is or where she lived. She is Persephone at rest below the earth; she is Proserpine at play above the ground. She is Ursula, the gentlest yet the rudest of little bears; a type in that, perhaps, of the moss rose, or of the rose *spinosissima*, with its rough little buds. She is in England, in Cologne, in Venice, in Rome, in eternity, living everywhere, dying everywhere, the most intangible, yet the most practical of all saints,—queen, for one thing, of female education, when once her legend is rightly understood. (xxxiii. 507)

Here, private preoccupations with Proserpina, with botany, with Carpaccio's St Ursula, display their origins in the death of Rose La Touche. This lecture, 'Protestantism: The Pleasures of Truth', was delivered in November 1884. Ruskin did not publish it, but E. T. Cook incorporated a detailed report into his edition of Ruskin's works. It includes the notorious reference to Protestants as pigs: ' "Here I have for you a type of the honest but not liberally minded Protestant", said Mr. Ruskin, disclosing a sketch of a little porker' (xxxiii. 509). This was too much. Ruskin was dissuaded from delivering his proposed lectures on 'The Pleasures of Sense' and 'The Pleasures of Nonsense'. His association with Oxford was almost at an end. Yet it was not the first time that Ruskin had used a pig to illustrate the English temper of mind. Cook's conjecture that the sketch Ruskin used was 'a copy from Bewick' (xxxiii. 509) is plausible, for such a copy appears as an illustrative figure in *Ariadne Florentina* (1876), the published version of the lectures on wood and metal engraving which Ruskin had delivered in Oxford in 1872. Ruskin speaks of Bewick's Englishness: 'No sight or thought of beautiful things was ever granted to him;—no heroic creature, goddess-born—how much less any native Deity— ever shone upon him. To his utterly English mind, the straw of the sty, and its tenantry, were abiding truth;—the cloud of Olympus, and its tenantry, a child's dream. He could draw a pig, but not an Aphrodite (xxii. 362). Here again, biographical considerations are relevant. Ruskin's father had chosen a boar's head as the crest of his family, and in *Praeterita* Ruskin speaks, with the blandness characteristic of that book, of the importance this had for him. His attack on the English in *Ariadne Florentina*, confirmed and emphasized in *The Pleasures of England*, is at least in part directed against himself.

As always for Ruskin, escape from personal bitterness seemed to lie in the eternal truths which he saw beyond himself. To create an Aphrodite might be no more possible for him than for Bewick; but he could at least recognize and demonstrate the sphere of spiritual significance of which the Greek Aphrodite was part. Greek mythology is important in Ruskin's final Oxford lectures because its wisdom could not be tainted or distorted either by his own threatening madness or the insanity of nineteenth-century England. For the true Greek spirit was not limited to classical art, literature, or architecture, any more than the true British spirit manifested itself in the industrial nightmare of London or Manchester. Just as Ruskin now saw St Ursula as an 'essentially British' (xxxiii. 491) saint, so he began to see the influence of Athena in the arches of the Norman church at Iffley (xxxiii. 478), or the presence of Hercules in the traditional lion of the British door-knocker (xxxiii. 500–2). It was Greek mythology, rather than Greek art, to which he turned. He was restating and emphasizing afresh what had long been central in his work. In 'Mythic Schools of Painting', the lecture on Burne-Jones and Watts that formed the second of his series on *The Art of England*, Ruskin refers to *The Queen of the Air* as a refutation of the idea that 'mythology is a temporary form of human folly' (xxxiii. 294). He now claims that *The Queen of the Air* did not go far enough towards stating that 'the thoughts of all the greatest and wisest men hitherto, since the world was made, have been expressed through mythology' (xxxiii. 294). It is above all to the mythology of Greek literature to which he directs his audience's attention:

And I believe that every master here who is interested, not merely in the history, but in the *substance*, of moral philosophy, will confirm me in saying that the direct maxims of the greatest sages of Greece do not, in the sum of them, contain a code of ethics either so pure, or so practical, as that which may be gathered by the attentive interpretation of the myths of Pindar and Aristophanes. (xxxiii. 295)

In speaking of what he described as the mythic art of Burne-Jones and G. F. Watts, Ruskin reasserts his misgivings about the art of the Greeks. The function of the modern mythic artist was a reflection of what Ruskin now saw as his own function. Burne-Jones could provide the interpretation of Greek mythology that no Greek artist could offer. In this his painting was comparable to what Ruskin was attempting in words:

And herein you see with what a deeply interesting function the modern painter of mythology is invested. He is to place, at the service of former imagination, the art which it had not—and to realise for us, with a truth then impossible, the visions described by the wisest of men as embodying their most pious thoughts, and their most exalted doctrines: not indeed attempting with any literal exactitude to follow the words of the visionary, for no man can enter literally into the mind of another, neither can any great designer refuse to obey the suggestions of his own: but only bringing the resources of accomplished art to unveil the hidden splendour of old imagination: and showing us that the forms of the gods and angels which appeared in fancy to the prophets and saints of antiquity, were indeed more natural and beautiful than the black and red shadows on a Greek vase, or the dogmatic outlines of a Byzantine fresco. (xxxiii. 296)

Ruskin is speaking of himself, not of Burne-Jones. This is still clearer when he comes to praise his friend for the extent of the scholarship, and breadth of imagination, that had enabled Burne-Jones to conflate the mythology of the ancient world with the legends of the Christian faith. Such an endeavour had of course been essential to Ruskin's mature work, but it is hard to see its equivalent in Burne-Jones's idealized and bloodless representations of standard mythological themes. Ruskin's response to Burne-Jones had always been personal. In this lecture, it touches autobiography:

It is impossible for the general public to estimate the quantity of careful and investigatory reading, and the fine tact of literary discrimination, which are signified by the command now possessed by Mr. Burne-Jones over the entire range both of Northern and Greek Mythology, or the tenderness at once, and largeness, of sympathy which have enabled him to harmonize these with the loveliest traditions of Christian legend. (xxxiii. 296–7)

It is still harder to see William Morris as foremost among a new school of comparative Greek mythologists. Yet Ruskin claims him as another ally, improbably associated with Lord Lindsay's *Sketches of the History of Christian Art* (1847). Lord Lindsay's work had been important to Ruskin, and here again his historical argument is based on circumstances of his own life. The syncretism of his approach to mythology and religion is mirrored in a confusion of generations in his own memory:

It is but fifty years ago that the value of the latter was again perceived and represented to us by Lord Lindsay, and it is only within the time which may be looked back to by the greater number even of my younger auditors, that the transition of Athenian mythology, through Byzantine, into Christian, has been first felt, and then traced and proved, by the penetrative scholarship of the men belonging to this Pre-Raphaelite school, chiefly Mr. Burne-Jones and Mr. William Morris. . . . (xxxiii. 297)

The supposed transition from Greek to Christian mythology was of more than academic importance to Ruskin. His first reverence for the Greeks had largely grown out of his admiration for the acceptance of human mortality that their mythological religion had seemed to express. Since the death of Rose, such an acceptance had no longer been tolerable to him. The renewed faith in eternal life which followed was a result of emotional necessity rather than doctrinal conviction. 'For all human loss and pain, there is no comfort, no interpretation worth a thought, except only in the doctrine of the Resurrection; of which doctrine, remember, it is an immutable historical fact that all the beautiful work, and all the happy existence of mankind, hitherto, has depended on, or consisted in, the hope of it' (xxxiii. 276–7). What Ruskin here characteristically calls 'an immutable historical fact' might more truthfully be seen as an intensely private belief. Ruskin could not work, or live, without trusting that he would see Rose again. The faith that was vital to him seemed a universal human need. The 'old Orphic song' (xxxiv. 313) of the Greeks, which he had taken up as his own in the humanist writings of the 1860s, was now no longer sufficient—or possible. Ruskin had written of this three years previously in *Fiction, Fair and Foul* (1880):

This is the root of all life and all rightness in Christian harmony, whether of word or instrument; and so literally, that in precise manner as this hope disappears, the power of song is taken away, and taken away utterly. When the Christian falls back out of the bright hope of the Resurrection, even the Orpheus song is forbidden him. (xxxiv. 313)

Ruskin saw the significance of the Greeks in terms that transcended the sadness of the song of Orpheus. In his first Oxford lectures, he had described a Greek school of art that extended from archaic vase-painting to the paintings of Turner. He now saw the imagery of the Christian Church as a part of the same school. It is the school of his own imagination, for in it he includes all that means 'more than it is in itself' (xxiv. 281)—all that was open to his own method of moral iconography. Ruskin claimed that

it is nearly impossible to find in the imagery of the Greek Church, under the former exercise of the Imagination, a representation either of man or beast which purports to represent *only* the person, or the brute. Every mortal creature stands for an Immortal Intelligence or Influence: a Lamb means an Apostle, a Lion an Evangelist, an Angel the Eternal justice or benevolence; and the most historical and indubitable of Saints are compelled to set forth, in their vulgarly apparent persons, a Platonic myth or an Athanasian article. (xxxiii. 486)

Because he perceived the origins of Christian symbolism in the Greek imagination, Ruskin tended to merge the mythological attributes of Greek religion with those of Christianity. He included Greek figures in the hierarchy of early mythical saints, which were, in his view, 'scarcely founded at all on personal characters or acts, but mythic or symbolic; often merely the revival, the baptized resuscitation of a Pagan deity, or the personified omnipresence of a Christian virtue' (xxxiii. 485). The 'most mythic' of all is St Sophia, 'the shade of the Greek Athena, passing into the "Wisdom" of the Jewish Proverbs and Psalms, and the Apocryphal "Wisdom of Solomon"' (xxxiii. 486). Ruskin was not alone in comparing religions in this way; but the focus on Athena has more to do with a private cosmology than participation in a scholarly movement. The death of Rose had driven him into an acceptance of the doctrine of Resurrection and had intensified his conviction of personality in the spiritual government of the world. Divine symbolism did not imply abstraction, for

Pallas cleaving the cloud, and Poseidon calming the sea, are as real persons to a Greek soul, in the great days of Greece, as Christ on the lake of Galilee, is to a Christian's—or was to a Christian's, in the great hour of Christendom, and you may rest absolutely on the general truth respecting Human Nature, that its fortitude and honour have hitherto depended (*ceteris paribus*) accurately on the intensity and simplicity of its trust in a Personal God. (xxxiii. 494 n.)

Athena had always dominated Ruskin's view of Greek religion, and he had defined the importance she had for him in *The Queen of the Air* (1869). He had completed that book with a disquisition on 'The Hercules of Camarina', which had included an interpretation of the meaning of the Nemean lion: 'The first monster we have to strangle, or to be destroyed by, fighting in the dark, and with none to help us, only Athena standing by, to encourage with her smile. Every man's Nemean Lion lies in wait for him somewhere' (xix. 417). Ruskin's own Nemean lion had taken a more definite shape in the years following 1869. He spoke of it again in the last of his published Oxford lectures, 'The Pleasures of Fancy', which appeared in *The Pleasures of England*. It is characteristic of these late lectures that Ruskin should now see the lion as a symbol at once Greek and Christian. Its origin, however, is to be found in Greek mythology. For Ruskin now sees the lion as 'the power of death on earth, conquered by Heracles, and becoming thenceforward both his helmet and aegis. All ordinary architectural lion sculpture is derived from the Heraclean' (xxxiii. 500–1). The list of five 'mythic lions' of which Ruskin asks his readers to 'recollect the meaning' presents a bizarre juxtaposition of cultures. The Nemean lion is set beside the lion of the tribe of Judah, the lion of St Mark, the lion of St Jerome, and the Egyptian lion of the Zodiac (xxxiii. 501). These five lions together 'will give

you, broadly, interpretation of nearly all Lion symbolism in
great art' (xxxiii. 501). This was the symbolism that had
declined into the familiar lion's head of the 'British door
knocker' (xxxiii. 501). Yet even here its Greek meaning had
survived, transformed by the mediation of Christianity.
Ruskin pointed to a vital connection 'between that last
degradation of the Leonine symbol, and its first and noblest
significance' (xxxiii. 501). Among the illustrative material for
'The Pleasures of Fancy' was a copy of a painting of a lion
from a medieval Bible believed to have been used by the
young King Alfred. Two Latin hexameters give the meaning
of the picture:

> Hic Leo, surgendo, portas confregit Averni
> Qui nunquam dormit, nusquam dormitat, in aevum.

Ruskin translates: 'This Lion, rising, burst the gates of
Death/This, who sleeps not, nor shall sleep, for ever' (xxxiii.
501). In the association with the door lies the link between the
golden lion of the youthful Alfred and the lion's head of the
British door-knocker. The lion was an image of Christ
himself, who, like Hercules, had broken through the doors of
the underworld: 'Now here is the Christian change of the
Heraclean conquest of Death into Christ's Resurrection'
(xxxiii. 502). The horror of the Greek Nemean lion had
become a sign of salvation. Such a transformation is an
indication of the peculiarly personal iconography underlying
Ruskin's late work. The apparent historicism of 'The
Pleasures of England' should not lead us to read them as
conventionally academic lectures, for in his last years Ruskin
was rewriting history according to the needs of his own
imagination.

Ruskin now saw the history of Europe in terms of opposition. There was an absolute antithesis between seeing and not
seeing, understanding and not understanding, the condition
of poet and that of dunce. No intermediate state seemed
possible. Ruskin's definitions of these polarities are often
unexpected. In the first of his lectures on *The Art of
England*, he speaks of 'the modern romantic school in
England' (xxxiii. 569). Focusing on the art of Rossetti and
Holman Hunt, Ruskin is concerned with Christian romance.

He picks Holman Hunt's picture *The Triumph of the Innocents* as a supreme representative of the school chiefly because it symbolizes the Christian doctrine of Resurrection. But this modern romanticism was not opposed to classicism. Ruskin explains in his sixth lecture on 'The Hill-Side':

I do not use the word Romantic as opposed to Classic, but as opposed to the prosaic characters of selfishness and stupidity, in all times, and among all nations. I do not think of King Arthur as opposed to Theseus, or to Valerius, but the Alderman Sir Robert, and Mr. John Smith. And therefore I opposed the child-like love of beautiful things, in even the least of our English Modern Painters, from the first page of the book I wrote about them to the last,—in Greek Art, to what seemed to me then (and in a certain sense is demonstrably to me now) too selfish or too formal,—and in Teutonic Art, to what was cold in a far worse sense, either by boorish dulness or educated affection. (xxxiii. 374–5)

It was Greek mythology, and not Greek art, that now shared in Ruskin's concept of romanticism. Greek myths were opposed to 'the prosaic characters of selfishness and stupidity'; as such, they were romantic. But Greek art, in its antagonism with Gothic, was included in his definition of classicism. In the third of his lectures on *The Art of England*, Ruskin chooses Frederick Leighton and Sir Lawrence Alma-Tadema as representative of 'Classic Schools of Painting'. Their classicism was by no means mythic. Ruskin warns his readers that the word 'classic' had many different meanings for him. He defines the meaning he intends in his lecture: 'And now in this following lecture, you must please understand at once that I use the word "classic", first in its own sense of senatorial, academic, and authoritative; but, as a necessary consequence of that first meaning, also in the sense, more proper to our immediate subject, of Anti-Gothic; antagonistic, that is to say, to the temper in which Gothic architecture was built' (xxxiii. 307). Leighton and Alma-Tadema are 'classic' chiefly in this second sense of the word. Ruskin disapproves. For such classicism gives no scope for expression of the personality which he saw as the basis of Greek mythology. Greek art allowed none of the vitality of the individual, for 'the glory of classic art is always in the body, and never in the face'[12] (xxxiii. 309n.). Gothic painting, on the other hand depends on the individuality of the face: '. . . it is really a true and extremely important consequence that all portraiture is essentially Gothic' (xxxiii. 316). Here again, Ruskin points to the transforming inter-vention of Christianity: 'The Greek . . . pourtrayed the body and the mind of man, glorified in mortal war. But to us is given the task of holier portraiture, of the countenance and the heart of man, glorified by the peace of God' (xxxiii. 325).

It is disconcerting to find Ruskin indicating the art of Francesca Alexander as a distinguished example of what this new art might achieve. Yet his condemnation of the superfici-ality of the Greek trappings in the classical paintings of Leighton and Alma-Tadema strikes home. In painting the 'classic' ideal of the body, they had missed the religious spirit of Greek culture. Ruskin reminds his readers of the religion of Homer: 'I said that the Greeks studied the *body* glorified by war; but much more, remember, they studied the *mind* glorified by it. It is the $\mu\hat{\eta}\nu\iota\varsigma$ $'A\chi\iota\lambda\hat{\eta}\sigma\varsigma$,[13] not the muscular force, which the good beauty of the body itself signifies' (xxxiii. 319–20). It is the mind of the Greeks that seemed to Ruskin to have escaped the modern classical painters. Ruskin directs his readers to a passage from the *Iliad*, in which Achilles is described standing on the Greek rampart, with Athena causing his figure to shine by casting her aegis round his shoulders.[14] The passage illustrates the importance of the associated ideas of light and of the proudly standing figure to the Greek imagination. It rests on

the association of light and cloud, in their terrible mystery, with the truth and majesty of the human form, in the Greek conception; light and cloud, whether appointed either to show or to conceal, both given by a divine spirit, according to the bearing of your own university shield, 'Dominus illuminatio'. In all ancient heroic subjects, you will find these two ideas of light and mystery combined; and these with height of standing—the Goddess central and high in the pediment of her temple, the hero on his chariot, or the Egyptian king colossal above his captives. (xxxiii. 320)

---

[12] From Cook's report. See xxxiii. 426n.
[13] 'the wrath of Achilles'.
[14] Homer, *Iliad*, xviii. 203–6, 225–7.

Ruskin points out that Alma-Tadema's paintings fail in exactly these two qualities of light and erectness:

Now observe, that whether of Greek or Roman life, M. Alma Tadema's pictures are always in twilight—interiors, ὑπὸ συμμιγεῖ σκιᾷ.[15] I don't know if you saw the collection of them last year at the Grosvenor, but with that universal twilight there was also universal crouching or lolling posture,—either in fear or laziness. And the most gloomy, the most crouching, the most dastardly of all these representations of classic life, was the little picture called the Pyrrhic Dance, of which the general effect was exactly like a microscopic view of a small detachment of black-beetles, in search of a dead rat.[16] (xxxiii. 320–1)

Here we arrive at the real impulse behind Ruskin's lecture on the 'Classic Schools of Painting'. He saw Alma-Tadema's exhibition at the Grosvenor Gallery[17] as a new manifestation of the false classicism of the Renaissance. Seizing on what seemed sensual in the ancient world, Alma-Tadema had, like the artists of the Renaissance, perverted the spirituality of its mythological religion. More than twenty years had passed since Ruskin had first insisted on the need to distinguish between the true spirit of the Greeks and its distorted reflection in the Renaissance. Now, he believed his work to have been in vain. Old lessons must be repeated, the fight taken up once more:

But it is absolutely necessary for me to-day to distinguish, once for all, what it is above everything your duty, as scholars in Oxford, to know and love—the perpetual laws of classic literature and art, the laws of the Muses, from what has of late again infected the schools of Europe under the pretence of classic study, being indeed only the continuing poison of the Renaissance, and ruled not by the choir of the Muses, but by the spawn of the Python. (xxxiii. 322)

The struggle had come to seem hopeless. Two months after his final resignation of the professorship at Oxford, Ruskin had again collapsed into madness.

[15] 'in mingled shade' (Plato, *Phaedrus*, 239 C).

[16] Alma-Tadema's *A Pyrrhic Dance* had enjoyed great success when first exhibited in London. See Vern G. Swanson, *Sir Lawrence Alma-Tadema: The Painter of the Victorian Vision of the Ancient World* (London, 1977), 60.

[17] This exhibition, sponsored by the Grosvenor Gallery in 1882, included 287 pictures painted by Alma-Tadema between 1840 and 1882. See Swanson, *Alma-Tadema*, p. 23.

8
Prosperpina: Myth and Science
(1875–1888)

The Spiritual Government of Plants

Ruskin's three late works on natural science, *Love's Meinie* (1873–81), *Deucalion* (1875–83), and *Proserpina* (1875–86), are now little read. Their similar dates, comparable modes of publication, and common inspiration in a long-standing interest in natural history, have tempted critics to speak of them all in the same dismissive breath. *Love's Meinie*, the slightest of the three works, grew out of a course of lectures that Ruskin delivered in Oxford in 1873.[1] *Deucalion*, which also contains material from Oxford lectures, has a more solid basis in study that Ruskin had pursued intermittently since boyhood. He believed that *Deucalion* would stand as a permanent contribution to geology. *Proserpina* was more experimental. He described his work on flowers as 'being merely tentative, much to be modified by future students, and therefore quite different from that of *Deucalion*, which is authoritative as far as it reaches, and will stand out like a quartz dyke, as the sandy speculations of modern gossiping geologists get washed away' (xxv. 403). However, *Proserpina* was, like *Deucalion*, founded on the interest of a lifetime. In the introduction which he wrote in 1874, Ruskin recalls 1842 as the year in which his study of botany began in earnest (xxv. 204). During those thirty-two years his concept of the function of botanical investigation had developed almost out of recognition. The studies of plants in *Proserpina* are an expression of the attack on materialism which is the central concern of his mature work. It is his most comprehensive attempt to realize the dream of an alternative science.

---

[1] This course consisted of 'The Robin' (delivered 15 Mar., repeated 20 Mar.), 'The Swallow' (delivered 2 May, repeated 5 May), and 'The Chough' (delivered 9 May, repeated 12 May). The lecture on the chough was never printed in Ruskin's lifetime, and the only substantial addition he made was a lecture on the dabchicks.

Proserpina raises in an acute form the question of value
and meaning in Ruskin's late work. It cannot be read as an
orthodox contribution to the dry and descriptive science of
botanical classification. Indeed, one of its first aims is to
attack such science, a fact characteristically deplored by the
liberal E. T. Cook.[2] *Proserpina* is openly personal and
polemic, and demands to be read on its own terms. In one
sense, it belongs to the old tradition of the gentleman
amateur naturalist. It is certainly true that Ruskin had no part
in the new professionalism in natural science that had grown
up since, as a boy, he noted geological formations in the Alps
and measured the blue of the sky with his cyanometer. Yet
Proserpina is genuinely innovatory. Though it discovers no
new facts, it does represent a new kind of scientific text.
Some have seen the book as too odd to have lasting interest.
Joan Evans speaks of Ruskin's natural science as the
'whimsical and fantastic systems of nomenclature and classification, that had no real basis except in his imagination'.[3]
Robert Hewison is more perceptive, noting that the late
works on natural history are 'important not just because his
private obsessions force their way through, but because they
demonstrate how consistent his interpretation of reality
was.'[4] *Proserpina* is indeed the culmination of the work of
thirty years. But its private obsessions cannot be ignored. To
trace the origins of *Proserpina* in the earlier books is to see its
fusion of autobiographical, didactic, and literary impulses as
part of an inexorable development. *Proserpina* represents a
climax in Ruskin's work, though it leads to its close.

  Like so much of the later work, *Proserpina* grew out of
Modern Painters. In 1844 Ruskin had discussed the science of
botany in his preface to the second edition of the first
volume of *Modern Painters*:

Every kind of knowledge may be sought from ignoble motives, and
for ignoble ends; and in those who so possess it, it is ignoble

---

[2] Cook and Wedderburn made no secret of their disapproval of this aspect of
Ruskin's work. In his editorial introduction to *Proserpina*, E. T. Cook notes that
'Ruskin chaffed men of science . . . and sometimes allowed himself in passages,
destined to stand, a freedom of contemptuous comment which his admirers must
deplore' (vol. xxv, p. xlvi).

[3] Evans, *John Ruskin*, pp. 356–7.

[4] Hewison, *Argument of the Eye*, p. 176.

knowledge, while the very same knowledge is in another mind an attainment of the highest dignity, and conveying the greatest blessing. This is the difference between the mere botanist's knowledge of plants, and the great poet's or painter's knowledge of them. The one notes their distinctions for the sake of swelling his herbarium, the other, that he may render them vehicles of expression and emotion. The one counts the stamens, and affixes a name, and is content; the other observes every character of the plant's colour and form; considering each of its attributes as an element of expression, he seizes on its lines of grace or energy, rigidity or repose; . . . Thenceforward the flower is to him a living creature, with histories written on its leaves, and passions breathing in its motions. (iii. 36–7)

It became Ruskin's aim to combine and reconcile the two kinds of knowledge. This is a task which he had attempted long before 1875. *Modern Painters* includes an extensive study of plants. The emphasis on their function as 'vehicles of expression and emotion', and on their characteristic 'colour and form', is evident throughout the description and analysis of their place in landscape and art. There is, however, little reference to flowers. In the fifth and final volume of *Modern Painters*, Ruskin explains why. He notes

that flowers have no sublimity . . . impressions of awe and sorrow being at the root of the sensation of sublimity, and the beauty of separate flowers not being of the kind which connects itself with such sensation, there is a wide distinction, in general, between flower-loving minds and minds of the highest order. Flowers seem intended for the solace of ordinary humanity: children love them; quiet, tender, contented, orderly people love them as they grow; luxurious and disorderly people rejoice in them gathered: they are the cottager's treasure; and in the crowded town, mark, as with a little broken fragment of rainbow, the windows of the workers in whose heart rests the covenant of peace. Passionate or religious minds contemplate them with fond, feverish intensity; the affection is severely calm in the works of many old religious painters, and mixed with more open and true country sentiment in those of our own pre-Raphaelites. To the child and the girl, the peasant and the manufacturing operative, to the grisette and the nun, the lover and monk, they are precious always. But to the men of supreme power and thoughtfulness, precious only at times; symbolically and pathetically often to the poets, but rarely for their own sake. They fall forgotten from the great workmen's and soldier's hands. Such men will take, in thankfulness, crowns of leaves, or crowns of thorns—not crowns of flowers. (vii. 119–20)

If Ruskin changed his mind, it was because he now associated flowers with Rose La Touche. He was in the habit of spelling Proserpina to himself without the initial 'P' and the second 'r', leaving *Rose*pina.[5] In the spring of 1866 he wrote to Burne-Jones: 'I'll come on Monday and then be steady, I hope, to every other day—Proserpine permitting. Did you see the gleam of sunshine yesterday afternoon? If you had only seen her in it, bareheaded, between *my* laurels and *my* primrose bank!'[6] (xxxvi. 504). In associating Proserpina with primroses, perhaps Ruskin recalled the passage from *The Winter's Tale* which he had quoted in the second volume of *Modern Painters* (1846) and from which he drew the epigraph for his work on botany. Myths of love and mortality are here fused in a way which haunts Ruskin's work:

> O Proserpina,
> For the flowers now that, frighted, thou let'st fall
> From Dis's wagon! daffodils,
> That come before the swallow dares, and take
> The winds of March with beauty; violets, dim,
> But sweeter than the lids of Juno's eyes,
> Or Cytherea's breath; pale primroses,
> That die unmarried, ere they can behold
> Bright Phoebus in his strength, a malady
> Most incident to maids . . .

Observe how the imagination in these last lines goes into the very inmost soul of every flower, after having touched them all at first with that heavenly timidness, the shadow of Proserpine's . . .[7] (iv. 225–6)

---

5 See *Brantwood Diary*, p. 110.

6 Other unpublished letters from Ruskin to Burne-Jones, preserved in the Fitzwilliam Museum, Cambridge, confirm this link between Proserpina and Rose La Touche. On 17 Aug. 1866, for instance, he wrote that he was 'afraid of the whole things [*sic*] turning out an Aylmer's field kind of business—Not that Proserpines die—but they might turn into grim evangelical preaching Proserpines, which would be worse' (Unpubl. letter, Fitz. MS Envelope 12). In Tennyson's *Aylmer's Field* parental interference in a love affair causes the death of Edith, the heroine, and subsequent suicide of her lover. I am grateful to Tim Hilton for directing my attention to this correspondence.

7 See Shakespeare, *The Winter's Tale*, iv, iv. 116–25.

Ruskin first projected a separate work on botany in 1866,[8] a year in which his life was dominated by his love for Rose.[9] In *Time and Tide* (1867) he wrote that he was 'writing a book on botany just now, for young people, chiefly on wild flowers' (xvi. 413). Eight years passed before the first part of *Proserpina* appeared, but he had not forgotten the idea. Flowers appear in *The Ethics of the Dust* (1866) and *The Queen of the Air* (1869). Soon after *The Queen of the Air* came out, Ruskin wrote to Charles Eliot Norton of his plan to publish a work on botany in the following year, to be called '*Cora Nivalis*, "Snowy Proserpine": an introduction for young people to the study of Alpine and Arctic wild flowers' (xxxvi. 597). This was postponed by his appointment as Slade Professor of Fine Art at Oxford. In his first series of lectures, however, he gave an indication of the kind of work he had in mind: 'Now what we especially need at present for educational purposes is to know, not the anatomy of plants, but their biography—how and where they live and die, their tempers, benevolences, malignities, distresses, and virtues' (xx. 101).

Ruskin saw plants in human terms. He called his work on flowers *Proserpina: Studies of Wayside Flowers, while the air was yet pure among the Alps, and in the Scotland and England which my Father knew*. Mythical reference combines with personal memory in this elegiac title. The Greek myth of Proserpina spoke of flowers, and this was of course why he had named his work after Demeter's daughter. But Ruskin also brooded on her kinship with death.[10] As long ago as

[8] See vol. xviii, p. xxxvi; xxvi. 569.

[9] On 10 Dec. 1865, he had seen Rose for the first time after three years' separation. On 2 Feb. 1866, he proposed marriage to her. The anniversary of this day was important to him for the rest of his life. Years later, he commissioned a picture of the rape of Proserpina from Burne-Jones. On 2 Feb. 1883, seventeen years after his proposal to Rose, Ruskin wrote to the artist: 'Also—if my Proserpine isn't begun, *please* begin it now if it is stopped—go on again—and if it is going on again, do a nice big bit as the Spring comes.—(N.B. Today. Black cloud over all. Black fog under it. Universal Snow on the ground. Steady rain from the Clouds, through the Fog, into the Snow.—and I'm all alone—unless Proserpine's here without my knowing it)' (Unpubl. Lett. Fitz. 175.X52; cf. xxxvii. 436–7). Burne-Jones's picture was never completed, though a detailed pencil study entitled *Pluto and Proserpine* hangs in the City Museum and Art Galleries, Birmingham.

[10] For an invaluable account of the origins and early development of the myth of Persephone, see Günther Zuntz, *Persephone: Three Essays on Religion and Thought in Magna Graecia* (Oxford, 1971). Ruskin was not the only Victorian for

1861, in a lecture on 'Tree Twigs', he had spoken of the Greek feeling for flowers: 'There is no Greek goddess corresponding to the Flora of the Romans. Their Flora is Persephone, "the bringer of death." She plays for a little while in the Sicilian fields, gathering flowers, then snatched away by Pluto, receives her chief power as she vanishes from our sight, and is crowned in the grave'[11] (vii. 478). Five years later the dark myth of Proserpina was again in his mind. Only a few weeks before the letter to Burne-Jones in which Rose is happily linked with Proserpina, he had written to Charles Eliot Norton in a mood of depression and uncertainty: 'I could get, and do get, some help out of Greek myths—but they are full of earth, and horror, in spite of their beauty. Persephone is the sum of them, or worse than Persephone—Comus'[12] (xxxvi. 501).

The double significance of Proserpina acquired tragic meaning for Ruskin when Rose La Touche died on 25 May 1875. He was studying the blossom of the hawthorn on the day she died. Three days later, he wrote to his neighbour at Coniston, Susan Beever:

I've just heard that my poor little Rose is gone where hawthorn blossoms go—which I've been trying to describe all morning, and can't get them to stay with me. It is very wonderful—as one, and another, flower 'is not'—to feel how fast summer is over and gone.

I've just left the second number of *Proserpine* to be printed. There were many little things going to be said in it, which nobody but she could have understood. I daresay I shall try to say them yet

whom the myth of Proserpina held a special fascination. For Swinburne, Proserpina was the supreme representative of the pagan ideal. His *Poems and Ballads* (1866) included 'The Garden of Proserpina', 'At Eleusis', and the notorious 'Hymn to Proserpina'—a poem which was important to Ruskin. On 12 Sept. 1866 Ruskin wrote to Edward Coleridge: 'I've got the original MS of the Hymn to Proserpine, and wouldn't part with it for much more than leaf gold' (*The Swinburne Letters*, ed. C. Y. Lang, 6 vols. (New Haven and London, 1959–62), i. 184). Rossetti began his brooding portrait of Jane Morris holding the pomegranate in 1872 and worked on successive versions of the picture until his death ten years later. Pater's evocative essay on 'The Myth of Demeter and Persephone' was published in 1876. Tennyson's 'Demeter and Persephone', which appeared in 1889, gave a Christian interpretation curiously at odds with the sombre tone of the myth.

[11] Ruskin returned to the theme in *The Queen of the Air*: 'Proserpine plays in the fields of Sicily, and thence is torn away into darkness, and becomes the Queen of Fate—not merely of death, but of the gloom which closes over and ends, not beauty only, but sin' (xix. 304).

[12] Quoted above, p. 93.

and think she's reading them. I daresay *you* will understand some of them, too.[13]

Ruskin made use of his study of the hawthorn blossom when analysing the function of the stem in the third part of *Proserpina*, in a passage given the precise date of Rose's death, 25 May 1875. The passage is shadowed by his loss, as he describes Rose through his description of the flowers:

White,—yes, in a high degree; and pure, totally; but not at all dazzling in the white, nor pure in an insultingly rivalless manner, as snow would be; yet pure somehow, certainly; and white, absolutely, in spite of what might be thought failure,—imperfection—nay, even distress and loss in it. For every little rose of it has a green darkness in the centre—not even a pretty green, but a faded, yellowish, glutinous, unaccomplished green; and round that, all over the surface of the blossom, whose shell-like petals are themselves deep sunk, with grey shadows in the hollows of them—all over this already subdued brightness, are strewn the dark points of the dead stamens—manifest more and more, the longer one looks, as a kind of grey sand, sprinkled without sparing over what looked at first unspotted light. And in all the ways of it the lovely thing is more like the spring frock of some prudent little maid of fourteen, than a flower . . . (xxv. 301)

Rose entered a world of spiritual presences. She took many forms,—not only that of Proserpina, but also of the Gothic saint Ursula, of Dante's Beatrice, of Ariadne, or the 'dear Greek princess' of Venice.[14] In 1880 he wrote in *Fors Clavigera*: 'I myself am in the habit of thinking of the Greek Persephone, the Latin Proserpina, and the Gothic St. Ursula as the same living spirit; and so far regulating my conduct by that idea as to dedicate my book on Botany to Proserpina; and to think, when I want to write anything pretty about flowers, how St. Ursula would like it said' (xxix. 385).

   This presiding spirit could take forms that were less benefi-cent. These too could be observed in their influence over plants. Some flowers seemed to Ruskin to be ruled by the

[13] Unpubl. letter, Bodl. MS Eng. Lett. c. 40, fo. 228. On 4 June 1875 he wrote to Carlyle: 'I . . . was away into the meadows, to see buttercup and clover and bean blossom, when the news came that the little story of my wild Rose was ended, and the hawthorn blossoms, this year, would fall—over her' (xxxvii. 167–8).

[14] For the Doge Selvo's legendary Greek wife, see *Brantwood Diary*, p. 102; see also p. 131, and cf. xiv. 427–8; xxiv. 274–6.

devil. In October 1874 he wrote of the proper management of gardens in *Fors Clavigera*, noting that it is 'not at all of camellias and air-plants that the devil is afraid; on the contrary, the Dame aux Camellias is a very special servant of his; and the Fly-God of Ekron himself superintends—as you may gather from Mr. Darwin's recent investigations—the birth and parentage of the orchidaceae. But he is mortally afraid of roses and crocuses'[15] (xxviii. 182–3). Ruskin loathed orchids. Two months before the first part of *Proserpina* was published, he wrote to his friend 'good Mr. Oliver of Kew'[16] (xxv. 331): 'My feeling about the orchids is complicated with many moral and spiritual questions wholly overwhelming to me . . . and I have notions which I dare not print for fear of the world's thinking me mad, and I never yet was so sure in my life as I am now—though threatened I think with brain disease from fatigue if I don't slack work.'[17]

But Ruskin cared little for what the world thought, and he did print his ideas about the spiritual government of plants. In his chapter on 'Brunella', for instance, from the ninth part of *Proserpina* (1885), he notes that if any of the petals of a flower

lose their definite character as such, and become swollen, solidified, stiffened, or strained into any other form or function than that of petals, the flower is to be looked upon as affected by some kind of constant evil influence; and, so far as we conceive of any spiritual power being concerned in the protection or affliction of the inferior orders of creatures, it will be felt to bear the aspect

[15] cf. xxv. 224, xxix. 108.

[16] Professor Daniel Oliver LL D, FRS (1830–96), was for many years Keeper of the Herbarium and Library at Kew; cf. xxix. 31, where Ruskin refers to 'the friend who is helping me in all I want for *Proserpina*,—Mr. Oliver.' Oliver had written of the orchids: 'The Order is of peculiar physiological interest from the circumstance to which Mr. Darwin has recently called attention, in that, with very rare exceptions, self-fertilisation of the flower is mechanically impossible, the species being consequently dependent upon extraneous (insect) aid to secure the transfer of the pollen to the viscid stigma. The special adaptations of the structure of the flower, especially of the form and position of the lip, column, pollen and stigma, designed to secure insect aid and also to insure the transfer of the pollen from flower to flower, are exceedingly curious and well illustrated in common British species' (Daniel Oliver, *Illustrations of the Principal Natural Orders of the Vegetable Kingdom: Prepared for the Science and Art Department of the Council of Education* (London, 1874), 121).

[17] Unpubl. letter, Bem. MS T. 30 (3 Feb. 1875).

of possession by, or pollution by, a more or less degraded Spirit.
(xxv. 466)

Proserpina expresses Ruskin's view of the world as a physical
manifestation of the struggle between powers of good and
evil. In the third part, published in March 1876, he contrasts
an ordered and lovely wood at Malham Cove with an over-
grown patch of woodland in ugly confusion at Brantwood.
Ruskin points out how 'in the waste and distressed ground,
the distress had changed itself to cruelty. The leaves had all
perished, and the bending saplings, and the wood of
trust;—but the thorns were there, immortal, and the gnarled
and sapless roots, and the dusty treacheries of decay' (xxv.
294). What follows is a reminder that the point of such
analysis is not scientific:

Of which things you will find it good to consider also otherwise
than botanically. For all these lower organisms suffer and perish,
or are gladdened and flourish, under conditions which are in utter
fidelity representative, of the conditions which induce adversity
and prosperity in the kingdoms of men: and the Eternal
Demeter,—Mother, and Judge,—brings forth, as the herb yielding
seed, so also the thorn and the thistle, not to herself, but *to thee*.
(xxv. 294)

The evil coexisting with the good of the earth is appointed
both for the trial and punishment of mankind. In a chapter of
1882, Ruskin refers back to his earlier thoughts on the
meaning of weeds:

Meanwhile the Thistle, and the Nettle, and the Dock, and the
Dandelion are cared for in their generations by the finest arts
of—Providence, shall we say? or of the spirits appointed to punish
our own want of Providence? May I ask the reader to look back to
the seventh chapter of the first volume, for it contains suggestions
of thoughts which came to me at a time of very earnest and faithful
inquiry, set down, I now see too shortly, under the press of reading
they involved, but intelligible enough if they are read as slowly as
they were written, and especially note the paragraph of summary
. . . on the power of the Earth Mother, as Mother, and as *Judge*;
watching and rewarding the conditions which induce adversity and
prosperity in the kingdoms of men . . . (xxv. 463)

Demeter, the 'Earth Mother' as Ruskin calls her, is the

mother of Proserpina and in the mythology of the Greeks is closely linked with her. The poppy is her flower, and thus comes to be associated with Proserpina herself. Ruskin reveals the personal significance that the poppy had for him in the chapter on 'The Flower' from the second part of *Proserpina*, issued in August 1875. He had commented on the poppy's tendency to shed its calyx quickly in *The Ethics of the Dust*, and it is to this point that he now returns. He notes that

nearly all other flowers keep with them, all their lives, their nurse or tutor leaves,—the group which, in stronger and humbler temper, protected them in their first weakness, and formed them to the first laws of their being. But the poppy casts these tutorial leaves away. It is the finished picture of impatient and luxury-loving youth,—at first too severely restrained, then casting all restraint away—yet retaining to the end of life unseemly and illiberal signs of its once compelled submission to laws which were only pain,—not instruction. (xxv. 260)

In representing the conditions which afflict the flower in its youth, Ruskin recalls the circumstances of his own upbringing. He would have been writing this chapter on 'The Flower' while he was recounting his own early childhood in *Fors Clavigera*, in an irregular monthly serialization that ended at about the time of Rose's death.[18] This may well have been one of the passages which he had mentioned to Susan Beever, 'which nobody but she could have understood'. In July 1875, two months after Rose La Touche died, Ruskin wrote an extended study of the poppy. Issued in the third part of *Proserpina*, in March 1876, it is the only chapter in the first volume devoted to the study of a particular flower. He insists that the poppy be seen in spiritual rather than material terms; that this is not only a more complete, but also a more accurate way of looking at the flower. It is not enough to note, with Sowerby's *Botany*, that the petals are of 'bright scarlet'.[19] In describing them as 'robed in the purple of

[18] This account, the germ of *Praeterita*, had begun in Oct. 1871. The last part appeared in May 1876. See xxvii. 167–71, 517–18, 617; xxviii. 101–2, 170–1, 271–5, 296–8, 316–19, 343–53, 385–91, 546–9, 602–5.

[19] J. E. Sowerby, *English Botany: Or, Coloured Figures of British Plants*, ed. J. T. B. Syme, with figures by J. Sowerby, J. deC. Sowerby, J. W. Salter, J. E. Sowerby, 3rd edn., 12 vols. (London, 1863–86), i. 88. The first edition of

Caesars', Ruskin fixes the moral quality of their colour; 'that the splendour of it is proud,—almost insolently so' (xxv. 287). What Ruskin has to say about the poppy is in part an extended and bitter reflection on his own pride, and the forms of ruin to which it had led.

Ruskin's disquisition on the poppy is, like all that he wrote after Rose's death, part of the complex and inward auto-biography that culminated in *Praeterita*. Yet he was not alone in simultaneously rejecting both orthodox Christianity and scientific naturalism. The second half of the nineteenth century saw a reaction against the triumph of science represented by men such as Huxley, Darwin, or Tyndall, whose work Ruskin had long opposed. It took the form of a more spiritual, though not necessarily more Christian, inter-pretation of the world.[20] Ruskin had contact with some of those who had expounded these ideas, notably with Oliver Lodge (1851–1940), the first principal of the University of Birmingham, who was both a psychical researcher and an eminent physicist,[21] and Frederick W. H. Myers (1843–1901), who, like Lodge, made an extensive study of psychical phenomena. Ruskin shared Myers's curiosity about spiritu-alism. But he differed radically from Myers in his appeal to the unchanging body of wisdom that he saw in the classic literature and mythology of the world. Myers had turned away from the Greek ideal that had inspired his youth. Writing of his early enthusiasm for Hellenism, he describes the visit that he had made to Greece in 1864, at the age of twenty-one:

For gazing thence on Delos and on the Cyclades, and on those straits and channels of purple sea, I felt that nowise could I come

Sowerby's *Botany*, which Ruskin describes as 'far the best' (xxv. 441 n.), describes the flower more vividly: 'Petals large, broad, crumpled, of a deep vivid scarlet, and with a rich silky gloss' (J. E. Sowerby, *English Botany* (London, 1790–1814), ix. 645).

[20] Ruskin was in correspondence with Lodge during the 1880s. Some of these letters are published in the Library Edition of Ruskin's works. Many others are to be found in the collection of MSS in the Ruskin Galleries at Bembridge, Isle of Wight.

[21] Ruskin may have been introduced to Myers by Prince Leopold (xxxvii. 199). It was probably in 1875, soon after the death of Rose had given him special reason to be interested in the spirit world, that he wrote to Myers that 'being sure there is a spirit world, I am so poor-hearted and cold that I never think I shall get to it' (xxxvii. 185).

closer still; never more intimately than thus could embrace that vanished beauty. Alas for an ideal which roots itself in the past! That longing cannot be allayed; it feels 'the insatiability which attends all unnatural passions as their inevitable punishment.' For it is an unnatural passion; the world rolls onward, not backward, and men must set their hearts on what lies before.[22]

Ruskin's standards, unlike Myers's, are defined by the past. His careful investigation of the poppy includes a consideration of the standard botanical name of the common European wild poppy, *Papaver rhoeas*. He suggests that this may be translated the 'swiftly ruinous' poppy,[23] because of the rapidity with which it sheds both calyx and corolla. He had already used this trait as an image of human frailty in 'The Flower'. The poppy is also often seen to droop, before it blooms and when the flower is filled with rain. This adds to the aptness of the epithet 'swiftly ruinous'. Ruskin recalls a passage from the *Iliad* in which the drooping head of a dying soldier is compared to that of a poppy after rain,[24] and compares translations of this passage from Chapman, 'a man of pure English temper, and able therefore to understand pure Greek temper', and Pope, 'infected with all the faults of the falsely classical school of the Renaissance' (xxv. 275). Underlying the analysis is the belief that there is a right way of looking at the world, that it is unchanging, that the Greeks had found it and expressed it in their mythology and their literature:

But note farther, in the Homeric passage, one subtlety which cannot enough be marked even in Chapman's English, that his second word ἤμυσε,[25] is employed by him both of the stooping ears of corn, under wind, and of Troy stooping to its ruin; and otherwise, in good Greek writers, the word is marked as having such specific sense of men's drooping under weight, or towards death, under the burden of fortune which they have no more strength to sustain; compare the passage which I quoted from Plato (*Crown of Wild Olive* §83): 'And bore lightly the burden of gold and possessions.' And thus you will begin to understand how the

---

[22] F. W. H. Myers, *Fragments of Prose and Poetry*, ed. Eveleen Myers (London 1904), 19.

[23] From ῥοή: 'a river, stream, or flood'.

[24] Homer, *Iliad*, viii. 306–8.

[25] ἤμύω: 'to bow down, or to fall'.

poppy became in the heathen mind the type at once of power, or pride, and of its loss . . .[26] (xxv. 276–7)

The Jews had shared the insight and expressed it in their scriptures. It had been passed on, in different form, to the Byzantines. It reached medieval Italy. The same wisdom was apparent in Chapman's translation of Homer. Ruskin follows the myth of the poppy throughout the literature and art of Europe, claiming that behind the ornamental use of the flower lies the symbolic meaning which the Greeks had expressed in their legend of Demeter and her lost daughter, and which is connected with that of the wheat-ear, the vine, the fleur-de-lys, and the acanthus. The reader is expected to see that the symbolism of these plants is close to Ruskin's central theme in *Proserpina*, for it expresses the meaning of the cycle of legends surrounding Demeter. References to the Bible, to botanical texts, to art, to Greek religion, or to weeds, jostle against each other in Ruskin's description of

the relation of weeds to corn, or of the adverse powers of nature to the beneficent ones, expressed for us readers of the Jewish scriptures, centrally in the verse, 'thorns also, and thistles, shall it bring forth to thee; and thou shalt eat the herb of the field' ($\chi \acute{o} \varrho \tau o \varsigma$, grass or corn), and exquisitely symbolized throughout the fields of Europe by the presence of the purple 'corn-flag', or gladiolus, and 'corn-rose' (Gerarde's name of Papaver Rhoeas) in the midst of carelessly tended corn; and in the traditions of the arts of Europe by the springing of the acanthus round the basket of the canephora, strictly the basket *for bread*, the idea of bread including all the sacred things carried at the feasts of Demeter, Bacchus, and the Queen of the Air. (xxv. 279–80)

Ruskin's chapter on 'The Leaf' shows how myth might refute the science of mythology, as it contradicted the science of botany. Describing two orders of leaves, the unbranched 'Apolline' and the aquatic 'Arethusan', he warns his readers that 'you must not attach any great botanical importance to the characters of contrasted aspects in leaves, which I wish you to express by the words "Apolline" and "Arethusan"; but their mythic importance is very great, and your careful observance of it will help you completely to understand the

[26] See xviii. 457.

beautiful Greek fable of Apollo and Daphne' (xxv. 242). Considering the origins of this myth, he rejects the theories of Max Müller:

There are indeed several Daphnes, and the first root of the name is far away in another field of thought altogether, connected with the Gods of Light. But etymology, the best of servants, is an unreasonable master; and Professor Max Müller trusts his deep-reaching knowledge of the first ideas connected with the names of Athena and Daphne, too implicitly, when he supposes the idea to be retained in central Greek theology. 'Athena' originally meant only the dawn, among nations who knew nothing of a Sacred Spirit. But the Athena who catches Achilles by the hair, and urges the spear of Diomed, has not, in the mind of Homer, the slightest remaining connection with the mere beauty of daybreak. Daphne chased by Apollo, may perhaps—though I doubt even this much of consistence in the earlier myth—have meant the Dawn pursued by the Sun. But there is no trace whatever of this first idea left in the fable of Arcadia and Thessaly. (xxv. 243)

Ruskin here reminds his readers of what he had said on this subject in *The Queen of the Air*. But he had thought out his views on the myth of Apollo and Daphne long before 1869. His first reference had been inspired by his study of Turner. Ruskin had written of Turner's picture *Apollo and Daphne* in his *Notes on the Turner Gallery at Marlborough House, 1856* (1857). He had suggested there that Daphne represents the life of foliage, not the dawn, as F. M. Müller had suggested in his essay on 'Comparative Mythology' in 1856.[27] Ruskin explains that 'Daphne was the daughter of the river Peneus, the most fertilizing of the Greek rivers, by the goddess Terra (the earth). She represents, therefore, the spirit of all foliage, as springing from the earth, watered by rivers;—rather than the laurel merely' (xiii. 149). The pursuit of Daphne by Apollo represents the sun burning the vegetation, which, appealing to its father the river for help, is kept eternally green by its moisture. 'So then the whole picture is to be illustrative of the union of the rivers and the earth; and of the perpetual help

---

[27] 'Any one who has eyes to see and a heart to feel with nature like the poets of old, may still see Daphne and Apollo,—the dawn rushing and trembling through the sky, and fading away at the sudden approach of the bright sun' (F. M. Müller, 'Comparative Mythology', p. 57).

and delight granted by the streams, in their dew, to the earth's foliage' (xiii. 150).

Ruskin expands his interpretation in his next reference to the myth. This is found in the lecture on 'Tree Twigs' (1861). He suggests there that Daphne may be seen as river mist. She is

the daughter of one of the great Arcadian river gods, and of the earth; she is the type of the river mist filling the rocky vales of Arcadia; the sun, pursuing this mist from dell to dell, is Apollo pursuing Daphne; where the mist is protected from his rays by the rock shadows, the laurel and other richest vegetation spring by the river-sides, so that the laurel-leaf becomes the type, in the Greek mind, of the benevolent ministry and vitality of the rivers and the earth, under the beams of sunshine; and therefore it is chosen to form the signet-crown of highest honour for gods or men, honour for work born of the strength and dew of the earth and informed by the central light of heaven; work living, perennial, and beneficent. (vii. 478)

The idea that the myth is concerned with the relation between the sun, the river's moisture, and their effect on vegetation is unchanged; and the interpretation of the myth of Apollo and Daphne which he develops in his chapter on 'The Leaf' is substantially the same as that given fifteen years earlier in 'Tree Twigs'. The moral implications hinted at in 1861 are, however, explicit in the text of 1875. Characteristically, they are supported by a parallel in the Bible. The trees in the Garden of Eden are watered, not by rivers or rain, but a '*mist* from the earth'[28] (xxv. 246), and the flourishing tree is a symbol of human life in the book of Ezekiel: 'Behold, the Assyrian was a cedar in Lebanon, with fair branches; the waters nourished him, and the deep brought him up, with her rivers running round about his planets'[29] (xxv. 246). The myth is urged on the reader not simply as a literary or even botanical image, though it is expressed in both literature and botany. The science put forward in *Proserpina* as an alternative to 'materialistic theories' will give results as tangible and practical as any of theirs, though it is founded on spiritual rather than physical truths. It is to be acted upon: 'Is it

[28] See Gen. 2:6.
[29] See Ezek. 31:3–4.

among these leaves of the perpetual Spring,—helpful leaves
for the healing of the nations,—that we mean to have our
part and place, or rather among the "brown skeletons of
leaves that lag the forest brook along"? For other leaves there
are, and other streams that water them,—not water of life,
but water of Acheron'[30] (xxv. 247–8). The forces that govern
plants govern the lives of men with equal inevitability.

Revisions of Authority

In a later chapter of *Proserpina*, Ruskin recommends that his
pupils should buy Louis Figuier's *Histoire des plantes* (1865),
and remarks that

> The botanists, indeed, tell me proudly 'Figuier is no authority'.
> But who wants authority? Is there nothing known yet about plants,
> then, which can be taught to a boy or girl, without referring them
> to an 'authority'?
> I, for my own part, care only to gather what Figuier can teach
> concerning things visible, to any boy or girl, who live within reach
> of a bramble hedge, or a hawthorn thicket, and can find authority
> enough for what they are told, in the sticks of them.
> If only *he* would, or could, tell us clearly that much; but like
> other doctors, though with better meaning than most, he has
> learned mainly to look at things with a microscope,—rarely with
> his eyes.[31] (xxv. 483–4)

Looking with eyes rather than with microscopes is Ruskin's
proclaimed method in *Proserpina*, as indeed in every other of
his works. When the authority of his own eyes and that of a
botanical author seem to be in conflict, he has no hesitation
in preferring the former. There is, however, another kind of
authority to which Ruskin constantly refers, though it bears
little resemblance to 'authority' in any usual academic sense.
The detailed visual observation which is the basis of his
method seems to be simply personal—as, for instance, in his
description of the cow violet (*Viola cornuta*): 'I perceive,
farther, that this disorderly flower is lifted on a lanky,
awkward, springless, and yet stiff flower-stalk; which is not

---

[30] See Coleridge, *The Ancient Mariner* (1798), vii. 566–7: 'The skeletons of leaves
that lag | My forest brook along'.
[31] See Guillaume Louis Figuier, *Histoire des plantes* (Paris, 1865).

round, as a flower-stalk ought to be, but obstinately square, and fluted, with projecting edges, like a pillar run thin out of an iron-foundry for a cheap railway station' (xxv. 397). But in Ruskin's view, what a flower-stalk ought to be, or ought not to be, is not a matter of opinion. It must be learned from the fixed standard of values embodied in the mythology, art, literature, and history of the world, which represents what Ruskin considered to be genuine 'authority'. So, in his chapter on the 'Viola', he speaks of the botanists with scorn and concentrates on the place of the violet in an older scheme of authority. In doing so, he reiterates his theory of the close relation between Greek mythology and the natural world. He explains why he has called the order of flowers to which the violet belongs 'Cytherides'; a name which refers primarily to the passage from *The Winter's Tale* which had provided the epigraph for his work.[32] Ruskin reminds his readers that in naming the Greek gods, 'you have first to think of the physical power they represent' (xxv. 415), and then shows how this is relevant to the passage from which he had named his order of violets. When

Homer speaks of Juno's dark eyes, you have to remember that she is the softer form of the rain power, and to think of the fringes of the rain-cloud across the light of the horizon. Gradually the idea becomes personal and human in the 'Dove's eyes within thy locks', and 'Dove's eyes by the rivers of waters' of the Song of Solomon.

'Or Cytherea's breath',—the two thoughts of softest glance, and softest kiss, being thus together associated with the flower: but note especially that the Island of Cythera was dedicated to Venus because it was the chief, if not the only Greek island, in which the purple fishery of Tyre was established . . . (xxv. 415–16)

The passage characteristically links the myths, literature, and history of the Greeks, the Bible, and Shakespeare in a web of associations and allusions. This is the authority of *Proserpina*.

Ruskin did not reject all scientific authority. But he frequently refers to peripheral or outmoded sources. In the eyes of a professional botanist, Dr Lindley's *Ladies Botany*, a

---

[32] 'violets, dim, | But sweeter than the lids of Juno's eyes | Or Cytherea's breath' (*The Winter's Tale*, IV. iv. 120–2).

work to which Ruskin often refers, would hardly have counted as a more substantial text than Figuier's *Histoire des plantes*. 'For without at all looking upon ladies as inferior beings, I dimly hope that what Dr. Lindley considers likely to be intelligible to *them*, may be also clear to their very humble servant' (xxv. 272), Ruskin remarks in '*Papaver rhoeas*'. He proceeds to present his list of names for various members of the poppy family, comparing his new system with that of 'present botany'. In his table of nomenclature, the science as practised in the ancient world is represented by Dioscorides, a Greek medical and botanical writer of *c*.100 AD.[33] Ruskin worked from the Greek text, and his references to Dioscorides suggest that he knew it well. But the authority of Dioscorides is given no more weight than 'present botany'. He too is to be replaced by the system of Ruskin's own Oxford school. Ruskin turns to the Greeks for their literature and mythology, and not for their science.

Despite his unconcern for academic opinion, Ruskin was uneasy about trespassing on the territory of classical scholars. Perhaps Liddell contributed to his uncertainty. In deference to the Dean, Ruskin does not insist on his favourite theory concerning the Greek violet (ἴον), which he believed to be in fact the iris. Liddell had warned that ἴον probably requires the digamma[34] in Homer, as, according to his *Lexicon*, it does also in Theocritus.[35] In a half-mocking note to his chapter on 'The Viola', Ruskin writes: 'I suppress, in some doubts about my "digamma", notes on the Greek violet and

[33] Ruskin had first encountered Dioscorides through his study of the history of painting. He refers to Eastlake's mention of Dioscorides, who had described the drying properties of certain vegetable oils, in his review of Eastlake's *History of Oil Painting* in 1848 (xii. 259–60). The first, and as yet only translation of Dioscorides' botanical writings, made by John Goodyer in 1655, was not published till 1934. See *The Greek Herbal of Dioscorides*, trans. John Goodyer (1655), ed. Robert T. Gunther, (Oxford, 1934).

[34] Originally the sixth letter of the Greek alphabet, the digamma (ϝ) later fell into disuse, and the sound which it represented gradually disappeared from literary Greek; though it left traces in the form of many Greek words. It was a consonant, probably correspondent in sound to the English 'w', and related to 'f' and 'v'. In postulating an initial digamma for ἴον, Liddell suggests a connection between that word and the Latin 'viola' which would be at odds with Ruskin's theory.

[35] The *Lexicon* also quotes Hesychius, a lexicographer of the 5th or 6th century AD, as giving 'γία (i.e. ϝ ία) ἄνθη, so that there can be no doubt of the connexion of ἴον with Lat. vio-la' See H. G. Liddell and R. Scott, *A Greek–English Lexicon*, 7th edn. (Oxford, 1883), 704.

the Ion of Euripides;—which the reader will perhaps be good enough to fancy a serious loss to him, and supply for himself'[36] (xxv. 405–6n.). The new system of names advocated in *Proserpina* was based on Greek and Latin. Ruskin wrote to Daniel Oliver that 'I am more and more satisfied every day that no nomenclature since Linnaeus's can stand, unless founded securely on Nature first, and then on the finest Greek, Latin, and English. This I shall—if I live—be partly able to do, and it will be completed by better scholars.'[37] Anxious about the security of his own Greek scholarship, Ruskin looked, rashly, to Liddell for help and reassurance;

My new botanical names of the great Floral Families are all to be Greek derivatives, either in the form *idae* or *ides*, but I'm not quite sure of myself in manufacturing them. I mean the *idae* to signify relation either of race, Rhodoidae, or to some protecting power, Artemidae, and the *des* (Naiades, Hesperides, Pleiades), groups expressive only of personal character and relation among the flowers themselves. Will the following names be admissable?

Cyllenidae (from Mt. Cyllene and Hermes)
Dionysidae
Helidae
Aesculidae
Vestalidae

I think the *des* will be all right if these are. (vol. xxv, p. xi)

We may assume they were not 'all right', for Ruskin changed the names of his five *idae* orders. This is one instance in which he was willing to bow to 'authority' in the usual academic sense of the world. For Ruskin, however, Liddell's academic jurisdiction was supported by an intimidating personal authority. Liddell had, after all, become Dean of the college in which Ruskin had been an undergraduate. Two days after writing this letter, he wrote to Liddell again: 'The most immediate anxiety with me is not to disgrace Oxford by any

[36] Ruskin does, however, achieve the distinction of a mention in Liddell's monumental *Lexicon*, in the entry for ἴον: 'Mr. Ruskin suggests that ἴον in Hom. may be the *blue* or *purple Iris*; and this would best agree with Pind. O. 6. 91, who speaks of ἴα with their ξανθαὶ καὶ παμπόρφυροι ἀκτῖνες' (Liddell and Scott, *Lexicon*, p. 704). A violet would not usually be spoken of as having the 'yellow and purple splendour' that Pindar refers to in his ode.

[37] Unpubl. letter, Bem. MS T. 30 (10 July 1875).

absurd mistake in these botanical names.'[38] Thanking Liddell
for his advice, Ruskin explains that

I felt as if they might seem to you only a form of continuous
fantasy remaining from my illness; nor do I myself look for the
slightest effect upon the scientific world while I live; but if I do live
a few years more the collation of what I have systematised for the
first time in Art Education with what I had learned of natural
science in pure love of it, and not in ambition of discovery, will
form a code of school teaching entirely separate from the technical
formalities of each several branch of science as now pursued, and
which I believe many parents and children will thank me for. (vol.
xxv. p. xli)

No such defensiveness is evident in *Proserpina* itself. Ruskin
rarely had cause for scholarly disquiet of the kind betrayed by
his letters to Liddell, for he did not often use Greek as a
source of scientific nomenclature, except for the classification of species. In the fifth part of *Deucalion* (1878), he wryly
instructs his pupils to use pure English, 'avoiding all
unnecessary foreign, especially Greek, forms of words
yourself, and translating them when used by others. Above
all, make this a practice in science. Great part of the supposed
scientific knowledge of the day is simply bad English, and
vanishes the moment you translate it' (xxvi. 260–1). Ruskin,
always uncomfortable about his uncertain command of
Greek, contended that the language was often used to
disguise ignorance rather than to communicate knowledge.
He remarked on the use of the world 'chlorophyll' in *The
Queen of the Air*: 'I wish they would use English instead of
Greek words. When I want to know why a leaf is green, they
tell me it is coloured by "chlorophyll," which at first sounds
very instructive; but if they would only say plainly that a leaf
is coloured green by a thing which is called "green leaf" we
should see precisely how far we had got' (xix. 355). He
returns to this point in his chapter on 'The Leaf', adding the
moral bias which defines his method in *Proserpina*. He
considers the colour of the laurel leaf:

think awhile of its dark clear green, and the good of it to you.
Scientifically, you know green in leaves is owing to 'chlorophyll,'

38 Unpubl. letter, Bodl. MS Eng. Lett. c. 42, fo. 202 (20 Nov. 1878).

or, in English, to 'green-leaf'. If may be very fine to know that; but my advice to you, on the whole, is to rest content with the general fact that leaves are green when they do not grow in or near smoky towns; and not by any means to rest content with the fact that very soon there will not be a green leaf in England, but only greenish-black ones. And thereon resolve that you will yourself endeavour to promote the growing of the green wood, rather than the black. (xxv. 232)

Yet Greek can illuminate, as well as obfuscate. Ruskin ponders the Greek word for 'leaf'. Noting that thinness is essential to the character of the leaf, he explains that the

Greeks called it, therefore, not only the born or blooming thing, but the spread or expanded thing—"πέταλον." Pindar calls the beginnings of quarrel, "petals of quarrel." Recollect, therefore, this form, Petalos; and connect it with Petasos, the expanded cap of Mercury. For one great use of both is to give shade. The root of all these words is ΠΕΤ (Pet), which may easily be remembered in Greek, as it sometimes occurs in no unpleasant sense in English.[39] (xxv. 230–1)

Ruskin proceeds to analyse further ideas which group themselves round this root ΠΕΤ, in its association with πέτομαι, to fly, and πότμος, fate, which he sees as 'Fate in its pursuing flight, the overtaking thing, or overflying Fate' (xxv. 231). He was in the habit of describing the girls who comforted and distracted his latter years as 'pets'. The pursuing flight of Fate, or Fors, as Ruskin habitually called it, preoccupied him increasingly as his mental health grew more unstable with advancing age. In passages such as these, personal references are barely concealed. Yet the Greek which expresses them serves also to distance them. For the Greeks were reassuringly remote in time. The analysis of their language could allay painful thoughts and unsettling emotions. As Ruskin grew older, however, he found it harder to exclude private distress from his writing. Notes made for a chapter on the cyclamen, unpublished during his lifetime, suggest that the difficulty may have contributed to his abandoning of the still unfinished *Proserpina*.

Ruskin saw the essential character of the cyclamen in its circularity, a trait which associated the plant with Demeter,

---

[39] See xix. 322; and Pindar, *Isthmian Odes*, viii. 43.

who ruled over the cycles of the seasons. The connection is seen in the cyclamen's 'subterranean stem, stooping flower, and buried, or at least hidden front', all of which gave 'ample reason for the dedication' (xxv. 542). Its colour provided another reason: 'there is a farther, though more subtle one, in its dark purple colour, which the Greeks always associated with death'. (xxv. 542). These were painful themes for Ruskin. The legends of Demeter inevitably bring to mind those of her daughter, and Demeter's association with death could not but recall the loss of Ruskin's own Proserpina, Rose La Touche. He had intended a 'treatise on the mythic meaning of spirals—of the wheel of Fortune, and nine spheres of fate, which I hope the reader laments the loss of', and had meant to relate this study to the 'evil circles' in the *Frogs* of Aristophanes (xxv. 542). Abandoning this plan, he writes that 'this only it is worth saying still, that the running round of the Dogs (Furies) in Aristophanes certainly means the tormenting recurrence of painful thoughts in a circle from which there is no escape' (xxv. 542). Such περίδρομοι κύνες[40] became inexorable for Ruskin after 1886, the year in which the tenth and last part of *Proserpina* was published. He never finished his chapter on the cyclamen, and his work on *Proserpina* came to an end. But in 1888, two years after what was to be the last part of his work on botany had appeared, the cyclamen was again in his thoughts. On his last journey to the Continent, he saw it growing on the rocks of Champagnole. In lines which are a moving conclusion to a lifetime's study of plants, Ruskin wrote of the cyclamen in association with his favourite myth of Apollo and Daphne:

I write these lines (1st Sept., 1888) at my old home at Champagnole, where but the day before yesterday I had a walk in the pine wood, and on rocks glowing with deep purple cyclamen above the glen of the Ain, which might well have been in the Earthly Paradise after Christ's kingdom shall be come. And in the actual sound of forests, and the murmur or whisper of the spring winds through budding branches and setting blossoms, there is a true Eolian song, addressed partly to the ear, but more to the heart and to the true and creative imagination. The fable of Apollo and Daphne, chief of those founded on the humanity of trees, and the

---

[40] 'circling dogs' (Aristophanes, *Frogs*, 472).

resultant acceptance of the laurel crown as the purest reward of
moral and intellectual power used nobly in the service of man, has
yet a deeper symbolism in its expression of the true love which may
be felt, if we are taught by the Muses, for the beautiful earth-bound
creatures that cherish and survive our own fleeting lives.[41] (xxxv.
641)

[41] The passage, intended for *Dilecta*, was first published in the Library Edition.

SELECT BIBLIOGRAPHY

A. Unpublished Sources

Marginalia

A substantial number of the classical texts used by Ruskin are now preserved in the Ruskin Galleries, Bembridge, Isle of Wight. Many of these are marked by Ruskin. I have cited the following annotated texts from Bembridge:

Lenormant, Ch., and De Witte, J., *Élite des monuments céramographiques: matériaux pour l'histoire des religions et des mœurs de l'antiquité*, 4 vols. (Paris, 1844–61).

Plato, *Platonis Scripta Graece Omnia*, ed. E. Bekker, 11 vols. (London, 1826).

Ruskin, John, *The Queen of the Air: Being a Study of the Greek Myths of Cloud and Storm* (London, 1869).

Letters and diaries

In the course of their work in preparing the Library Edition of Ruskin's works, E. T. Cook and Alexander Wedderburn made typescript copies of many letters that were not finally included in their edition. These copies, bound into 21 volumes, are now preserved in the Bodleian Library. Ruskin's editors also made a more complete transcript of his diaries than that which was eventually published; this too is preserved in the Bodleian Library:

Bodl. MS Eng. Lett. c. 32–52.
Bodl. MS Eng. Misc. c. 209–49.

The papers of Henry Acland are preserved in the Bodleian Library. I have referred particularly to the correspondence between Acland and H. G. Liddell:

Bodl. MS Acland d. 69; d. 82; d. 90; d. 92; d. 96; c. 2.

Correspondence between Ruskin and his cousin, George Richardson, is preserved in the Bodleian Library. I have cited the following letter:

Bodl. MS Eng. Misc. e. 182, fo. 6.

I have cited letters from John James Ruskin to his son, from Ruskin to Daniel Oliver, and from Ruskin to Eliza Fall; these are to be found in the Ruskin Galleries, Bembridge:

Bem. MS C4.
Bem. MS T. 30.
Bem. MS BX111.

Correspondence between Ruskin and Edward Burne-Jones is preserved in the Fitzwilliam Museum, Cambridge. I have cited the following letters:
Fitz. MS Envelope 12.
Fitz. MS X52.
Correspondence between Ruskin and Professor John Stuart Blackie is preserved in the National Library of Scotland, Edinburgh. I have cited the following letters:
Edinburgh MS 2624, fo. 15.
Edinburgh MS 2643, fo. 136.

Notebooks and other manuscript sources

A number of Ruskin's notebooks are preserved in the Ruskin Galleries, Bembridge. I have cited the 'Myth Book', containing material on Greek mythology, and a notebook which refers to Egyptian mythology. For an excellent account of the 'Myth Book' see Robert Hewison's unpubl. B. Litt. thesis, listed below.
Bem. MS 45.
Bem. MS 17.

Unpublished theses

Burstein, Janet, 'Journey Beyond Myth: The Progress of the Intellect in Victorian Mythography and Three Nineteenth Century Novels', Ph.D. (Drew University, 1975).

Claiborne, Jay Wood, 'Two Secretaries: The Letters of John Ruskin to Charles Augustus Howell and the Rev. Richard St. John Tyrwhitt', Ph.D. (The University of Texas, 1969).

Clegg, Jeanne, 'Ruskin and Venice', D.Phil. (Oxford, 1979).

Fitch, Raymond E., 'The Golden Furrow: Ruskin and the Greek Religion', Ph.D. (The University of Pennsylvania, 1965).

Hewison, Robert A. P., 'Some Themes and their Treatment in the Work of John Ruskin 1860–71, with Special Reference to *Unto This Last*, *Sesame and Lilies*, and *Queen of the Air*', B.Litt. (Oxford, 1972).

Shrimpton, N. G., 'Economic, Social, and Literary Influences upon the Development of Ruskin's Ideas to *Unto This Last* (1860)', D.Phil. (Oxford, 1976).

Unrau, John, 'A Study of Ruskin's Architectural Writings', D.Phil. (Oxford, 1969).

Williams, Catherine, 'Ruskin's Late Works c. 1870–1890, with Particular Reference to the Collection Made for the Guild of St. George', Ph.D. (London, 1972).

Yoder, Albert Christian, 'Concepts of Mythology in Victorian England', Ph.D. (The Florida State University, 1971).

B. Primary Sources

Anon., 'An Analysis of the Egyptian Mythology', *Monthly Review*, 92 (July 1820), 225–42.

Anon., 'The Ethics of the Dust', *Saturday Review*, 30 Dec. 1865, 819–20.

Anon., 'Mythology and Religion of Ancient Greece', *Foreign Quarterly Review*, 7 (1831), 33–8.

Anon., 'An Oxford Lecture', *Nineteenth Century*, 3 (Jan. 1878), 136–45.

Anon., 'Ruskin's "Queen of the Air"', *Saturday Review*, 21 Aug. 1869, 257–9.

Anon., 'The Principle of the Grecian Mythology: Or, How the Greeks Made their Gods', *Fraser's Magazine*, 49 (Jan. 1854), 69–79.

Anon., 'The Queen of the Air', *Spectator*, 17 July 1869, 852–3.

Apollodorus, *The Library*, trans. Sir J. G. Frazer, 3 vols. (Loeb edn.; London and New York, 1921).

Aristophanes, *The Acharnians, The Knights, The Clouds, The Wasps*, trans. B. B. Rogers (Loeb edn.; London and Cambridge, Mass., 1960).

—— *The Lysistrata, The Thesmophoriazusae, The Ecclesiazusae, The Plutus*, trans. B. B. Rogers (Loeb edn.; London and Cambridge, Mass., 1924).

Aristotle, *Aristotelis de Rhetorica Libri Tres: Ad Fidem Manuscriptorum Recogniti in Usum Academicae Juventutis*, ed. J. G. Buhle (Oxford, 1833).

—— *The 'Art' of Rhetoric*, trans. John Henry Freese (Loeb edn.; London and Cambridge, Mass., 1926).

—— *The Nicomachean Ethics*, trans. H. Rackham (rev. Loeb edn.; London and Cambridge, Mass., 1968).

—— *The Nichomachean Ethics of Aristotle: with English Notes*, ed. John S. Brewer (Oxford, 1836).

—— *On the Soul, Parva Naturalis, On Breath*, trans. W. S. Hett (Loeb edn.; London and Cambridge, Mass., 1935).

Arnold, Matthew, *The Complete Prose Works of Matthew Arnold*, ed. R. H. Super, 11 vols. (Ann Arbor, 1960–77).

Arundale, Francis, and Bonomi, Joseph, *The Gallery of Antiquities: Selected from the British Museum* (London, 1844).

Atlay, J. B., *Sir Henry Wentworth Acland: A Memoir* (London, 1903).

Bacon, Francis, *The Works of Francis Bacon*, ed. J. Spedding, R. L. Ellis, and D. D. Heath, 7 vols. (London, 1858–61).

Blackie, John Stuart, *Classical Literature in its Relation to the Nineteenth Century and Scottish University Education: An Inaugural Lecture Delivered in the University of Edinburgh* (Edinburgh and London, 1852).

—— *Horae Hellenicae: Essays and Discussions on Some Important Points of Greek Philology and Antiquity* (London, 1874).

Blackie, J. S., *On the Living Language of the Greeks and its Utility to the Classical Scholar: An Introductory Lecture Delivered in the University of Edinburgh* (Edinburgh and London, 1853).

—— *University Reform: Eight Articles Reprinted from the Scotsman Newspaper; with a Letter to Professor Pillans* (Edinburgh, 1848).

Bruce, James Manning, 'Ruskin as an Oxford Lecturer', *Century Magazine*, 33 (Feb. 1898), 590–4.

Bunsen, C. C. J., *Egypt's Place in Universal History*, trans. C. H. Cottrell, 5 vols. (London, 1848–60).

Carlyle, Thomas, *The Works of Thomas Carlyle* (Centenary Edition), 30 vols. (London, 1897–9).

Catullus, *The Poems of Gaius Valerius Catullus*, trans. F. W. Cornish (Loeb edn.; London and Cambridge, Mass., 1913).

Champollion, Jean François, *Panthéon égyptien: collection des personnages mythologiques de l'ancienne Égypte* (Paris, 1823–5).

Chaucer, Geoffrey, *The Works of Geoffrey Chaucer*, ed. F. N. Robinson, 2nd edn. (London, 1957).

Clinton, Henry Fynes, *Fasti Hellenici: The Civil and Literary Chronology of Greece from the Earliest Accounts to the Death of Augustus*, 3 vols. (Oxford, 1834).

Coleridge, S. T., *Poems*, ed. E. H. Coleridge, 2 vols. (Oxford, 1912).

Collingwood, W. G., *The Life and Work of John Ruskin*, 2 vols. (London, 1893).

Cook, E. T., *The Life of John Ruskin*, 2 vols. (London, 1911).

Cox, George William, *The Mythology of the Aryan Nations*, 2 vols. (London, 1878).

Crawford, Alexander William (Lord Lindsay), *Sketches of the History of Christian Art* (London, 1847).

Crowe, J. A., and Cavalcaselle, G. B., *A History of Painting in North Italy*, 2 vols. (London, 1871).

—— *A New History of Painting in Italy from the Second to the Sixteenth Century*, 3 vols. (London, 1864).

Cullimore, Isaac, 'The Trinity of the Gentiles: Egyptian Mythology: An Analytical Essay in Four Chapters', *Fraser's Town and Country Magazine*, 20 (July–Sept. 1859), 1–10, 200–11, 326–32.

Dante Alighieri, *The Divine Comedy of Dante Alighieri*, trans. J. D. Sinclair, 3 vols. (rev. edn.; London, 1948).

Description de L'Égypte: ou recueil des observations et des recherches qui ont été faites en Égypte, pendant l'expédition de l'armée française, 9 vols. (Paris, 1809–30).

Diodorus Siculus, *The Library of History*, trans. C. H. Oldfather, C. H. Sherman, *et al.*, 12 vols. (Loeb edn.; London and Cambridge, Mass., 1933–67).

Dioscorides, *The Greek Herbal of Dioscorides*, trans. John Goodyer (1655), ed. Robert T. Gunther (Oxford, 1934).

Euripides, *Ion, Hippolytus, Medea, Alcestis*, trans. Arthur S. Way (Loeb edn.; London and Cambridge, Mass., 1971).

Fergusson, J., *Tree and Serpent Worship* (London, 1866).

Figuier, Guillaume Louis, *Histoire des plantes* (Paris, 1865).

Gladstone, W. E., *Juventus Mundi* (London, 1869).

—— *Studies on Homer and the Homeric Age*, 3 vols. (Oxford, 1858).

Green, John Richard, *The Letters of John Richard Green*, ed. Leslie Stephen (London, 1901).

Grote, George, *A History of Greece*, 8 vols. (London, 1846–56).

Grove, Sir William, *The Correlation of Physical Forces* (London, 1846).

Gurney, E., Myers, F. W. H., Padmore, F., *Phantasms of the Living*, 2 vols. (London, 1886).

Hamilton, William, *Discussions on Philosophy and Literature, Education and University Reform* (London, 1852).

Herbert, George, *The Works of George Herbert*, ed. F. E. Hutchinson (Oxford, 1941).

Hesiod, *The Homeric Hymns and Homerica*, trans. Hugh G. Evelyn-White (rev. Loeb edn.; London and Cambridge, Mass., 1954).

Hewlett, H. G., 'The Rationale of Mythology', *Cornhill Magazine*, 35 (Apr. 1877), 407–23.

Hoare, J. N., 'The Religion of the Ancient Egyptians', *Nineteenth Century*, 4 (Dec. 1878), 1105–20.

Homer, *The Iliad*, trans. A. T. Murray, 2 vols. (Loeb edn.; London and Cambridge, Mass., 1960).

—— *The Odyssey*, trans. A. T. Murray, 2 vols. (Loeb edn.; London and Cambridge, Mass., 1963).

Hyginus, *Hygini Fabulae*, ed. H. I. Rose (Leyden, 1963).

Juvenal, *Juvenal and Persius*, trans. G. G. Ramsey (Loeb edn.; London and New York, 1918).

Kearie, Annie, *Early Egyptian History for the Young* (Cambridge, 1861).

Kingsley, Charles, *The Life and Works of Charles Kingsley*, 19 vols. London, 1903).

Knight, Richard Payne, *An Account of the Remains of the Worship of Priapus* (London, 1786).

—— *An Inquiry into the Symbolical Language of Ancient Art* (London, 1818).

La Touche, Rose, *John Ruskin and Rose La Touche: Her Unpublished Diaries of 1861 and 1867*, ed. Van Akin Burd (Oxford, 1979).

Lenormant, Ch., and De Witte, J. *Élite des monuments céramographiques: matériaux pour l'histoire des religions et des mœurs de l'antiquité*, 4 vols. (Paris, 1844–61).

Liddell, H. G., and Scott, R., *A Greek–English Lexicon*, 7th edn. (Oxford, 1883).

Lindley, John, *Ladies Botany: Or a Familiar Introduction to the Study of the Natural System of Botany*, 2 vols. (London, 1834–7).

Lucian, *The Works of Lucian*, trans. A. M. Harmon, K. Kilburn, and M. D. MacCleod, 8 vols. (London and Cambridge, Mass., 1913–67).

Millingen, James, *Ancient Coins of Greek Cities and Kings* (London, 1831).

Müller, Carl Otfried, *Ancient Art and its Remains: Or a Manual of the Archaeology of Art*, trans. John Leitch (London, 1847).

—— *The History and Antiquities of the Doric Race*, trans. H. Tufnell and G. G. Lewis, 2 vols. (London, 1830).

—— *Introduction to a Scientific System of Mythology*, trans. J. Leitch (London, 1844).

Müller, Friedrich Max, 'Comparative Mythology', in *Oxford Essays: Contributed by Members of the University* (London, 1856), 1–87.

—— *Lectures on the Science of Language*, 1st Ser. (London, 1861).

—— *Lectures on the Science of Language*, 2nd Ser. (London, 1864).

Myers, F. W. H., *Fragments of Prose and Poetry*, ed. Eveleen Myers (London, 1904).

Oliver, Daniel, *Illustrations of the Principal Natural Orders of the Vegetable Kingdom: Prepared for the Science and Art Department of the Council of Education* (London, 1874).

Ovid, *Metamorphoses*, trans. Frank Justus Miller, 2 vols. (Loeb edn.; London and Cambridge, Mass., 1916).

Pater, Walter, 'A Fragment on Sandro Botticelli', *Fortnightly Review*, 14 (Aug. 1870), 155–60.

—— *Studies in the History of the Renaissance* (London, 1873).

—— *Works of Walter Pater*, 10 vols. (London, 1910).

Pindar, *The Odes of Pindar*, trans. Sir John Sandys (rev. Loeb edn.; London and Cambridge, Mass., 1946).

Plato, *Charmides, Alcibiades I and II, Hipparchus, The Lovers, Theages, Minos, Epinomis*, trans. W. R. M. Lamb (rev. Loeb edn.; London and Cambridge, Mass., 1955).

—— *Cratylus, Parmenides, Greater Hippias, Lesser Hippias*, trans. H. N. Fowler (rev. Loeb edn.; London and Cambridge, Mass., 1953).

—— *Euthyphro, Apology, Crito, Phaedo, Phaedrus*, trans. H. N. Fowler (Loeb edn.; London and Cambridge, Mass., 1953).

—— *Laws*, trans. R. G. Bury, 2 vols. (Loeb edn.; London and Cambridge, Mass., 1961).

—— *Lysis, Symposium, Gorgias*, trans. W. R. M. Lamb (Loeb edn.; London and Cambridge, Mass., 1975).

—— *Platonis Scripta Graece Omnia*, ed. E. Bekker, 11 vols. (London, 1826).

—— *The Republic*, trans. Paul Shorey, 2 vols. (rev. Loeb edn.; London and Cambridge, Mass., 1963).

—— *Timaeus, Critias, Cleitophon, Menexenus, Epistles*, trans. R. G. Bury (Loeb edn.; London and Cambridge, Mass., 1961).

Plutarch, *Parallel Lives*, trans. Bernadotte Perrin, 11 vols. (Loeb edn.; London and Cambridge, Mass.; 1914–26).

Pope, Alexander, *The Twickenham Edition of the Poems of Alexander Pope*, gen. ed. John Butt, 11 vols. (London, 1961–9).

Roberts, David, *Egypt and Nubia*, 3 vols. (London, 1846).

Rosellini, Ippolito, *I Monumenti dell'Egitto e della Nubia*, 11 vols. (Pisa, 1832–46).

Ruskin, John, *The Brantwood Diary of John Ruskin: Together with Selected Related Letters and Sketches of Persons Mentioned*, ed. Helen Gill Viljoen (New Haven and London, 1971).

—— *Dearest Mama Talbot: A Selection of Letters from John Ruskin to Mrs Fanny Talbot*, ed. Margaret Spence (London, 1966).

—— *The Diaries of John Ruskin*, ed. Joan Evans and J. H. Whitehouse, 3 vols. (Oxford, 1956–9).

—— *The Froude–Ruskin Friendship: As Represented through Letters*, ed. Helen Gill Viljoen (New York, 1966).

—— *The Letters of John Ruskin to Lord and Lady Mount-Temple*, ed. John Lewis Bradley (Columbus, Ohio, 1964).

—— *The Queen of the Air: Being a Study of the Greek Myths of Cloud and Storm* (London, 1869).

—— *The Ruskin Family Letters: The Correspondence of John James Ruskin, his Wife, and their Son, John, 1801–1843*, ed. Van Akin Burd (Ithaca and London, 1973).

—— *Ruskin in Italy: Letters to his Parents, 1845*, ed. Harold I. Shapiro (Oxford, 1972).

—— *Ruskin's Letters from Venice: 1851–1852*, ed. John Lewis Bradley (New Haven, 1955).

—— *The Winnington Letters: John Ruskin's Correspondence with Margaret Alexis Bell and the Children at Winnington Hall*, ed. Van Akin Burd (London, 1969).

—— *The Works of John Ruskin* (Library Edition), ed. E. T. Cook and Alexander Wedderburn, 39 vols. (London, 1903–12).

Scott, Sir Walter, *Minstrelsy of the Scottish Border*, 2 vols. (London and Edinburgh, 1802).

—— *The Poetical Works of Sir Walter Scott*, ed. J. Logie Robertson (Oxford, 1904).

Shakespeare, William, *The Riverside Shakespeare*, textual ed. G. B. Evans (Boston, 1974).

Smith, William, *Dictionary of Greek and Roman Biography and Mythology*, 3 vols. (London, 1844–9).

Sophocles, *Ajax, Electra, Trachiniae, Philoctetes*, trans. F. Storr (Loeb edn.; London and Cambridge, Mass., 1978).

Sophocles, *Oedipus the King, Oedipus at Colonus, Antigone*, trans. F. Storr (Loeb edn.; London and Cambridge, Mass., 1912).

Sowerby, J. E. *English Botany*, 36 vols. (London, 1790–1814).

—— *English Botany: Or, Coloured Figures of British Plants*, ed. J. T. Syme, 3rd edn., 12 vols. (London, 1863–86).

Strauss, David Friedrich, *The Life of Jesus: Critically Examined by Dr. David Friedrich Strauss*, trans. Mary Ann Evans, 3 vols. (London, 1846).

Swinburne, A. C. *The Complete Works of Algernon Charles Swinburne* (Bonchurch ed.), ed. Sir Edmund Gosse and Thomas James Wise, 2 vols. (London and New York, 1925–7).

—— *Poems and Ballads* (London, 1866).

—— *The Swinburne Letters*, ed. C. Y. Lang, 6 vols. (New Haven and London, 1959–62).

Symonds, John Addington, *The Letters of John Addington Symonds*, ed. Herbert M. Schueller and Robert L. Peters, 3 vols. (Detroit, 1967–9).

—— *Studies of the Greek Poets*, 1st Ser. (London, 1873).

—— *Studies of the Greek Poets*, 2nd Ser. (London, 1876).

Tennyson, Alfred, *The Poems of Tennyson*, ed. Christopher Ricks (London, 1969).

Tylor, E. B. *Primitive Culture: Researches into the Development of Mythology, Philosophy, Religion, Art, and Custom*, 2 vols. (London, 1871).

—— *Researches into the Early History of Mankind and the Development of Civilization* (London, 1865).

Tyrwhitt, Richard St John, 'Ancilla Domini: Thoughts on Christian Art', *Contemporary Review*, 4 (Apr. 1867), 340–58.

—— 'The Greek Spirit in Modern Literature', *Contemporary Review*, 29 (Mar. 1877), 552–66.

Valerius Maximus, Valeri Maximi Factorum et Dictorum Memoralibium Libri Novem, ed. C. Kempf. (Leipzig, 1888).

Wilkinson, John Gardner, *Manners and Customs of the Ancient Egyptians*, 6 vols. (London, 1837–41).

Williams, Rowland, 'Bunsen's Biblical Researches', in *Essays and Reviews* (London, 1860), 50–93.

Winckelmann, Johann Joachim, *Reflections on the Painting and Sculpture of the Greeks*, trans. Henry Fuseli (London, 1765; repr. Scolar Press, London, 1972).

Wordsworth, William, *The Poetical Works of William Wordsworth*, ed. E. de Selincourt and H. Darbishire, 5 vols. (Oxford, 1940–9).

Xenophon, *Memorabilia and Oeconomicus*, trans. E. C. Marchant (Loeb edn.; London and Cambridge, Mass., 1923).

Young, Edward, *The Complete Works of the Rev. Edward Young . . . to which is Prefixed a Life of the Author by John Doran*, ed. James Nichols, 2 vols. (London, 1854).

C. Secondary Sources

Ball, Patricia, *The Science of Aspects: The Changing Role of Fact in the Work of Coleridge, Ruskin and Hopkins* (London, 1971).

Bloom, Harold, *The Ringers in the Tower: Studies in the Romantic Tradition* (Chicago and London, 1971).

Brown, Samuel E. 'The Unpublished Passages in the Manuscript of Ruskin's Autobiography', *Victorian Newsletter*, 16 (Autumn 1959), 10–18.

Burstein, Janet, 'Victorian Mythography and the Progress of the Intellect', *Victorian Studies*, 18 (Mar. 1975), 309–24.

Chase, Richard Volney, *The Quest for Myth* (Baton Rouge, La. 1949).

Chaudhuri, Nirad Chandra, *Scholar Extraordinary: The Life of F. M. Müller* (London, 1974).

Claiborne, Jay Wood, 'John Ruskin and Charles Augustus Howell: Some New Letters', *Texas Studies in Literature and Language*, 15 (Fall 1973), 471–98.

Clegg, Jeanne, *Ruskin and Venice* (London, 1981).

Crook, J. Mordaunt, *The Greek Revival: Neo-Classical Attitudes in British Architecture 1760–1870* (London, 1972).

DeLaura, David Joseph, *Hebrew and Hellene in Victorian England: Newman, Arnold and Pater* (Austin and London, 1969).

Dorson, Richard M., 'The Eclipse of Solar Mythology', in *Myth: A Symposium*, ed. Thomas A. Sebeok, 2nd edn. (Bloomington and London, 1965), 25–63.

Drake, Gertrude G., 'Ruskin's Athena, Queen of the Air', *Classical Bulletin*, 51 (Dec. 1974), 18–24.

Evans, Joan, *John Ruskin* (London, 1954).

Feldman, Burton, and Richardson, Robert D., *The Rise of Modern Mythology: 1680–1860* (Bloomington and London, 1972).

Fellows, Jay, *The Failing Distance: The Autobiographical Impulse in John Ruskin* (Baltimore and London, 1975).

Fitch, Raymond E., *The Poison Sky: Myth and Apocalypse in Ruskin* (Athens, Ohio, and London, 1982).

Frye, Northrop, *Anatomy of Criticism: Four Essays* (Princeton, 1957).

Guthrie, W. K. C., *A History of Greek Philosophy*, 5 vols. (Cambridge, 1962–78).

—— *The Greeks and their Gods* (London, 1950).

—— *Orpheus and Greek Religion: A Study of the Orphic Movement* (London, 1935).

Hewison, Robert A. P., *John Ruskin: The Argument of the Eye* (London, 1976).

—— ed., *New Approaches to Ruskin: Thirteen Essays* (London, 1981).

Hilton, Tim, *John Ruskin: The Early Years* (New Haven and London, 1985).

Horne, Herbert P., *Alessandro Filipepi Commonly Called Sandro Botticelli: Painter of Florence* (London, 1908).

Jenkyns, Richard, *The Victorians and the Ancient Greeks* (Oxford, 1980).

Kirchhoff, Frederick, 'A Note on Ruskin's Mythography', *Victorian Newsletter*, 50 (Autumn 1976), 24–7.

—— 'A Science Against Sciences: Ruskin's Floral Mythology', in *Nature and the Victorian Imagination*, ed. U. C. Knoepflmacher and G. B. Tennyson (Berkeley, Los Angeles, and London, 1977), 246–58.

Kirk, G. S., *Myth: Its Meaning and Functions in Ancient and Other Cultures* (Cambridge, Berkeley, and Los Angeles, 1970).

Kissane, James, 'Victorian Mythology', *Victorian Studies*, 6 (Sept. 1962), 5–28.

Kitchin, G. W., *Ruskin in Oxford and Other Studies* (London, 1904).

Landow, George P., *The Aesthetic and Critical Theories of John Ruskin* (Princeton, 1971).

Leon, Derrick Lewis, *Ruskin: The Great Victorian* (London, 1949).

Levey, Michael, 'Botticelli and Nineteenth Century England', *Journal of the Warburg and Courtauld Institutes*, 23 (1960), 291–306.

Manuel, Frank, *The Eighteenth Century Confronts the Gods* (Cambridge, Mass., 1959).

Messmann, Frank J., *Richard Payne Knight: The Twilight of Virtuosity* (The Hague and Paris, 1974).

Murdoch, Iris, *The Fire and The Sun: Why Plato Banished the Artists* (Oxford, 1977).

Pevsner, Nikolaus, 'Richard Payne Knight', *Art Bulletin*, 31 (1949), 293–320.

Rose, H. J., *A Handbook of Greek Mythology* (London, 1928).

Rosenberg, John D., *The Darkening Glass: A Portrait of Ruskin's Genius* (London, 1963).

Ruthven, K. K., *Myth* (London, 1976).

Sherburne, James Clark, *John Ruskin or the Ambiguities of Abundance: A Study in Social and Economic Criticism* (Cambridge, Mass., 1972).

Simmonds, Michael, 'Ruskin, Apemantus, and his Father', *Notes and Queries*, NS 26 (Aug. 1979), 308–10.

Strauss, Leo, *Xenophon's Socratic Discourse: An Interpretation of the Oeconomicus* (Ithaca and London, 1970).

Swanson, Vern G., *Sir Lawrence Alma-Tadema: The Painter of the Victorian Vision of the Ancient World* (London, 1977).

Thompson, Revd Henry L., *Henry George Liddell D.D., Dean of Christ Church, Oxford: A Memoir* (London, 1899).

Townsend, Francis G., *Ruskin and the Landscape Feeling* (Urbana, Ill., 1951).

Tuckwell, Revd William, *Reminiscences of Oxford* (London, 1900).

Turner, Frank Miller, *Between Science and Religion: The Reaction to Scientific Naturalism in Late Victorian England* (New Haven and London, 1974).

Vermeule, Emily, *Aspects of Death in Early Greek Art and Poetry* (Los Angeles, 1979).

Viljoen, Helen Gill, *Ruskin's Scottish Heritage: A Prelude* (Urbana, Ill., 1956).

Ward, W. R., *Victorian Oxford* (London, 1965).

Wilenski, R. H., *John Ruskin: An Introduction to Further Study of his Life and Work* (London, 1933).

Wind, Edgar, *Pagan Mysteries in the Renaissance* (London, 1958).

Wortham, J. D., *British Egyptology 1549–1906* (Norman, 1971).

Zuntz, Günther, *Persephone: Three Essays on Religion and Thought in Magna Graecia* (Oxford, 1971).

Zwerdling, Alex, 'The Romantic Mythographers and the Romantic Revival of Greek Myth', *Proceedings of the Modern Language Association*, 79 (1964), 447–56.

INDEX